The Theater of Narration

The Theater of Narration

From the Peripheries of History to the Main Stages of Italy

Juliet Guzzetta

NORTHWESTERN UNIVERSITY PRESS
EVANSTON, ILLINOIS

Northwestern University Press
www.nupress.northwestern.edu

Except where otherwise noted, this title is licensed under the Creative Commons Attribution-NonCommercial-NoDerivatives 4.0 International License (CC BY-NC-ND). Read the license at https://creativecommons.org/licenses/by-nc-nd/4.0/legalcode.

This book is freely available in an open access edition thanks to TOME (Toward an Open Monograph Ecosystem)—a collaboration of the Association of American Universities, the Association of University Presses, and the Association of Research Libraries—and the generous support of Michigan State University. Learn more at the TOME website, available at openmonographs.org.

Copyright © 2021 by Northwestern University. Published 2021 by Northwestern University Press. All rights reserved.

Printed in the United States of America

10 9 8 7 6 5 4 3 2 1

Library of Congress Cataloging-in-Publication Data

Names: Guzzetta, Juliet, author.
Title: The theater of narration : from the peripheries of history to the main stages of Italy / Juliet Guzzetta.
Description: Evanston, Illinois : Northwestern University Press, 2021. | Includes bibliographical references and index.
Identifiers: LCCN 2021008536 | ISBN 9780810143869 (paperback) | ISBN 9780810143876 (cloth) | ISBN 9780810143883 (ebook)
Subjects: LCSH: Italian drama—20th century—History and criticism. | Italian drama—21st century—History and criticism. | Historical drama, Italian—20th century—History and criticism. | Historical drama, Italian—21st century—History and criticism.
Classification: LCC PQ4153.H3 G89 2021 | DDC 852/.051409—dc23
LC record available at https://lccn.loc.gov/2021008536

For my love,

Joshua Yumibe Guzzetta

Our daughters,

Livia Leigh and Raffaella Fara

And my best friends,

Franny and Elissa

La storia riguarda tutti, perché tutti hanno una propria prospettiva sulla storia. Perché tutti vivono nella storia, anche se ne abitano solo la periferia.

(History concerns everyone, because everyone has their own perspective on history. Because everyone has a place in history, even if only on the periphery.)

—Ascanio Celestini

CONTENTS

ILLUSTRATIONS

ACKNOWLEDGMENTS

Many moons ago when my mom left this earth, one of the thoughts that most haunted me was that I felt too few people knew her brilliance. Where was the state service? Where were the flags at half-mast? Where was the declaration of a national holiday in her memory? It was a feeling that distills the ways in which the private world can overshadow the shared public one. When I discovered the theater of narration only a year or two later, it reaffirmed for me what I had begun to realize then: everyone's individual stories do hold monumental weight, electricity, and potential even if they never reach beyond a select body of listeners. Initially I thought the theater of narration was about the many lives of stories, but actually it is about the many people whose lives are connected by their private stories, personal stories that bind the public histories so many of us share. The first person I wish to acknowledge is the person with whom my story began, a beginning that was already more than halfway through her own story. Her loving memory is written in these pages.

As the theater of narration has also taught me, what might appear the ending to a story is sometimes a new beginning. I understood this to be true when I met my partner, Josh, to whom I dedicate this work. In walking with each other down one path that was coming to an end, we found ourselves on an entirely new course. Our shared experiences and life together have been the happiest days I have known, and I am humbled by his generosity, intellect, and, well, he makes me laugh too. In the many stages of this study all those qualities continually manifested as we discussed my ideas, challenges, and goals. Our Livia, independent and joyous, and our Raffaella, achingly sweet and surprisingly stubborn, distract me from my work and will me into their wondrous present and remind me that the two are connected. I dedicate this study to them as well. The other member of our immediate family needs acknowledgment too. Augustus Stellan, or Gus ("Gas" in Italy), has sat at our feet patiently on many long flights, accompanied me to a number of libraries, archives, and interviews in Italy, and proves the aphorism that when you rescue an animal, the animal rescues you. The family bridging the one to whom I was born with the one that I helped create are my two best friends, Frances Sullivan and Elissa Crum. We have been together for all Dickensian time, and they are pillars of my world. Paul Levesque has cheered for me since high school soccer games through my professional life, and I thank him for his steady encouragement and love.

Family friends, kind and kindred spirits, mentors and colleagues have supported me throughout this project. They have contributed to my thinking in this study and my intellectual formation more broadly. For upward of a decade Giorgio Bertellini has been a North Star; Vincenzo Binetti held the pulse of an era of shared interest, and Nadine Hubbs remained a Zen sage open to consultation on a range of matters. Sara Ritchey, the best friend of my partner for many years before I knew him, is now one of *my* best friends. She is also a mentor, role model, beloved "guardian Sara" to our children, and helpful reader of these pages. Pat O'Donnell, golfer extraordinaire, sensitive observer, and prolific scholar, has supported my work in many ways. Nancy Marino, gone too soon, read everything I ever gave her and returned it to me with comments on almost every page, usually in less than three days. She was a fellow New Yorker and mentor. Justus Nieland, first a loyal friend, is also a model colleague. He has taught me a great deal as a teacher and scholar, and at the poker table as well. I thank him for his support these many years in more ways than I probably know. I have long admired Sarah Wohlford, who is incisive, thoughtful, and brilliant. She brings a little mountain range to Michigan.

At Michigan State University I am especially grateful to friends and colleagues Robin Silbergleid, Divya Victor, Zarena Aslami, Tamar Boyadjian, and Leonora Paula for their intellect and compassion. My colleagues in Italian and in theater and performance studies have been wonderful collaborators and generous readers of my work. Thank you, Carmen De Lorenzo, Valentina Denzel, Jennifer Toby, Jyotsna Singh, Ann Larabee, Dan Smith, and Ann Folino White. I also wish to thank Steve Arch, David Stowe, Cara Cilano, Marshall Olds, Helene Weldt-Basson, Doug Noverr (in memoriam), Rocio Quispe-Agnoli, and Tony Grubbs, for their support as chairs over the years. I would like to acknowledge the many other colleagues who are special to me: Yelena Kalinsky, Coco Logan, Ellen McCallum, Jeff Wray, Tama Hamilton Wray, Judith Stoddart, Josh Lam, Swarnavel Pillai, Bill Vincent, Yomaira Figueroa, Kaveh Askari, Kristin Mahoney, Sheila Contreras, Salah Hassan, Marcia Aldrich, Ken Harrow, Danny Méndez, Scott Boehm, Andaluna Borcila, Anna Pegler-Gordon, Senta Goertler, Lily Woodruff, and Stephanie Nawyn. I have learned much from Jennifer Mojica Santana and appreciate her help in the final hours of this project. From my life in Ann Arbor at the University of Michigan, a special thanks to Peggy McCracken, Ken Garner, Larry La Fountain-Stokes, EJ Westlake, Alison Cornish, Glenda Dickerson (in memoriam), and Christi Merrill. Friends and colleagues at other universities with whom I have collaborated on related projects or who have kindly offered feedback on various drafts of these pages and to whom I offer my gratitude include Ombretta Frau, Elena Past, Gerardo Guccini, Paolo Puppa, Stacy Wolf, Charlotte McIvor, and Andrew Sofer. A number of friends from other walks have also seen me through this project's many forms and other related vicissitudes: Amélie Baudot, Lesley and Mike McWilliams,

Pam Ostrager (in memoriam), Letizia Randaccio (in memoriam), Tova Shaban, Bob Burgoyne, Chris Lamonte, Alan Heller, Carole André Smith, Peace Sullivan, Will Cullinan, and my fellow Eastcheap Rep thespians Molly Kidder, Luke Rosen, Sally Jackson, Chris Chaberski, Pete Chenot, Phil Easley, and Kelly O'Day. Turin would not be my Italian home without Monica Spinella, Katia Gravili, Luisa Gori, Guido Marcodini, Debora Perretti, Luciana Regina, Patrizia Prinzivalli, la famiglia Cigagna, Enrico Guglielminetti, Barbara Gugliuzza, Lorenzo Rogna, Roberta De Martini, Costanza "Connie" Carena, Giaime Alonge, and my best theatergoing partner, friend, and colleague, Federica Mazzocchi.

Finally, this book would not exist without its protagonists. I have benefited personally and professionally from the narrators whose projects inspired these pages. It has been an honor to spend over a decade discovering and rediscovering their important work, and I am ever grateful for the time that many of them took to welcome me for interviews and conversation before or after countless shows, into their homes to sift through their archives, and in continued correspondence. I met Laura Curino by chance after the director Alessandro d'Alatri casually gave me her phone number when we were chatting at an Italian conference at Yale University in 2007. He had just directed her in a play. When I called her out of the blue two months later since we just happened to coincide on a visit in Milan, she welcomed me to a workshop, after which we talked for more than four hours over *negroni sbagliati* and maybe a few Gauloises. (The rest, of course, is history.) One day her personal archive will be part of the special collections at an important library. I am honored to be the first scholar to have sorted through those many materials. Thank you, Laura, and Federico Negro, for your warmth and generosity, your friendship, and your faith in my work. Giuliana Musso has been especially gracious, and I thank her for her friendship and trust in my work as well. I am also grateful to Marco Baliani, Ascanio Celestini, Lella Costa, Mariella Fabbris, and Saverio La Ruina for our meaningful meetings. Thank you, finally, to Davide Enia, Gabriele Vacis, and Marco Paolini.

There are a number of institutions that have supported the work that resulted in this book and I am grateful for their structures, and to the members of the committees who allowed me to benefit from them. During graduate school, the US Fulbright Scholar Program supported the research that kick-started this project for a year in Italy. The Mellon Summer School for Theater and Performance Research at Harvard University helped me work through some of my theoretical arguments. I am grateful for the research culture at my home institution, Michigan State University. Both the Summer Faculty Fellowship awarded by the College of Arts and Letters, and especially my junior research leave, brought me back to Italy, where I completed the research for this manuscript, and provided valuable writing time. I am especially grateful to the Consul of Italy in Detroit, Maria Manca, and my friend and colleague Pierluigi Erbaggio for helping us make these trips possible. As a graduate student at the University of Michigan, Ann Arbor, I had many generous funding opportunities for what was eventually the important preliminary research for this work through the Center for World Performance Studies, the Rackham Graduate Student Research Award, the Center for European Studies Research Award, the International Institute Research Award and as a fellow at the Public Humanities Institute. I would also like to recognize the American Association for Italian Studies and the American Society for Theatre Research, where I have found inspiration and collegiality and where I first worked through many aspects of this project. Finally, I thank Northwestern University Press. Gianna Mosser first encouraged this project, and later Patrick Samuel, Maia Rigas, Anne Tappan Strother, and especially Trevor Perri walked me through the process with generosity and patience. I am grateful for the smart suggestions and close reading by Christi Stanforth during the project's copyediting stage. The two anonymous reviewers were encouraging and supportive, while also offering thoughtful ways to make this book better: thank you, especially.

Our lives seem small, and in many ways they are. There is nothing like writing the acknowledgments to your first book to make you realize, with awe and humility, that there are so many chance encounters, fortuitous circumstances, and people whose lives intersect with yours and nudge along new experiences and perceptions. Together our narratives tell their own history. May we remember to listen.

For the section "Teatro Settimo's Lingering Influence: Celestini's *Radio clandestina* (2000)" in chapter 1, I have revised portions from Juliet Guzzetta, "Ethical Considerations in Ascanio Celestini's *Radio clandestina*," in *La riflessione etica nel teatro italiano contemporaneo*, ed. Cristina Perissinotto and Patrizia Piredda (Naples: Guida Editori, 2019), 233–57. In the section "Multiple Media Performance in *Santa Bàrbera*" in chapter 5, I have revised Juliet Guzzetta, "A Voice of Her Own: Feminism and Subjectivities for a Modern Santa Bàrbera," in *A Window on the Italian Female Modernist Subjectivity: From Neera to Laura Curino*, ed. Rossella M. Riccobono (Newcastle, UK: Cambridge Scholars, 2013), 187–201.

The Theater of Narration

Introduction

✦

The Past and the Players

In Italian, *storia* is the word for both "history" and "story," emphasizing the narrative foundations of history. Amid the rich artistic and intellectual potential in this overlap, the contemporary Italian theater practice known as *teatro di narrazione*, or the theater of narration, delivers a method of historical recuperation that hinges on this nuance. Narrators, so named to distinguish themselves from actors, demonstrate how telling a story can perform an act of history making. They revisit historical events of national importance from local perspectives, emphasizing the ways in which ordinary people can exert substantial influence on the legacies of the past. The method's potency lies not only in its ability to render meaningful the great and tragic histories of Italy on an intimate scale, but also in its pedagogical stance, which demonstrates how personal histories shape the collective past. The practice conveys this by playing on the dialogic dimension of storytelling, suggesting that audience members in the present are already in constant dialogue with public figures and events that personally affected them. Together, through this multitude of voices, they have the agency to shape what becomes history.

Laura Curino, one of the pioneering narrators, opens her exceptionally successful play *Camillo Olivetti: Alle radici di un sogno* (*At the Roots of a Dream*, performed in repertory since 1996) by declaring, "This work is dedicated to Adriano Olivetti."[1] Her insistence on the word "work," she explains, stems from a memory of her parents, when, in their native Piedmontese dialect, they complimented a performer by noting that he *worked* well, rather than commenting that he *acted* well. Their remark, she continues, helped her to recognize a connection between art and work, which is a dominant theme in the play as well as a reflexive statement regarding her own art and work. Maintaining this duality, she explains that the play concerns two dreams. The first is the dream of Camillo Olivetti, founder of the company that engineered typewriters, a company that he and later his son Adriano would grow into an industry that not only invented the laptop of yore but also sustained a worker-centric ethos with employee benefits beyond the imagination of any Fortune 500 today.[2] Her other dream, she adds, was typical for children of Fiat factory laborers like herself: they wished that their fathers worked for Olivetti.

One of the major theater of narration pieces, Curino's *Camillo Olivetti* deploys several key characteristics of the practice even in those opening minutes. Without making any bold political claims, Curino invites her audience to reflect on the idea of work, which she will explore throughout the entire play as she recounts the early days of the celebrated Olivetti family. She also stakes her personal investment when she shares the memory from her childhood and will continue to use autobiography at different points, creating an intimacy with her audience and setting her positionality in relation to the main topic. Even though he was eventually a national hero for Italian industry, Camillo (and Adriano) Olivetti came from the Alps in the Northwest near Turin and near to where Curino has spent her entire life. She situates herself as the best person to tell his story because she is an insider. Relatedly, she emphasizes the regionalism of this national figure, even translating the Piedmontese into standard Italian for her audience. Finally, she references a specific community, that of Italian factory workers, of which she can also speak intimately as the daughter of a Fiat worker. While every narrator has a personal aesthetic, most of their stories contain all of these elements in varying degrees: political engagement with a topic or figure of national importance; elements of autobiography; and a focus on a specific community such as factory workers, students, the mentally ill, the women of a small southern town, midwives, and many more.

Developing from the work of Laboratorio Teatro Settimo, a theater collective in Italy's industrial North just outside Turin that began in 1974 with Curino a founding member, the theater of narration eventually veered away from the group work and visual stimuli of Teatro Settimo toward solo performances and a minimalist aesthetic. In its pluralistic breadth, the theater of narration frequently juxtaposes the frenetic noise of the many with the single presence of one person onstage. Narrators both write and perform their shows, often inhabiting multiple points of view through a variety of characters, while at the same time portraying themselves as more neutral storytellers. With the first solo shows appearing in 1987, it was another decade before the theater of narration rose to critical and popular acclaim when Marco Paolini's *Il racconto del Vajont* (*The Story of Vajont*, recounting the 1963 disaster at the Vajont dam) was televised nationally in 1997.[3] After nearly four previous years of performances on Italian stages and in public and private spaces across the country, the success of *Vajont* televised inaugurated an additional mode of exhibition for the narrators in which their work could reach millions. The practice has only continued to grow in popularity, challenging the boundaries of the solo performance genre and the oratorical gesture with performances from rural playhouses to major theaters across Italy and a sustained presence on Italian national television.

One reason it is important to recognize Teatro Settimo's early work as the fertile ground from which many of the most powerful narrative theater pieces grew is its link to the 1970s. This was a painfully violent and fraught period in Italy's past. It was a long decade of letdowns, but also one of major social, intellectual, artistic, and legal achievements. As will become evident, one main attribute of the theater of narration is the way narrators build on Italian intellectual currents of the 1970s, both intentionally and not, including their attention to minor authors, microhistories, and subaltern narratives. By combining historical methods with performance practices that also seek to reinvigorate political awareness and a renewed sense of community, narrators demonstrate how historical ideologies operate across systems of discourse and artistic expression. Understanding the theater of narration through 1970s culture establishes the extent to which this performance practice works to bridge collective and personal histories. Narrators often guide their audiences along this journey in the context of their lived experiences.

For sake of clarity, critics began categorizing narrators into two generations. Marco Baliani (born 1950, Piedmont, but moved as a young boy to the outskirts of Rome), Lella Costa (born 1952, Milan), Laura Curino (born 1956, Turin), and Marco Paolini (born 1956 Belluno, Veneto) are some of the founding "first-generation" narrators, while Ascanio Celestini (born 1972, Rome), Davide Enia (born 1974, Palermo), Giuliana Musso (born 1970, Vicenza, though Udine since early adulthood), Mario Perrotta (born 1970, Lecce, Puglia), and Saverio La Ruina (born 1960, Castrovillari, Calabria) have ushered forth a "second generation." The visionary director Gabriele Vacis (born 1955, Settimo Torinese) who was also a founding member of Teatro Settimo, worked with several of these leading narrators on some of their most successful productions both in an editorial role and as director including with Costa, Curino, and Paolini. Notably, as a single group, they are geographically diverse, and have all performed across the country. In addition to their work as narrators, many also pursue more traditional actors' paths in films and television dramas and on the stage. Some have authored novels (Baliani, Celestini, and Enia) and have explored directing (Baliani and Musso), and many also continue to teach through formal affiliations or in workshops.

Much like historians and ethnographers, narrators frequently visit archives to research their topic, conduct interviews, reflect on their own life experiences, and, with all this material, devise their scripts and performance notes. In fact, as this study argues, narrators explicitly share several methodological approaches with Italian micro- and oral histories as they developed in the postwar era, including the preference for narrative structures, the uses of autobiography and ethnography, and the emphasis on the ordinary and every day in understanding the past. In putting these historical methodologies in conversation with the theater of narration, it becomes clear that narrators not only employ microhistorical techniques to develop their works, but they also perform the very practice of microhistory, insofar as they focus their projects on single individuals, specific aspects of historical events, and local topics. Their practice adds to the ways in which theatrical approaches both represent the past and urge audience members to reassess their own personal relationships to history's grand narratives. If the theater of the absurd pondered the existential failure of human communication, and the theater of cruelty reasserted the necessity of fuller sensory experiences, then the theater of narration entreats ordinary people to rewrite the annals of popular history through their own lived experience. Although the social, economic, and cultural order has transformed in Italy and globally since the 1970s, it is still crucial, and more critical than ever, that underprivileged groups reclaim their experiences by giving voice to them.

While the theater of narration is first and foremost a performance practice, this study examines a second and crucial role: theater of narration as historical praxis. Though previous investigations have framed the theater of narration as a mode of witnessing, contextualized it within postwar avant-garde theater, and interpreted it as an extension of the Italian tradition of the actor-author, no studies have given due process to the complex relationship that the genre shares with practices of history and historiography.[4] One of the more significant results of this historical framework is its far-reaching epistemological implications. Live performance privileges oral transmission of knowledge, but it can also signify the less certain *search* for knowledge (and not just its dissemination) through other means than the written word. While narrators often incorporate document-based archival work into their productions, they supplement those more traditional sources with oral accounts, their own memories, and even their imaginations. Rather than emphasizing the extent to which history is key to their art, this study reads creativity as an integral part of the historical process, encouraging a reconsideration of Western epistemology that relies so heavily on what performance scholar Diana Taylor has framed as the "writing = memory/knowledge equation."[5] Since the 1970s, narrators have drawn extensively on the vast range of subaltern materials that Taylor urges scholars and students of performance studies to include in their archive: everything from song and speech to nonverbal embodied expression. Their methodology then bridges techniques in both historical inquiry and performance studies in their very productions where they perform how, also, the theatrical = memory/knowledge.

In terms of style, the theater of narration avoids the techniques of traditional stage productions that employ elaborate costumes, set design, and character development. Though its most common incarnation is a one-person show, written and performed by the same person, occasionally there are musicians onstage, and in very rare circumstances there are other actors too, as in Laura Curino's second Olivetti play, *Adriano Olivetti: Il sogno possibile* (1988; *The Dream That Is Possible*). The topics of some of the best-known pieces include episodes from the Allied invasion of Sicily in 1943, the 1963 landslide at the Vajont Dam in northeastern Italy, the kidnapping and eventual assassination of Prime Minister Aldo Moro in 1978 on the same day that the Mafia murdered a young Sicilian named Giuseppe "Peppino" Impastato who spoke out against them, and the hardships of temporary workers on short contracts at a call center in suburban Rome circa 2005. No matter the topic, the narrator stands at a lectern or sits in a chair, looks directly into the audience, and tells a story.

To some extent, this theater was born out of political engagement, known in Italy as *impegno*: artists, intellectuals, and ordinary people worked to redefine what it meant to be political in a late twentieth-century world that had not yet emotionally recovered from an economically and politically tumultuous century of war and disaster. From the social uprisings of 1968 through the 1980 Bologna train station bombing (which killed eighty people), the long 1970s, in which impegno was perhaps at its strongest, influenced the first generation of narrators, who came of age in a climate of daily violence and struggles. This time marks the formative years for that first generation of narrators, who were born in the 1950s and thus finished high school, attended university, and began their professional lives in the 1970s. Although only a few plays deal directly with any actual events from the decade, the vast majority echo the urgency and influential thinking of that time. The impact of the 1970s, along with the methodological proximity to microhistory, distinguish this theater from other monologist performances and speak to a dormant yet humming contemporary political unrest in Italy, which began with the leadership of Silvio Berlusconi in 1994 and continued through the inauguration of the euro currency and its various financial and cultural anxieties in the 2000s, and continuing through the 2010s and 2020s with the rise of neoliberalism and populism.

In fact, one attribute that connects the many works within the theater of narration is the way in which narrators recast moments of violence and struggle in Italian history into much more dynamic and complex narratives rather than one-sided tragedies. Their critical method is not merely an ancillary detail, but central to the practice, and performative in its own way. In constructing national histories, narrators demonstrate that asking questions and exercising due diligence leads to a plurality of perspectives. In nearly every production, narrators question authority and interrogate why circumstances unfolded in the ways they did. They ask how people remember, whom they privilege, and why they favor certain perceptions, gently suggesting alternative readings and, ultimately, alternative ways of constructing history.

One of the main objectives of this book, then, is to explore how narrators "do" history: how they perform voices from the past, how they re-create events through those voices, and how they invite their audiences to join in their conversations through a dialogic practice of historical construction against the backdrop of everyday experiences. If to further historical understanding is to reconcile the past to the present, narrators can bridge that distance by shifting the terms from the macro perspective to the micro within a community of distinct voices. Through the accessibility, indeed familiarity, of ordinary people, including themselves, narrators challenge hegemonic notions of national memory and demonstrate how the complex dynamics of individual lives lead to multivalent experiences of the past.

The Formal and the Theoretical

In terms of its theatrical influences, as the next chapter explores in more depth, the theater of narration emerged from several key European traditions but was also influenced by American groups like the Living Theater and experimental forms of performance art, such as happenings. In the works of Dario Fo and Franca Rame, and particularly Jerzy Grotowski, narrators gravitated toward engagement with subaltern experience and subjectivity, as well as voicing collective history through individual performers, as Fo and Rame did. There are also traces of Bertolt Brecht's dialectic impulses toward an epic theater that aimed to educate as much as entertain, and especially his didactic early plays, the *Lehrstücke*. Despite these clear inspirations, some of which several leading narrators have publicly discussed, this theater is very much its own practice, and one that defies concise definitions. The theater of the poor, the theater of the oppressed, and even the theater of the absurd suggest political directions in their very names, yet the theater of narration, to both its benefit and detriment, refuses to declare a position. One distinguishing feature of the theater of narration is that it pivots between political activism and the desire to resist labels and a political system.

In addition to the sociopolitical climate and the artistic influences that contributed to the development of the theater of narration, an intellectual trend of the 1970s in Europe and the United States is perhaps what had the greatest impact on the practice. Fueled by studies such as Michel Foucault's macroanalyses across disparate disciplines and Lynn Hunt's work questioning how theory operates in historical practice, several areas from literature to anthropology and, above all, history saw shifts from the focus on the canonical to the unknown, from major voices to minor ones, paving the way for the New Historicism of the early 1980s pioneered by Stuart Hall and Stephen Greenblatt. To both counter and complement these developments, a concern with the minute evolved, establishing the practice of microhistory through the work of Natalie Zemon Davis, Emmanuel Le Roy Ladurie, and, especially important for the first generation of narrators, Carlo Ginzburg and Giovanni Levi.[6] Assigning value to the common voices of the past echoes throughout the theater of narration in the little-known protagonists of its plays, and in the metonymic focus on smaller moments within great events. Microhistory also privileges the story and an acute awareness of the researcher's subjectivities, other characteristics that transferred to narrative theater. The techniques of these historians often involve the kind of expansive research for which Taylor advocates by including the repertoire, which the narrators also employ.

Unlike Fo and Rame, who very much rooted their theater in the present, the theater of narration occupies a more reflective space in which narrators gravitate toward traumatic past events and reframe those through the eyes of the ordinary people who lived trauma as part of their daily experience. Questions of war (World Wars I and II and, more recently, the war in Afghanistan) and how to process its tragedies surfaces in a number of plays. Themes of class struggle are also present in most productions either overtly or subtly, with narrators giving voice to the working poor and middle classes. Narrators have also confronted trauma from domestic terror—including marital abuse and organized crime, especially by extraparliamentary groups during the 1970s—as a large-scale problem. By choosing to confront these specific major events, the theater of narration reveals how they still haunt the public at large.

As much as the topics of the plays provide insight into what troubles the Italian psyche, the absence of other topics points to areas that are either of lesser concern to the main narrators or Italians generally, or perhaps too controversial—indeed, too present—to address in a style that is more pensive than polemical. Though narrators revise the dominant historical narratives in more inclusive and complex ways, at times the practice can feel too attracted to the past when there are such important current sociocultural issues and the analogy to those present crises is not as clear as it could be. Addressing a larger variety of populations with more frequency would richly diversify the people whom the narrators represent. For example, awareness of women's plights occasionally surfaces in plays that address childbirth, sex work, and abortion—but not with anything like the candor in Franca Rame's plays and performances. Further, narrators rarely incorporate women's issues into the larger narratives of war and class that are central to so many productions. Given the powerful work of feminists in Italy, particularly from the postwar period to the present, both in practical legal advancements and in widely praised theoretical arguments, representation of women's stories is urgent.

There is also a dire need for Italian stages to address the country's history of colonialism and relatedly, though more crucially, the present migration crisis, including the fear and racism that has accompanied the many migrants who have found their way into Europe through Italy via treacherous journeys. Film and literature have far more examples of works that depict migrant struggles, and, even better, of works that create a space where migrants to Italy themselves tell their own stories of past and present.[7] By contrast, Italian theater lags far behind, though the theater of narration, with its didactic intimate style, and its emphasis on peripheral voices, would be an especially suitable form to reflect on both Italian colonialist history and what it means today to be a person of color in Italy. A handful of more recent narrative theater projects confront migration, race, and racism, though most are still shy in attempting the type of direct analysis with which the theater of narration typically operates.

Finally, for such an unspectacular style, the genre has been surprisingly successful across all of Italy—from Palermo to Turin, Rome to Venice—where the most celebrated narrators have presented their works on urban stages as well as in the small-town squares of many rural centers. Some of their success is due to the ways that they have disseminated their practice beyond the stage through other modes of distribution. Many works are also adapted into published scripts that sell with DVDs and are widely distributed by major publishing houses such as Einaudi. Some pieces are nationally televised, and there are also instances in which major weeklies such as *L'Espresso* have sold series of the theater of narration DVDs over several months in their (slightly pricier) papers.[8] There is also a cultural element at work in their success as municipalities pay for summer theater festivals in town squares, mountain refuges, abandoned industrial structures, and city parks and as narrators take part in these local efforts where people who are not necessarily theater aficionados will pass a summer evening acquainting themselves with the practice. The lack of expense and ease in mounting productions makes it particularly attractive, and though it requires great skill, both writing and performing offer precious freedoms. With its continued and increasing presence on Italian stages by a growing number of artists who are taking the form in new directions, the theater of narration is proving to be a long-standing and prominent form of expression.

Examining how *storia* functions as a critical concept within the theater of narration is fundamental to appreciating the breadth of the art form. While the performance practice might not be an obvious interlocutor with the discipline of history, understanding its engagement with history reveals its core objectives. This study considers "history" in the way that Michel de Certeau refers to it, "in the sense of 'historiography.' " Certeau's understanding of history emphasizes its intrinsic qualities of performance that align with his definition. As he puts it, "By 'history' I mean a practice (a discipline), its results (a discourse), and the relation between them."[9] The idea of exchange that takes place in this definition is of particular interest to this project as it relates generally to the notion of performance, and specifically to the mechanisms at work in the theater of narration.

In the general sense, Certeau is quick to define practice as a discipline, which suggests something static and demarcated, yet the term "a practice" also connotes an actor at work (the historian) practicing a craft (history), or "doing" history in the parlance of performance scholar Richard Schechner, who has famously described performing as "doing," which he defines as "the activity of all that exists."[10] In Schechner's view, what moves any particular activity into a realm of performance, as opposed to "just doing," is when some thing or being *shows* doing by "pointing to, underlining, and displaying doing."[11] Specific to the theater of narration, the performative aspect of the practice, or the way in which narrators highlight what they are doing (and what they are doing is historical inquiry), relates to Certeau's definition of the results of a practice as a discourse. For narrators "showing doing," or performing the histories that they revisit, takes the form of oratorical dialogic discourse. This presentation of dialogue as a form of historical exploration and recuperation is a key attribute of the theater of narration.

The general framework of the theater already emphasizes the idea of exchange between the performer and audience. What is striking about this dynamic in the theater of narration is that narrators themselves embody the basic theatrical exchange that takes place between the person onstage and in the audience by performing in the solo mode while they also perform acts of dialogue. In the tension they bring as solo artists inhabiting other voices, they demonstrate how dialogue, indeed the exchange of ideas and positions between people, can lead to new ways of experiencing the past, a greater understanding of one's proximity to the past, and the ability to shape stories of the past. Through the act of dialogue, and particularly the act of dialoguing with the past, the theater of narration also offers its audiences a new relationship to the present that is rooted in community and being in the presence of others.

As with performance, the making of history is an act in the present, since it also includes making sense of history, even while the subject is located in the past. While the interdependence of past and present is a recurring theme in Certeau's writing on history, it is also relevant in the theater of narration. For Certeau, "historiography is always about the present and always takes place in the present. So, just as the past is excluded from and returns to haunt the present, the present returns to haunt writing about the past."[12] This rapport with time reverberates with the dialogic element that is so integral to narrative theater's ability to stage the complex relationship between history making and the present. This temporal interplay between time present and time past is also dialogic, like the relationship between narrators, their audiences, and the past voices that narrators evoke. Such conversation creates a rich and heterogeneous tapestry, which depicts past and present in ever-changing concert with each other. As with any other theatrical performance, the experience of history is ephemeral, yet ongoing.

On the most meta level, the relationship between the practice and its results, the last part of Certeau's definition of historiography, emerges in the pedagogical positioning within the theater of narration and shares some similarities with how Schechner articulates the objective of performance studies as "explaining 'showing doing'" or explaining a performance.[13] Narrators make historical discoveries through both traditional means (the archive) as well as through more imaginative or "ephemeral" means (in the words of Diana Taylor) when they connect their documentary findings with anecdotes from oral accounts or their own memories, and then when they share these historical findings in performance (and text, in many cases, when they publish a script). During their performances they often perform this process. When they incorporate themselves into the narrative, they demonstrate the subjective renderings of history. From this position, they show how an imagined history pairs with documented history. As they stage different voices, they offer both a revised history, as well as a primer for the audience to continue these exercises in historical revision in their own lives. Insofar as they model their techniques (the combination of documentary and imagined history; the incorporation of oneself in that history; the inclusion of different perspectives), their performances are pedagogical because they share with audiences how they can also do what they are witnessing onstage, echoing Schechner's designation of "explaining 'showing doing.' "

Like other art forms that engage history, the theater of narration constantly negotiates the relationship between evidence and imagination. When narrators embellish a sequence with poetic detail, they construct a communal memory based on common experience. While these "partial truths" and "hybrid" sequences allow narrators to enhance continuity and tone, they especially serve to demonstrate the importance of one's own history in collective histories by way of identification and imagination.[14] In stitching together a shared history with renderings that are familiar and general though specific in the context, they dramatize the overlapping spaces between history and narrative, private and public experience. Giuliana Musso, for example, emphasizes the exhaustion of the early twentieth-century midwife working through the night by adding her journey peddling up and through the muddy hills of Friuli to the laboring woman. This early description sets up the character as tenacious, determined, creative, and smart, with her own upward journey into the night mirroring the audience at the beginning of their journey into the play. Musso ends the narrative with the midwife once again on her bike, now gliding down the hills peacefully toward rest in a satisfying denouement.[15] These details, clearly imagined yet relatable in their physicality and their mental states, perform that connection between history and narrative, layered in the Italian *storia*.

Filling in the narratives that emerge from the archives with imagined detail also entails acknowledging the deficits inherent in whose voice the archive has preserved. Paolini references his own awareness of silencing at the beginning of *Vajont* when he shares how the dominant account of the landslide that focused on tragedy motivated him to conduct his own inspection on what caused the disaster. In this awareness there is a methodological connection to the work conducted by historians of slavery such as Michel-Rolph Trouillot and Marisa Fuentes who investigated the relationship of historiography to power within the historical narrative that centered archival research. Trouillot cautions that the archives are structures of power, and when they are the sole building blocks that compose history, the result is a dangerous one-dimensional narrative. By examining fragments of archival evidence, Fuentes shows how the archives actively refuse to reveal details of specific individuals such as enslaved women in Barbados.[16] By centering the silences and distortions that surround the dispossessed lives of slaves, Trouillot and Fuentes point to the need for more expansive approaches to historical recuperation. In its most activist impulses, which have compelled critics to sometimes refer to the theater of narration as civic theater (*teatro civile*), particularly in the cases of Paolini and Celestini, the practice is reaching toward an awareness of these macro power dynamics writ large.

The well-known connections that Certeau has made between history and fiction and that Hayden White further developed also consider notions of truth and reality in other ways. Like Trouillot, White argued that if historians relied on the documentary record to design the past, then a superficial version of "reality" would emerge, but he offers the hypothetical as a space of promise. If historians were to add to the "actuality" a consideration of what "could possibly be," then "the rest of the real" might begin to take shape: "Something like this may have been what Aristotle had in mind when, instead of opposing history to poetry, he suggested their complementarity, joining both of them to philosophy in the human effort to represent, imagine and think the world in its totality, both actual and possible, both real and imagined, both known and only experienced."[17] As narrators contemplate the role of the imagination, mixed with the subjectivity of one's own experiences, and the objective to empower silenced voices, they broach a history of what was possible, a hypothetical history. This history of dreams may never have come to fruition, but it is re-presented to the audience as a way forward for them if they endeavor to rewrite histories from more perspectives, including the difficult task of negotiating one's own.

Finally, one of the most exciting aspects of the theater of narration is its implicit argument for the necessity of physical presence in the production of historical accounts, nodding toward embodiment as a means of conducting history. Both Diana Taylor and Rebecca Schneider have written highly influential works exploring the corporeal presence that the stage (or other sites of performance) demands. The playing space becomes its own library, and those within that space have the ability to disseminate information through a powerful embodied language. In problematizing the document-centric traditional view of the archive, Schneider posits considering the body, not the library stacks, as the keeper of historical insight. For her, in performance, "the place of residue is arguably *flesh* in a network of body-to-body transmission of affect and enactment—evidence, across generations, of impact."[18] When narrators recall specific historical acts, these affective remains embark on a "body-to-body" transmission from the narrator to the audience member, inviting a simultaneous rather than chronological experience.[19]

One aspect of the emphasis on embodied practices that is relatively unique to the theater of narration is the prominence of dialogue as a method of historical inquiry. The narrators employ multiple dialogic interactions: between themselves and the audience; between the characters that they portray; and among the methods of historical analysis such as the archival document met with the imagined scenario. This idea invokes the incredible potency of the body as both enactor and subject acted on, which Saidiya V. Hartman explores in her study on slavery.[20] While these accounts focus on trauma, the residue of that trauma bares affective remnants, which eventually take the place of the bodily trauma altogether. The narrators, in the flesh, before their audiences, with their own lived experiences surfacing in various ways and crafting complex discourses of historical recuperation, are also rallying for performance as a productive mode of knowledge-making.

While White and Certeau primarily allude to fiction prose when they invoke the relationship between narrative and historiography, and while other historians have furthered their provocations, live performance offers distinctive benefits.[21] In the specific context of the Shoah and the failures of the French Revolution, Freddie Rokem underlines the theater's unique ability to create a site of powerful confrontation in a safe place that is contained both spatially (by the site of the performance) and temporally (by its length): "What may be seen as specific to the theatre in dealing directly with the historical past is its ability to create an awareness of the complex interaction between the destructiveness and the failures of history, on the one hand, and the efforts to create a viable and meaningful work of art, trying to confront these painful failures, on the other."[22] He continues to explain that what is at work in these productions is "the restorative potential of the theatre," which opens up the possibility of counteracting some of the harm and pain of the past. Another part of this journey to the past in the theater of narration is the demonstration that one can counteract history not only in a theater, with its ritualistic and creative powers, but elsewhere as well: such an ability is within everyone in the stories they share and the perspectives they bring. The health of history and the diversification of the historical record depends on the public's courage and ability to create history together.

The Long 1970s: 1968–80

Lead is an attractive bluish-silver metal when freshly cut. Only when exposed to air does it turn into the dull gun-metal gray for which it is more widely known. While the dominant view of the 1970s in Italy is notoriously tarnished with bullets and blood, constantly reinforced with the moniker "the years of lead," a more varied perspective has increasingly begun to emerge in cultural representations.[23] This historical context is vital to understanding the nuances of the theater of narration; in return, the act of contextualizing the practice within this decade contributes to a much-needed nuanced reading of the period. The long 1970s was a tumultuous decade that did indeed witness much violence but also saw meaningful social progress. It would be impossible and even unethical to disregard the physical and psychological terror of the period, but one aim of this project, in addition to acknowledging that terror, is to demonstrate how the long decade also saw positive social changes and cultural initiatives, including the theater of narration itself. In that regard, this study performs its own dialogue with the long 1970s in the hopes of recasting it in a more complex and nuanced light than its infamous label affords.

One could argue that the long 1970s began as early as 1966, when students in the small northwestern town of Trento organized to occupy the university.[24] Their efforts were successful. Beyond the administration meeting the students' demands, the greater payoff for the students was the realization that they had power and influence over institutions. Student uprisings and university occupations continued throughout 1966 and 1967, notably in Turin, Milan, and Rome. On March 1, 1968, the famous Battle of Valle Giulia in Rome symbolized the high point of student protests, sparking numerous solidarity actions on campuses around the country. On that late winter day, near the Spanish Steps, close to four thousand people gathered to take over the Architecture School of the University of Rome in the large Villa Borghese park when they were met by heavily armed police. The students fought back. The sheer number of individuals involved and the level of violence during this event signals the beginning of the long 1970s. From that moment, a plethora of social groups across all party lines, from the extreme Left to the Right, both official and extraparliamentary, protested and fought for various causes, from the legal right to divorce and abortion care to employment protections.[25]

The reason for most of the student protests across the country at that time, including at Valle Giulia, was the so-called Gui bill (named after minister of education Luigi Gui) then under review in Parliament, which would have imposed various limits and restrictions on degree programs. Students were also reacting to the controlling nature of government and growing bureaucracy. At Valle Giulia, what marks the event's place at the beginning of the long 1970s is not just its violence but also its symbolic importance as "a kind of collective initiation in conflict with the state."[26] When actual change was slow to come despite the extent to which students had managed to cripple the higher education system across Italy, paving the way for what they had hoped was a clean slate, they slowly began to form alliances with other social groups, including union workers and political organizations. Thus, when the workers revolted across the North in the "Hot Autumn" (as the period came to be known) of 1969, students were there in solidarity. Similar to students, workers were not only interested in material improvements on their lives such as better pay and fewer working hours; they also had ideological grievances that challenged the organization of labor and authoritative systems within factories.[27]

The other bookend of the decade is August 2, 1980, when a bomb exploded at the Bologna train station. At the time it was the deadliest attack in postwar Western Europe, killing eighty-five people and injuring more than two hundred. Although following judicial rulings it is widely believed that members of Far Right neofascist groups were responsible, there were several false leads and controversies, including guilty judgments later reversed, only to be reinstated. The stuttering hesitancy to the investigation left space for doubt (or denial) of whom the perpetrators actually were, which continues to haunt the episode.[28] While the years between the Battle of Valle Giulia and the Bologna Massacre are marked with brutal acts of violence and terrorism, there were also peaceful protests, new laws that aimed to improve human rights, the formation of collectives, the proliferation of public art, and the blossoming of small-print magazines. All of this confusion and creativity, violence and triumphs for social justice constituted the formative years of the first generation of narrators and still surfaces in a number of ways in productions of the second.

The enduring relevance of the 1970s in other cultural productions demonstrates the mystery in which this period continues to remain shrouded, as well as its psychic proximity to the present.[29] Many of these artistic renderings reference two major efforts known as the "strategy of tension" and the "historic compromise" that have assumed their own mythological status, wrapped in and out of conspiracy theories, betrayals, and secrecy.[30] Given the classical melodramatic potential of these themes, it might seem challenging to sift through to a more realist perspective. Further complicating such an attempt is the political climate that unfolded in the dawn of the new millennium. Several literary critics and cultural historians, including Marco Belpoliti, Enrico Palandri, Ruth Glynn, and Adalgisa Giorgio, argue that much perspective on the 1970s is contaminated by the political situation wrought by the center-right government of Silvio Berlusconi (prime minister of Italy from 1994 to 1995, 2001 to 2006, and 2008 to 2011). The same can be said for the center-right and hard-right populist parties, in particular the Lega Nord, that gained momentum during the 2010s, largely riding a wave of anti-immigration sentiments, and entered the 2020s in a politically strong position. Given the resulting tension and anxiety, it is especially challenging to analyze the long 1970s in a way that envisions the period cohesively.[31] Despite this, and maybe also because of it, the ongoing desire among intellectuals and artists to better comprehend those years reveals itself not just in artistic productions but also through a wide range of histories and memoirs, many by people formerly on the frontlines of violent protests. All of these projects, including the plays in the theater of narration that are directly and indirectly in conversation with the long 1970s, demonstrate a wide-ranging attempt to memorialize individual experiences, investigate the motivations behind the era's violence, and, in particular, to create a lucid narrative of this variegated past.

Given the confusion, obfuscation, violence, and social progress both during and surrounding the long 1970s, the very act of confronting that time reveals some of the political nuances in the theater of narration. By the 1990s, when the theater of narration grew exponentially, the overt politics of Fo and Rame and the protest energy of the 1970s was no longer a viable method to rouse a populace. This was a decade in which the degradation of certain populations, especially women, and the propaganda of complacency and distraction (a situation certainly not unique to Italy) wrought by Berlusconi's reign was commonplace.[32] This single individual controlled six out of seven national television channels—as private owner of three and as head of the government, which also owned three—in addition to privately owning major publishing houses such as Mondadori. In the words of the author and critic Enrico Palandri, Italians have been brainwashed by a "cheerful violence" in which "junk shows" outshine accounts of the current political climate, rife with xenophobia and other exclusionary practices. Ordinary people face a propaganda barrage when they attempt to examine the present honestly, let alone the past.[33] The theater of narration found its path out of the tumult of the 1970s, cutting through the temptation to look away from all the social issues that it brought to the foreground. The introspective, reflective, and inviting tone of the theater of narration, as opposed to directly proselytizing, was a way through the prejudices of Berlusconi's and later the Lega Nord's platforms. As those governments impose top-down assessments of what the country looks like and which policies it should pursue, the theater of narration combats not just their dominant vision but especially their dominant method of spoon-feeding the populace.

In other words, the theater of narration proposes a new way of feeling the past that includes questioning, critique, and agency in the creation of public histories. Baliani's *Corpo di stato* (1998; *Body of State*) is an excellent example of grappling with the very real terror that surrounded Italians on a national level during the 1970s while also showing how daily choices and everyday living experiences were in conversation with the larger crises during the period. By interweaving personal memories with the public event of Moro's kidnapping and assassination as well as the brutal murder of the anti-Mafia public citizen Peppino Impastato, Baliani forefronts his own place as a youth during those years. Even when narrators do not directly evoke the long 1970s, their opposition to the complacency that followed it through their rigorous critical methods forever links them to it as a time in which civic engagement was more commonplace.

Narrators also conjure the 1970s by way of theme, such as Curino's Olivetti plays (debuting in 1996 and 1998, respectively) that contemplate factory work, entrepreneurship, and, allegorically, women's labor. There is no direct reference to the 1970s, yet the leitmotifs indelibly link the piece to that period. Similarly, Celestini's tragic *Pecora nera* (*Black Sheep*; 2005, that he turned into a film in which he stars, wrote, and directed in 2010), takes a fictional, and often comedic reckoning with Italy's mental health history. Celestini, narrating in the first person, recounts the story of an impoverished boy who is eventually locked away for thirty years in a state-run insane asylum where he is isolated, tied up, forced to take medication, and subjected to electroshock therapy. He reminisces ironically about the "fabulous 60s" when the boy came of age, but it was during the 1970s that the treatment of the mentally ill became a major human rights issue, largely thanks to the work of the psychiatrist Franco Basaglia. One of the most celebrated legal victories of the 1970s, and certainly one of the most positive changes to emerge from that decade, is the "180 Law" for mental health reform, which ordered the closing of all insane asylums for reasons of cruelty, paving the way for a community-oriented approach to mental illness.[34] Despite such progress, the questions of how society treats the mentally ill in the present, who sees them, and who listens to them, also haunt the project. Still, in revisiting the horror and the achievement, Celestini reminds his audience not only of the cause at hand but of a time that witnessed tangible action on the issue.

Finally, the intellectual practices that emerged as products of the political and cultural ferment of the long decade surface in the theater of narration. This last category marks the turn toward engagement with and criticism of minor authors, particularly the use of methodological alternatives such as microhistory, with influence from the Annales school and its notions of history "from below," bringing the theater of narration in conversation with historiography. While the Annales school was macrohistorical in its orientation, looking at long-term processes of historical change, the emergence of microhistory along with social history in the 1960s is related insofar as it was a reaction against its tendency to favor large institutional structures. Since the Annales scholars promoted replacing the study of leaders, politics, and wars with inquiries on the lives of ordinary people, agriculture, commerce, communication, and the like, it shares important common ground with the specific microhistory that emerged from the pages of the scholarly journal *Quaderni storici* (*Historical Notebooks*, first issued in 1966) through the work of its editors, including Carlo Ginzburg, Edvardo Grendi, Giovanni Levi, Edward Muir, and Guido Ruggiero. One valuable aspect of these practices is their interdisciplinary tendencies. Making connections across fields and reaching across boundaries characterizes this era and resonates in the theater of narration as narrators embrace storytelling with methods taken from ethnographic and historical disciplines.

The literary critic Marco Belpoliti offers a creative portrayal of the environment at the University of Bologna in the 1970s, demonstrating this turn toward the minor that the narrators absorbed. He connects the disciplines of literature, history, and sociology in his reading of the city's intellectual environment by analyzing the work of the Bolognese scholar Piero Camporesi, who himself focused on minor authors. In particular, he praises Camporesi's 1970 introduction to Pellegrino Artusi's 1891 *La scienza in cucina e l'arte di mangiar bene* (*The Science of Cooking and the Art of Eating Well*) not only for his sound argument that it represented a unifying text for the (then) new nation in terms of language as much as gastronomy, nor for the resurrection of this turn-of-the-century text from a minor author, but also because Belpoliti praises Camporesi's introduction for his ability to incorporate elements of the contemporary cultural climate. He believes that Camporesi was responding specifically to literary critic Alberto Asor Rosa's 1965 *Scrittori e popolo* (*The Writer and the People*) and, moreover, that he conjured something of the atmosphere of the late 1960s when students occupied the piazzas with their slogans and the buzz of their excitement and energy.[35]

Tantamount to how narrators make the past relevant in the present, Belpoliti creates a dialogic historiographical pattern synchronizing diachronic voices, while highlighting the importance of a minor author. In praising Camporesi's resourceful thinking to interpret a cookbook as an important text in the national/regional discourse of the postunification years in the late 1800s, and noting that at the same time Camporesi uses it to engage debates on the reconstruction of populism in literature that Asor Rosa had recently analyzed, Belpoliti initiates, or better yet continues, a dialogue. This dialectical process of placing a historical episode directly in conversation with an aspect of contemporary thought to reveal an entirely new idea that relates to both echoes in the theater of narration's own dialogic practices. Recognizing these overlapping techniques emphasizes the broad and inclusive breadth that the form attempts.

As a political and intellectual divergence from nineteenth-century historiography that promoted an exclusionary logic, it is no wonder that microhistory emerged the same year that students began occupying universities. Ginzburg describes the old model of history thus: "The affirmation of a national identity, the advent of the bourgeoisie, the civilizing mission of the white race, and economic development furnished a unifying principle to historians of both a conceptual and narrative order." Microhistory, overlapping with ethnography, broke away from this tradition by looking at subjects widely considered unimportant and themes that were previously ignored or dismissed as inferior. In doing so, historians concentrated on contradictions and pluralities of viewpoints. The atmosphere of the long 1970s is critical to this new way of thinking. As Levi explains, the unpredictability of sociopolitical events during those years, which rendered many revolutionary efforts inadequate, also led to "redefining concepts and profoundly analyzing existing tools and methods." In part, he adds, those changes grew out of Marxist tendencies, since the study of an ordinary person recognizes a certain freedom within oppressive and normative systems.[36]

The influence of microhistory on the theater of narration is fourfold: regard for narrative, the researcher's (or narrator's) involvement in the story, the so-called "method of clues," and the emphasis on marginalized people. The return of the narrative was widely discussed in history circles beginning with a much-cited article published in 1979 by historian Lawrence Stone, who attempted to trace these developments while also noting interdisciplinary influences, especially from anthropology.[37] As Belpoliti points out, both

Camporesi and Ginzburg took delight in the pleasures of narration, particularly in crafting their own voices via literary technique.[38] In reflecting on his oeuvre, Ginzburg himself recalls that he had taken great care in considering the relationship between research hypothesis and narrative strategies and that, for example, his best-known study, *Il formaggio e i vermi* (1976; *The Cheese and the Worms*), "does not restrict itself to the reconstruction of an individual event; it narrates it."[39] This is where microhistory overlaps with the postmodern theories of White and others, offering productive ways to consider the theater of narration. Ginzburg's use of the word "restrict" as the opposite of what narrating does suggests both flexibility and the hypothetical, for which White advocated since they were beyond the typical "reconstruction."

Archive, Ethnography, and Architecture

One of the main clues that led me to pursue the connection between the theater of narration and microhistory was in the personal archives of Laura Curino. As I sorted through many remnants of the early career of this artist and several others with whom she worked, some of whom would later also become key figures in the theater of narration (e.g., Marco Paolini and the director Gabriele Vacis), the extensive origins of the practice began to emerge. The records from her archives have been extremely meaningful for this project for a variety of reasons and have heretofore been unavailable for any researcher to review. Like Ginzburg, I am inclined to acknowledge my own subjectivities and biases in this study, which are a result of the friendship I developed with Curino, as well as my instincts to diversify this theater history by privileging the records of a female performer who is at the same time honored as a founder of the practice, while also sidelined for the many complex reasons related to her gender and the difficulty for Italian societies (as in others) to accept that a woman, a writer, an actor (and not the director) was just as and maybe even more influential to the success of the theater of narration as some of the leading men. Certainly, they too feature prominently in my study of the practice.

Over several years, as I maintained contact with Curino, I also began meeting with other leading narrators often more than once, including Marco Baliani, Ascanio Celestini, Lella Costa, Giuliana Musso, and Saverio La Ruina. Slowly I began to realize that the value in meeting these artists extended beyond hearing what they had to say about their projects. In the midst of my second meeting with Baliani, I became aware that my questions for him had less and less to do directly with his work and were much more geared toward his political beliefs and how they evolved over the years. When I began interviewing Musso, I started to notice that following the curves of our conversations I myself was sharing personal and private memories that I normally would not. What was happening during these meetings? As much as their research was ethnographic, so mine contained elements of ethnography.

It was after my interview with Celestini—whom I found almost indistinguishable from his onstage persona, although his onstage persona had previously seemed to me the most embellished of the narrators—that I had that "ah-ha" archives moment. His replies to my questions were the most narrative: he responded in long stories, and in the midst of one, I realized that I was interested not only in his answers but also in *how* he answered.[40] It had been that way all along. I was following where the artists took the conversation, and the connections they themselves were making to their work. I was observing their physical gestures, their delivery and word choice, and comparing the persona they presented to me one-on-one with the persona they presented onstage. I reflected on the anecdotes they offered as though I were reading certain pages in their journals, except that they rather than I chose what to share. Ultimately both Curino and Musso provided me with actual documents from their personal archives, but all of the narrators who met with me, I realized, were themselves their own archives. Ginzburg expresses concern about his subjectivity in the power dynamic as researcher eliminating documents and investigating others, but when the archive is also the source of inquiry, the research becomes a more egalitarian effort. Indeed, these meetings shaped the way I understand the theater of narration, but they also tell their own story about archival research.

The recent interest in "performing the archives" in which theater artists both incorporate findings and reproduce aspects of their actual archival visits in performance is indicative of the richly layered experience of archival research.[41] Tacking in a slightly different direction, the theater and performance scholar Elin Diamond analogizes performance to archival research, demonstrating the performances that researchers initiate as they encounter archival works, from the moment they walk into an archive dressed a certain way, to the near-bowing (the "unwonted curtsy") as they accept an offering from a librarian who places the materials in their hands, to the affective experience of excitement and awe, and perhaps disappointment too, as they begin reviewing the materials.[42] If a performance emerged from my archival experience of this project, then my role was as an ethnographer in the field. The repeated occasions to spend time together in diverse realms from mundane everyday experiences to the festive energy of postshow gatherings, along with the continued company and conversation, provided a window for me to understand the work of these artists from an intimate perspective. These moments mostly provided me with a hunch. They gave me an impression, and that impression then led me to pursue specific lines of inquiry.

As an example of how information passed between us, in one of Curino's most celebrated productions she tells the story of the typewriter engineers and cultural entrepreneurs Camillo Olivetti and his son Adriano Olivetti. She does so largely from the perspectives of Elvira Sacerdoti, the mother of

Camillo, and Luisa Revel, his wife, the mother of Adriano. One of the most important materials for her in writing these scripts was a collection of letters from Camillo and Adriano that both Sacerdoti and Revel had kept, offering Curino a direct account of their business as it was developing. These were preserved and bound into a limited number of copies by the Olivetti archive, and Adriano's daughter Laura gave one to Curino. As she and I sat in her library looking through the bound copy together, she matter-of-factly remarked, "But we have almost nothing about the lives of Sacerdoti and Revel." With a wry smile she added, "Because the men saved none of the letters that their mothers and wives wrote to them. It's the women who save the letters of men." This comment inspired me to reflect on gender more closely in these plays, which I eventually argued propose bold critiques of gender in the ways that Italians memorialize the Olivetti men.[43]

With this comment Curino also performed a gendered reading of archival practices. Why did she save the many materials that she did about her own work as well as that of her theater company Teatro Settimo, and why was I, a young American woman, the first person to sort through them after close to forty years of storage? Was saving those materials a political act, consciously or not, to create a record that could attest to her work as a woman in theater? Had she internalized a primary message that the genre she helped create preaches: small personal histories matter on national—and international—stages? She must have always had a hunch, and wanted to believe that her voice, and the work of the company she helped found, would hold a lasting relevance. And maybe the distance that someone from another country would bring, someone who nonetheless demonstrates a cultural competency in Italy, was appealing. She also might have wanted a woman to be the person who could begin to tell her story. Perhaps, with these kinds of comments, she encouraged in me a desire to tip the scales of Italian theater history to a more equitable balance in gender representation.

As I organized her archival materials by date into folders, they began to paint a picture of the intellectual origins of what would become the theater of narration. Similar to the historians Trouillot and Fuentes, the theater scholar Samuel Ravengai notes that "while the archive is a repository of survivals of the past, it also acts as a closet that erases or closes out other knowledges."[44] Curino's archive opened up some of the very few records of the Laboratorio Teatro Settimo, the theater company that she founded with other friends in their late teens and early twenties in 1974. Resulting from the analysis of these documents, this study privileges Teatro Settimo and its members as the prototype of the theater of narration more than any other theater company or individual. A number of these young artists, including others with whom they collaborated over the years, such as Marco Paolini, would go on to create the seminal pieces of the form, many working with director Gabriele Vacis, who was also a founding member of Teatro Settimo. The findings in Curino's private collection provide the framework and evidence for the arguments concerning Teatro Settimo in this study. For example, in an old cardboard box I discovered a 1981 document that offers the theoretical rationale for a performance and education project that Curino's company wanted to produce in their hometown outside Turin. In the document, the company defends the relevance of local history by citing works by Marc Bloch, Michel Foucault, Umberto Eco, Heinrich Böll, Jean Baudrillard, and especially Carlo Ginzburg, the center around whom the ideas of the others rotate. This is what sparked the idea for me to think more deeply about the relationship between history and the theater of narration.

The documents that Curino kept include publicity pamphlets from early projects, applications to local city council explaining some of the company's performance pieces intended for public spaces, mission statements wherein the group articulated their artistic goals, and references to other groups during the mid-1970s with whom they associated, all of which begins to re-create the incipient stages of the theater of narration and shed light on what it meant to be a young artist during the tumultuous period of the 1970s. Some of the earliest documents from 1974 that discuss public space show how the young students aimed to create not just a new community theater but, indeed, a new community. This is why the discovery of the company's early declarations and ruminations in Curino's private collection are so important. By considering them in tandem with my meetings with the most influential narrators, the origins and intricacies of the theater of narration become clear.

The paramount characteristics that define the theater of narration guide this study. Rather than a specific text or narrator as the main subject of each chapter, a key theme of the practice itself is the focus, while various narrators and productions help illustrate the tendencies of the genre. This type of organization is most suitable to exploring the broader implications within the theater of narration in part because the practice does not emerge from a linear tradition of performance history; rather, it intersects and overlaps with social movements, academic debates about narrative, and other styles within the performing arts. Therefore, an examination that intermingles and teases out the central features of the theater of narration reveals the complex nuances of the sophisticated conversation that the practice is endeavoring more than dividing chapters chronologically or by narrator would.

Close readings of specific plays that had their debuts between 1987 and 2009, most of which are still performed in repertory, serve as primary examples to support the main ideas in each chapter, as well as introductions to some of the seminal texts in the practice. This study also identifies and examines a number of plays that debuted as recently as 2018 in order to articulate new directions as the form continues to evolve. Several key attributes provide the framework for the chapters and demonstrate how certain formal features translate into theoretical provocations. The formal aspects of these performances also exist at the crossroads of several fundamental theoretical issues in performance studies broadly including the primacy of the text, the challenge of representation, the responsibility of the actor, new performance spaces, different ways of interacting with the audience, and the deconstruction of temporal, spatial, and ideological coordinates of performances.[45]

This study takes its examples primarily from the main narrators who founded the practice: those who first laid the roots in the late 1970s (Baliani, Costa, Curino, Paolini), and the highly successful and creative second-generation narrators who took it in new directions in the early 2000s (Celestini, Enia, La Ruina, Musso). Since the 2010s, with the theater of narration becoming more and more of a mainstream practice, there are more recent narrators who follow the genre's attributes and push them in different directions. Elvira Frosini and Daniele Timpano, who have worked together and individually, experiment with screens, technology, and web interaction (Timpano) and a dance-oriented style of physical performance (Frosini). Although they are not frequently present in these pages, they, and others, are what critics might one day refer to as a third generation who developed the form in new ways.

Besides the occasional cursory acknowledgment, most studies on the theater of narration neglect to mention Teatro Settimo, which began in Settimo Torinese, seven kilometers outside Turin, as the name attests, in 1974. An investigation of this group, which in one way or another connects to almost all the principal narrators who developed the practice, is essential. The first chapter begins with an analysis of the theatrical traditions within and outside Italy that influenced the theater of narration, bringing to light some of the ways in which narrators learned to engage in a variety of social issues through dramaturgical expression, but its heart lies at the foothills of the Alps surrounding Turin, with Teatro Settimo. The company produced shows that were aesthetically very unlike what would become narrative theater, with their larger casts, detailed costumes, and character portrayals. Nevertheless, the philosophy of the group, focusing on the stories of ordinary people, set the groundwork for the streamlined genre that many of the Teatro Settimo artists later developed.

Thanks to the willingness of narrators to spend time with me, and of Curino and Musso to share their personal archives, there are a number of new resources that shed light on this early period. Among those is evidence of how microhistory and ethnography influenced the themes and styles of Teatro Settimo's productions. The first chapter pays particular attention to the work of microhistorians Carlo Ginzburg and Giovanni Levi in relation to Teatro Settimo and the theater of narration, with additional inquiries into oral history. To that end, the works of Luisa Passerini and Alessandro Portelli demonstrated methodologies in how to research, record, and interpret private histories that are linked to large national or even international events like World War II, using tactics that became fundamental to the theater of narration, especially with the second-generation narrators. Ascanio Celestini's

Radio clandestina (*Clandestine Radio*, debuting in 2000 and continuing in Celestini's repertory of performances more than twenty years later) demonstrates this clearly, while various notes and reviews offer a glimpse into Teatro Settimo's earliest productions more closely aligned with microhistory.

Centering on the idea of a "culture laborer," the second chapter interrogates the concept of the narrator, arguing that the essence of the narrator is less that of an author-actor, which is skill-based, and more the artistic interpretation of a civil servant, which is ethos-based. Exploring the frequent incorporation of their own lives in the stories about local events of national importance, this chapter pursues the idea that rather than simply incorporating autobiography, narrators enact autoethnographies. They attempt a distanced critical position as they reflect on the relationship between their own individual lives and a major event opening many possibilities for their relationship to the audience. One of the main benefits of performing autoethnographies is that it creates a pathway for their dialogic historiography. In using themselves as examples, the narrators demonstrate for the audience the ways in which many voices, including their own, influence local and national memories.

The third chapter focuses on the language of the theater of narration. With the 1970s as a background, it begins with various politicized constituencies, such as students and workers, and how they mobilized and shifted language from the formality of public engagement to the accessibility of the private. As in other countries, this was the decade of "your body is a battleground," and the theater of narration's linguistic dexterity reflects the multidimensionality of numerous subjectivities. Orality—the comprehensive dimensions of verbal communication—is critical here. Through methods including the use of colloquial expressions, dialects, and physical language, narrators have tailored an orality that allows them to experiment with different registers of dialogue. Yet there is a fascinating tension in the malleability of orality in their work. In most instances in which narrative theater plays have been published, the text easily reads like prose. This chapter demonstrates that the ways in which narrators engage with the written word is another aspect of their dialogic privileging, since they use their published text as an additional mode of communication.

Even if the theater of narration's philosophy largely originated in Turin with Teatro Settimo, the geographic diversity of principal narrators since 2000 is notable. In addition to the Teatro Settimo members, narrators hail from the South, in Sicily (Enia), Calabria (La Ruina), and Puglia (Perrotta); to the central, via Rome (Celestini and Baliani); to the northeast, outside Venice (Musso, Paolini); and back to the northwest, but this time in Milan (Costa). The fourth and penultimate chapter focuses on issues of geographic territory and performance sites, which are fundamental to the theater of narration in their ability to underscore the local politics that inspired some of the earliest productions, as well as formulate broader notions of national identity through the retelling of local events. The venues in which narrators perform range from traditional proscenium stages to abandoned train stations and speak to questions of distinct locality and geographic variance. Turning again to the private archives that depict the work of Teatro Settimo, a variety of documents describe a deep awareness and concern with the public spaces of their hometown, Settimo Torinese. They depict a profound underlying rapport between location, community, and environment.

The fifth chapter examines how the genre interacts and experiments with other media, particularly screens. Since the national state-run television station RAI2 aired the live performance of *The Story of Vajont* on October 9, 1997, the thirty-fourth anniversary of the tragedy, narrators have consistently televised productions on national channels, aired shows on radio stations, and Ascanio Celestini has created two feature-length film productions for theatrical release based on previous narrative theater projects. Additionally, straying from its characteristic simplicity, several live productions have incorporated screens upstage that include images from historical events, or abstract visual graphics. This chapter addresses how these developments in exhibition alter or evolve the original texts.

In the conclusion I confront the link between the theater of narration's historical practice and its subtle politics. It contemplates popular trends in European and (the ever-influential) American politics, from Brexit in the UK and the rise of the Five Star Movement in Italy (begun by a comedian, Beppe Grillo) to the election of Donald Trump, exploring the tensions in giving voice to publics and the ways in which doing so can lead to brands of nationalism that are inconsistent with the magnanimous values inherent in the notion of democratic ideals. These considerations contemplate how an art form that embraces supplementing documentary evidence with oral histories and imaginative ones might be compromised in an era of fake news.

Through a combination of research, ethnography, and storytelling, the theater of narration reorients traditionally dominant perspectives of the Italian nation toward individual experiences and asks what these can reveal about the broader society. By embracing the practices of microhistory and oral history, and with a lingering political consciousness derived from the social conflicts of the 1970s, narrators produce an innovative kind of community-theater that also serves as a form of historical recuperation. They offer not just *another* perspective on past events, but an unending plurality of perspectives. At times professorial in their delivery, they suggest that every ordinary citizen has the agency and, indeed, the duty to construct national narratives by engaging in conversation. Through these acts of dialogue, beginning with oneself, the theater of narration demonstrates that the ordinary person is not simply a witness to history but a participant in its creation.

Chapter 1

✦

Origins of a Practice

With the magnificent Alps reigning in the near distance, the small town of Settimo Torinese was an industrial wasteland in the postwar period. Deprived even of its own name, it identified itself only as seven (*sette*) kilometers from Turin. With the rapid increase of factories around the Piedmont capital in the postwar years, many southerners flocked to the region for work. As Laura Curino documents in her 1987 *Passione*, the first full-length play in what would be called the theater of narration at a later day, her eventual hometown was built seemingly overnight to accommodate the infusion of laborers, including her father, who became a Fiat employee. When she and her parents moved from Turin in 1965, half the city had yet to be built, so in the meantime her school was in someone's home where the windows were closed at all times to stave off the dust and fumes from the nearby construction, the tire factory (Pirelli), the makeup factory (L'Oréal), and the coffee factory (Lavazza). The themes of work and industry would have a major influence on her life and would become the subject of several of the most renowned plays of the theater of narration, including her two-part series on the celebrated Olivetti family.

The creation of the theater company Laboratorio Teatro Settimo was an organic process of serendipity that involved a group of high school and university students who came to know each other through their mutual interest in theater and discovered a shared passion to confront and improve their environmental surroundings in the manufacturing cities of the North. Examining the work of this company as a foundation to the theater of narration is vital to understanding the heart of the practice for two related reasons. First, most of the prominent narrators from both the first and second generation either are among Teatro Settimo's founders, joined or worked with the company at some point, or studied with members of the company. Second, an analysis of the artistic and intellectual theories that the company members explored and upheld, the social issues that were important to them, the books and artists that inspired them, greatly clarifies and enriches how to understand the goals and accomplishments at the core of the theater of narration even as it has and continues to evolve.

A study of Teatro Settimo also offers a microhistory of the way that socially minded peaceful artists struggled to respond to and engage with the political atmosphere around them during the tumultuous 1970s. The mission statements, letters to cultural ministers, and working papers of Teatro Settimo from Curino's private archive that depict a burgeoning company at the dawn of its formation also reveal a commitment to civic engagement on a local level and a dedication to classical dramatic texts from the perspective of minor characters, which would become two key themes in the theater of narration. It also demonstrates why narrators continue to embrace the poetics of narration instead of more spectacular productions, and, importantly, suggests why audiences across Italy from major cities to rustic towns continue to attend these intellectually rigorous performances. Ultimately, a better understanding of Teatro Settimo presents the opportunity to assess the goals of the theater of narration, whether or not it has met them, and the extent to which they have evolved over the years and across generations.

The only leading narrator from the first generation who did not work closely with Teatro Settimo, though he did correspond with them, is Marco Baliani, who was born in Piedmont but grew up in Rome. Nonetheless, his early projects have significant commonalities with the company, such as collaborative ventures and performances in children's theaters. Some of Baliani's work is even more directly in conversation with the 1970s in terms of theme, including two of his most famous pieces, *Corpo di stato* (1998; *Body of State*) and *Kohlhaas* (1990), which explicitly echo rhetoric and leitmotifs of the decade. He was also among the most political of the narrators, partaking in protests and meetings during the occupation of university buildings in the early 1970s when he was also a student.

In addition to Baliani, Lella Costa, from Milan, ages into this first generation but, perhaps because of a lack of affiliation with any theater company, which would have provided her with the scaffolding of interlocutors and more opportunity to experiment, her shows have never garnered the same attention as those of Curino, Paolini, and Baliani. As early as 1987 with *Adlib* and 1988 with *Coincidenze* (*Coincidences*), she began performing short solo pieces that fall somewhere between skits and narrative theater in length and in texture. She was tenacious and consistently worked in a style near the theater of narration, but also her own, never collaborating or following quite the same path as the central narrators of the practice and of this study. Further alienating, her tone and subtle references in her plays to the likes of T. S. Eliot and Marcel Proust locate her in an aristocracy, whereas narrators, erudite as they too are, have aimed to remain a part of the general populace. Midcareer she began to work with Gabriele Vacis, who directed her most successful piece and the one closest to the theater of narration: her rendition of *La Traviata*. The affiliation with Vacis aligned her with the genre both artistically and popularly and loosely connects her to Teatro Settimo. She has also dedicated a significant portion of her work to television and film and is very active with sociopolitical organizations such as Emergency, a coalition that helps build hospitals in developing countries.

In a creative experiment that fell short of its potential, in 2016 she debuted *Human*, a show she cowrote and costarred in with Baliani, who would also direct it. What makes this an important piece for these two first-generation narrators is the way they employ elements of the theater of narration while also exploring other modes of performance. In addition to Baliani and Costa, the cast included four other actors, as well as musicians. This is one of the few productions on Italian stages that concerns the migrant crisis in Italy and Europe. The cast meditates on the human condition in many forms, narrating the harrowing struggles of a migrant crossing the treacherous strait of Mediterranean between the northern tip of Africa to the southern reach of Europe and portraying a slew of Italian characters, from youthful students who want to help to older locals who fear the migrants.

As Baliani and Costa open the show dramatically lit and facing the audience in direct address offering quick-paced poetic monologues, they stand like two pillars on opposite ends of the stage, setting up the playing space between them, where the scene action will take place, and demonstrating the epic narrative mode as one of the play's commanding structures. Coming on the heels of *Trincea* (2016; *Trench*), Baliani's expressionistic homage to World War I that explores the life of an average soldier, *Human* embraces different poetic registers, signaling Baliani's thirst as a director to push the theater of narration's possibilities to include larger casts, more traditional uses of mise-en-scène, and narrative modes that feature scenes, different characters, and sketches, as well as the original monologue form. It opens the possibility for the return to collaborative methods and experimentation most easily recognizable in the work of Teatro Settimo and might lead to a different iteration of the narrative form that he helped popularize.

Costa's distinct experiences from the other principal narrators throughout her career suggest that for the first generation who were responsible in establishing the genre, the camaraderie of working with others was generative to their creativity and intellectual formation, even if they did go on to found a practice that celebrated the solo artist. There is also a gendered aspect that shadows the women, particularly in the first generation but also in the second, as it remains difficult to be a woman in theater—especially on one's own—in Italy (and elsewhere). The cases of two other Teatro Settimo founders, Lucilla Giagnoni and Mariella Fabbris, especially attest to this disparity. If healthy, their careers have never reached the heights of Curino's or even Costa's, though that should not discount the possibility that they had other priorities. Smartly, Curino, and later Costa, continued to work with Vacis, who became one of the most famous and respected directors in Italy. This affiliation undoubtedly helped the careers of both Curino and Costa, since their gender put them at a disadvantage.

In the second generation of narrators, there is more variation in terms of artistic training and formation. The Sicilian narrator, Davide Enia, was a student of Curino's in the late 1990s while studying at the Università Cattolica del Sacro Cuore in Milan and thus learned the Teatro Settimo techniques in direct lineage. From 2010 to 2018, beginning with the publication of the small text *Mio padre non ha mai avuto un cane* (*My Father Never Had a Dog*), he took time away from performing to write novels, and in 2017 the libretto for Mozart's unfinished opera *L'oca del Cairo* (*The Goose of Cairo*). Only in 2018 did he return to the stage with *L'abisso* (*The Abyss*), a strictly narrative theater piece that he adapted from his book *Appunti per un naufragio* (2017; *Notes on a Shipwreck*), another work that addresses the European migrant crisis but is very different both stylistically and tonally from *Human*. In *Appunti per un naufragio* Enia attempts to confront some of the many complicated facets of racism and empathy that this emergency has brought to light. Though he stops short of actually giving voice to migrants, he nonetheless brings their cause to theaters across the whole country, encouraging honest discussion and exposing some of the many conflicted feelings Italians have about their role in this dire world crisis.

Giuliana Musso, who trained classically in the theater, graduating from the famed Scuola d'Arte Drammatica Paolo Grassi (created by Grassi and Giorgio Strehler), has remained firmly committed to writing and performing, though she has also explored directing and other acting projects. She comes to the practice from northeastern Italy (originally Vicenza, later Udine) and at one point was set to take over Paolini's megahit *Vajont*, but at the last minute this project never came to fruition. Even though Enia has expanded his work beyond the theater of narration, he and Musso have strong ties to the practice of first-generation artists. Finally, the Roman Ascanio Celestini, whose civic theater resembles the more politically charged moments in Paolini's, came into the theater of narration while performing street theater and, like Baliani, arrived at this mode of expression outside of the direct inspiration of first-generation Teatro Settimo narrators. He has also explored different projects, publishing novels and writing, directing, and acting in several films.

In tracing a genealogy, this chapter not only explores the origins of the theater of narration to reveal its theoretical sophistication but also performs its own historical revision by reframing the typically fraught 1968–80 period in Italy. As much as Teatro Settimo was responding to that long decade, it was also part of the decade's response to current crises in Italy and globally. This chapter thus begins with the theatrical influences that emerged just before and during that period, demonstrating how narrators learned to negotiate an artistic practice in politically fraught climates to create a form with international interlocutors in other solo theaters. The focus then moves to Teatro Settimo as a fundamental influence on the theater of narration, especially through its repurposing of historical methods to create a theatrical form of historical commentary. To emphasize the ways in which narrators translated these methods over time, a case study of second-generation narrator Ascanio Celestini's *Radio clandestina* (2000) illustrates how the next generation nonetheless absorbed the main ideas of Teatro Settimo, cementing the legacy of the theater of narration.

Italian Theater History and New Performance Methods

Thinking broadly about performance, Elin Diamond asserts that even while each act is a distinctive event in its own unique temporal space, it nonetheless harbors imprints of previous acts.[1] These acts might be long forgotten, but they live on in the life of new performances. Indeed, this logic follows in the theater of narration, which builds on many cultural, historical, and social traditions both within and outside Italy. Echoes of theater traditions that both extend centuries into Italian practices and cross national boundaries, especially between the United States and Europe, contribute to this complex form of storytelling. Among these many methods and individuals that haunt the practice, there are three particularly significant influences for Teatro Settimo and, eventually, the narrators. The theater of Dario Fo has been most frequently associated with the theater of narration and is indeed fundamental, but the theater of Franca Rame is also a central influence, and it is a mistake to credit only Fo. In addition, the theater of Jerzy Grotowski and Eugenio Barba was particularly important for its group work and Poor Theater. At the same time, the practice of *animazione teatrale* (theatrical animation) inspired both socially conscious and ethnographically inclined methods within the practice.

The first generation of narrators came of age during the long 1970s, in a cultural climate that encouraged both experimentation and a reconciliation with historical aesthetic practices and national histories. In 1966, in what is commonly considered the period of postwar crisis of Italian theater, practitioners and critics alike declared that there was a profound need for renewal. Their response was to create *il teatro nuovo* (the new theater)—a close cousin of Grotowski's Poor Theater and Barba's "third theater"—which was largely led by Carmelo Bene, Carlo Quartucci, Mario Ricci, and Franco Quadri. The theater of narration embraced various aspects of these mid-twentieth-century theatrical currents, including even the post-avant-garde, in terms of its frequent use of metadialogue, but ultimately focused on their capacity to both witness and communicate a living history.[2] In the mid-1970s, amid a richly experimental cultural climate digesting and fueling social movements, and with the energy of young students, the practice's founders explored different ways in which they could create a theater with those possibilities. Beyond its symbiosis with these performance practices, this frenetic atmosphere speaks to the hybrid dynamic of the theater of narration and to the way its mode of storytelling accentuates the comedic performer, the tragedian, the orator, and even the musician.

Dario Fo and Franca Rame

Against the rise of the director, the twentieth century saw a constellation of talented satirists, from Ettore Petrolini (1884–1936) to Franca Valeri (1920–2020), Luigi "Gigi" Proietti (1940–2020), and, more famously, Franca Rame and Dario Fo.[3] In the latter half of the twentieth century, one-person shows grew ever more common, with work by Paolo Rossi (born 1953), Daniele Luttazzi (born 1961), and Roberto Benigni (born 1952) among others who, despite sharing some techniques with their narrative theater contemporaries, perform more in the stand-up comedic practice that favors short skits as opposed to an overarching story. They exemplify the different paths that narrators could have taken. Of all these Italian artists who frequently or exclusively practice a soloist form of theater, the monologuist work of Fo and Rame, who performed together, with a company of actors, and in soliloquy, is the most influential. Some critics have even dubbed Fo the "grandfather" of the theater of narration, drawing stylistic parallels with minimalism, though acknowledging the very different formal aspects and acting techniques (Fo is much more animated and physical than the narrators). Paolini even publicly acknowledged Fo's inspiration at the end of his highly influential televised performance of *Vajont* in 1997, a broadcast that coincidentally occurred just days after Fo won the Nobel Prize in Literature.

Critics have somewhat overstated the inspiration of Fo on the theater of narration, and certainly understated that of Rame's, but there are some commonalities between their theater and the theater of narration that are too palpable to ignore. It is important to remember that Fo and Rame have been hugely influential across the globe, both for their performances and their plays, frequently cited as the most performed living playwrights for nearly four decades until their deaths in 2013 (Rame) and 2016 (Fo). For young theater artists growing up in Italy in the 1960s and '70s, such as the first-generation narrators, it would have been impossible not to be influenced in some way by the work of Fo and Rame, and for the practice that became the theater of narration, this inspiration is visible in form as well as theme and philosophy. Two of the rarely addressed ways in which the pair meaningfully influenced the narrators' work were through their understanding of how politics is personal, and through Rame's oeuvre.

Fo and Rame's ability to combine routines from the everyday with complex political ideas, in a style that resembled the long-standing Italian storytelling tradition known as *affabulazione*, underscored the value of narrative as a tool for digesting current events. Similar to how microhistorians were working with narrative to depict history more richly, Fo and Rame tapped into the rich heritage of folk and oral culture in order to unpack current events and to appreciate their relevance in a more personal way. Commedia dell'arte is particularly pertinent to their mode of storytelling, trickling down to the narrators who practice the commedia's signature loose sketch techniques.[4] Following the commedia process of a basic story map with a beginning, middle, and end rather than a fully scripted play is common practice for several narrators, as it was for Fo. Celestini notes, "I don't have a script I know by heart, but I know the character's story, and I tell it in the same way that someone can describe the details of a car crash they've been in."[5] Paolini also articulates his improvisational methods in a similar fashion: "I always have a rhythm in my head." For both, the payoff in following a commedia sketch model relates back to audience rapport and community building, which was certainly a primary goal of Fo and Rame's political theater. Celestini has stated that the "dirtiness" of extemporaneous performing can lead to more direct encounters with the audience.[6] Similarly, Paolini has noted that parroting a script left little room for him to engage with spectators, so he does not commit any of his texts to fixed memory.[7]

Part of Fo and Rame's genius was also moving beyond tradition to recognize the rich culture of the everyday. Various encounters with narrative performance decorated Fo's youth, but he was particularly charmed by the fishermen, glassblowers, and itinerant vendors whom he affectionately referred to as the "*fabulatori* of my childhood."[8] It is no coincidence that his and Rame's theater, and later that of the narrators, would be linked to traditions, Gramscian in their feel, in which everyone, no matter their profession or class, was the beholder of a captivating tale. Even without an explicit political objective, just this idea imbues ordinary people with agency and importance, an objective in both the theater of Fo and Rame and the theater of narration.[9]

Fo and Rame's 1969 *Mistero buffo* is often cited as the piece that most influenced narrators because of formal similarities such as the use of monologue, the stark set and costume (usually Fo is simply dressed in black), and the audience interaction through direct address, making the event an opportunity for dialogue, debate, and even confrontation.[10] *Mistero buffo* consists of twelve mini-*canovacci* divided into two sections of commentary and then biblical accounts of the Passion; Fo and Rame link the monologues through didactic commentaries (descriptions, analyses) that create a continuous, dialectical exchange between the past and present, history and the current moment, culture and politics. Interrupting the metanarrative by smaller moments allows Fo and Rame to connect medieval fiction and contemporary realism—a formal technique that narrators also invoke.[11] However, while *Mistero buffo* is a montage of scenes with staccato switches between the Passion tales and contemporary commentary, the theater of narration prefers a much smoother experience in which scenes flow from one to the next in a single overarching story that has a beginning, middle, and end. *Mistero buffo* was, after all, a significant play for theater globally, not just in Italy, giving permission to artists to approach structures, like the Catholic Church, that seemed untouchable and prod them from all angles of satire, physical comedy, and serious discourse. In the case of Rame's monologue in *Mistero buffo*, uttered in an archaic Italian dialect, it also embraced tragedy.

When discussing the significance of *Mistero buffo* on the theater of narration, Rame needs to be at the core of the discussion. All too frequently in both scholarship and popular commentary on Fo and Rame, critics do not give due consideration to Rame but instead focus uniquely on Fo and even credit him as sole author for works that she largely devised.[12] This emphasis on Fo, especially regarding the influence of *Mistero buffo*, is also true for the majority of writings that contextualize the theater of narration solely in his work rather than projects on which they collaborated. Rame's tragic monologue from *Mistero buffo* is but one instance that exemplifies how *their* work was influential on the theater of narration in part thanks to *her* work. Laura Curino, for example, who often incorporates a consciously feminist approach in her plays, directly references Fo and Rame at the end of her 1987 play *Passione*, but then goes on to portray her own version of Rame's Maria monologue from *Mistero Buffo* in a layered and nuanced performance that is part homage, part original interpretation.[13]

Rame's celebrated monologues regarding women's conditions collected in *Tutta casa, letto e chiesa* (*All Home, Bed and Church*, or *It's All Bed, Board, and Church*, with several plays translated in the other collections *Female Parts* and *A Woman Alone*) and performed in various combinations or just one at a time, experiment with narration and monologue in ways that are much closer to the theater of narration than to Fo's comedy.[14] Rame inhabits characters, yet her women tell their stories rather than acting them. Of the narrators, Giuliana Musso perhaps most closely follows this method. While Rame explicitly explored themes of married life, motherhood, and working outside the home, she also addressed more universal themes, and certainly never lost an opportunity to critique capitalism when she could. In *Alice nel paese senza meraviglie* (*Alice in Wonderless Land*), she proselytizes about the pitfalls of consumerism not just as a threat to physical health but as a force of destruction for one's authenticity and uniqueness. While similar themes that deride the unhealthy modern model of working conditions creep up in Curino's *Passione* and *Olivetti* plays, what is especially notable is the dialectic of intermingling character portrayals and narrative to arrive at social commentary. This recipe seeped into much of the theater of narration, even as different narrators balance those three features in various ways.

The other dynamic to Rame's work that is fundamental to the theater of narration is the sometimes painful proximity between writer and subject matter. Though this relationship is not always overt in the work of Rame or narrators, even when it is subtle it adds complexity to the play. For Rame, that rapport characterizes some of her tragic monologues. There is no better example than her wrenching *Lo stupro* (1975; *The Rape*), in which she drew on her traumatic personal experiences after she was kidnapped, tortured, and gang-raped in 1973 by a neofascist group that was discovered much later to have been commissioned by several high-ranking Milanese police officials in retaliation for some of her activism and charged theater. Even with this very personal piece, however, she still follows the formula in which the character narrates the experience, leading to very clear sociopolitical objectives. The degree of autobiography varies widely in the theater of narration, as it does in Rame's theater, but it is a central characteristic in a number of their critically acclaimed plays and owes a gentle recognition to the ways in which Rame worked with it.

Ultimately the majority of narrators refined Rame's character emphasis by engaging less with portrayals and more with narration. Substituting character with narrator, especially when the narrative is imbued with autobiographical detail, allows the practice an even simpler model for audience members to pass into the hands of, if not the masses, then surely the many. Having repopularized the monologuist traditions that had regained stature with Fo and Rame, together Fo and Rame and the narrators created a template that has ongoing potential. With the added but central benefit that the form practices a "poor theater" (one that does not require any elaborate costumes, a set, or even other actors), it is able to reinvent itself in ways that neither Fo nor Rame, nor even the narrators continuing their work today, might have ever imagined.

Grotowski and Barba

While Fo and Rame never relied on elaborate costly productions, narrators owe their minimalist style to Jerzy Grotowski (1933–99) and his invention of a Poor Theater, which was rooted in social issues from the 1960s and 1970s. Grotowski and his student Eugenio Barba influenced Teatro Settimo artists, most notably with their theories on the rapport between the actor and spectator, as well as their leftist political undertones, grounded in the post-1968/69 moment, which they expressed differently than Fo and Rame. As Grotowski explains in his seminal *Towards a Poor Theatre*, two key questions preoccupied him: What is unique about theater? And what can it offer that new technologies (film and television) cannot? His response was to create the Poor Theater, an effort to determine the most organic form of theater. In seeking the fewest requirements needed to make a production, he discovered that "theatre can exist without makeup, without costume and scenography, without a separate performance area (stage), without lighting and sound effects, etc." What it cannot exist without, however, is an actor and a spectator in "perceptual, direct, 'live' communion."[15] By Grotowski's definition, the theater of narration is also a Poor Theater, independent of the spectacular tropes of the stage, privileging a direct rapport between the narrator and the audience member.

Grotowski and Barba's most direct influence was on Teatro Settimo, particularly regarding the interpersonal. Their experimental theaters were founded through working with actors or performance groups, and the theater of narration built on that sense of workshop by enlisting the public to help articulate a (re)vision of a particular event.[16] While Barba's work on presence might linger in the performances of narrative theater, he also had a direct influence insofar as Vacis, Paolini, and the theater scholar Gerardo Guccini all met in 1981 at one of Barba's famous two-month all-day intensive workshops for artists and critics with guests from around the world run by his International School of Theatre Anthropology in Volterra. That year, Grotowski was among those guests. Vacis characterizes his impact in theater as "revolutionary," noting his focus on the centrality of the actor-spectator relationship, without the mediation of other technologies. In a book reflecting on a 1991 ten-day Grotowski seminar in Turin that Teatro Settimo, the University of Turin, and the Teatro Stabile of Turin organized, Vacis emphasizes that the theater is one of the few contemporary places where one must physically exist.[17] Such hyperawareness of sharing present space points to a conceptualization of performance not as an instrument that mimics reality, but as a method of communication with didactic intentions, speaking to the pedagogical atmosphere that some theater of narration performances create.

A transcript from a 1976 Grotowski interview in the Laura Curino Private Collections further serves as testament to the group's interest in the artist. It praises Grotowski for having created a theater that had "a sense of liberation, of the search for truth."[18] For a group like Teatro Settimo, which sought to create a collective memory for their hometown, Grotowski's views enabled them to pare down their objectives to focus on the human rapport. Much of their work in rewriting stories plays on the intimacy of direct communication that Grotowski articulated in his definition of theater and its advantages over technology. Just as the theater of narration is not as overtly political as the plays of Fo and Rame, it is also less focused on challenging conventional theater than Grotowski and Barba were. Combining the two, narrators aim less to revolutionize the people or theater practices, and more to locate an effective mode of communication with popular audiences.

Animazione teatrale

The pedagogical theater movement called animazione teatrale (theatrical animation) was also highly influential to the development of the theater of narration, specifically with respect to audience rapport. Giuliano Scabia, a leader in the animazione experiments, was also drawn to narrative, but in different ways than Rame, who let her characters lead, or even the microhistorian Carlo Ginzburg, who was reconstructing the past. This movement, which used theater as a means to educate in civic discourse and social awareness, often in lower-income areas, brought a Brechtian perspective to the members of the Teatro Settimo, some of whom knew Scabia and worked with him directly, thinking of narration as a way to engage audience more didactically than fantastically.

The practice itself was woven into events of 1968, which spurred many to think of theater as a pedagogical tool, and not just as cultural entertainment or a mode of representation.[19] Although animazione was popular in both northern Italy and France, it was very much an Italian phenomenon. Cued by social conflict throughout the 1970s, only in Italy did the form grow from a more generic mixture of education and performance to an art with overt didactic and pedagogic relevance that was connected to the political and cultural movements marked by 1968 and after.[20] In addition to actor and director Giuliano Scabia, the leading animators include Loredana Perissinotto, who went on to teach at the University of Turin, and Pierantonio Barbieri, who acted but was perhaps better known as a director. In 1969, these three artists formed a company called Il Gruppo di Ricerca dell'Animazione Italiana (Research Group for Italian Animation) in Turin and as such, along with the scholar Gian Renzo Morteo—whose university lectures Curino would attend while she was still in high school—they largely shaped the form of animazione teatrale.

Broadly, animazione encouraged an approach focusing on theater as a sociopolitical tool capable of ameliorating the everyday experiences of the underprivileged. Reaching its apex during the mid-1970s in urban and suburban areas, it emphasized working with the community, particularly in schools, and resonated most profoundly within the early works of Teatro Settimo in their commitment to their own localities. In several working-class quarters of Turin, the first animazione experiments used techniques that emphasized the elimination of the text, improvisation, structural intermittency, audience participation, gestural expressiveness, lucidity (transparency), and "poor" materials for scenery and technology such as lighting.[21] For the theater of narration, it was a logical progression, at least technically, with Poor Theater, in which shows do not depend on large budgets and aim to create an intimate rapport between audience members and performer.

Similar to the theater of narration, the task of articulating what exactly animazione is grows cumbersome thanks to the several hybrid qualities it embodies. As Morteo notes in his manual on animazione, a copy of which Curino kept in her personal archives, part of the pleasure and satisfaction of the practice is *not* strictly defining it. The phenomenon, Morteo asserts, developed from a social necessity for cultural interventions on a local level, where the action in a play is no longer a "representation" from "real life" but rather is an event in itself.[22] Instead of creating a plot with characters as their performance material, animators began with actual people and a specific conflict in their lives. The idea of creating an event out of the ordinary demonstrates the desire to solicit action on a public level that stretches beyond the boundaries of a dramatic representation. Narrators develop this idea into a practice that explicitly encourages symbolic acts of dialogue between the audience and performers.

Global Interlocutors

A brief comparison of contemporary theatrical practices that share commonalities with the theater of narration (as opposed to ones that influenced its development) will situate and distinguish the theater of narration among its peers, namely other solo theaters. In particular, the theater of narration will call to mind different monologist and research-based theaters from an eclectic range of countries and times. Performance scholar Carol Martin theorizes many of these as belonging to a theater of the real. She largely credits the zeitgeist of the 1970s as well, namely in the United States, with its struggles toward authenticity in an age of deceit (Vietnam, Nixon) as inspiring practices that also sought to devise a transparent reality.[23] Performance traditions that overlap are far and wide, from the orations of classical Rome to West African griots. For Anglo-American audiences, documentary theater is a closely related cousin with its echoes of New Deal–era experiments such as Living Newspaper productions (which have their own associations in Fo and Rame's theater). In some of the seminal documentary theater productions, Anna Deavere Smith or members of the Tectonic Theater Project focus on a local issue of national importance and offer points of discussion through multiple perspectives. Similar to narrative theater works, these productions are meticulously researched and aim to put a cacophony of voices into conversation with each other, reconstructing the past through dialogue. As theater scholar Ryan Claycomb has written, these plays work to construct multiple perspectives that will incite new dialogue.[24] Much like Rokem, who asserts theater's restorative potential "to counteract the destructive forces of history," Claycomb also argues for the remedial potential of these plays.[25] That these plays focus less on the historical actions and more on a discourse that encapsulates a variety of perspectives puts them and the theater of narration in a similar category.

The two practices also share a leftist bent without declaring any political affiliation. In his book on documentary theater, Gary Fisher Dawson acknowledges that European soloist theater has traditionally been more overtly antihegemonic than its American counterparts but that, increasingly, American documentary theater also aims to challenge authority, even if its plays claim to function merely as conduits for discussion.[26] Their very composition is as democratic in method as any assembly of voices. Further, the authors conceive these plays because they feel there is a need to revisit an event, suggesting a dissenting opinion from the dominant discourse. Claycomb adds that the associations with 1930s Living Newspapers by the Federal Theatre Project automatically imbue the works of artists such as Smith with a left-leaning feel, even if she, like the Italian narrators, claims political neutrality.[27]

While similar in those important ways, the theater of narration also displays distinct differences. First, it is Italian, and while the themes of its plays are of interest across borders, their subjects are national, and local. That does not mean that it cannot translate across borders, but it is important to interrogate its relationship to its country of origin. Second, most plays have a classical Aristotelian plot arc with a clear beginning, middle, climax, dénouement, and end. The universality of their themes, mixed with this classical mode of storytelling, at times lends these performances a slightly mythic tone, or an air vaguely reminiscent of a fairy tale. Their "documentary" status, then, is much more fluid, even while they are heavily researched and employ documentary techniques. They rely much less on oral history, however, than does documentary theater broadly, and certainly in comparison to artists such as Smith, whose work is also known as verbatim theater for its precise use of oral accounts. Finally, narrators often include themselves among the other voices, emphasizing the importance of the mercurial nature of subjectivity. In documentary theater, this is the exception, such as in the works of Spalding Gray, rather than the rule. To that end, the breadth of voices that narrators encompass can be much wider, incorporating perspectives from different parts of the country and different time periods, making a much stronger statement for any ordinary voice and the continuing relevance of such a viewpoint. These free-flowing aesthetic tendencies are suggestive of the fact that different authors have their own styles and poetics, but they also recall the experimental atmosphere of other artistic practices in the 1970s.

Finally, the theater scholars Gerardo Guccini and Claudio Meldolesi employ the term "epic performance," harking back to Brecht, as a way to refer to many solo practices, including the theater of narration, and in a more Anglo-American context, also the theater of the real, documentary theater, tribunal theater, and so on.[28] Their aim, much like Martin's, was to create an umbrella term that could capture the many solo styles of performance that are primarily narrative. According to their terms, one key characteristic of epic performance is an extratextual dimension. Interestingly, this is strongest among the many nonprofessional actors who explore a manner of presentation onstage. Though some are better known than others, there is a significant group of people who are not trained as actors but who have occasionally embraced the oratorical. The diversity of professional backgrounds here is notable: the performers range from mathematicians and astrophysicists (Piergiorgio Odifreddi, Margherita Hack) to journalists and former judges (Marco Travaglio, Gherardo Colombo).[29]

In a last example, epic performance would include the internationally known writer and journalist Roberto Saviano, famous for his reportage against the Neapolitan mafia, the Camorra, in his 2006 book *Gomorrah*, which was made into a neo-documentary-style film in 2008 directed by Matteo Garrone. In the early 2010s, Saviano regularly appeared in television specials in which he described his investigations, placing himself as both a Neapolitan and journalist, at the center of his works. This interweaving of autobiography within a larger narrative is a common trait in the theater of narration, yet in this specific example Saviano has a much more direct political agenda than most narrative theater pieces do. Further teasing out the distinctions between these different modes of performance, from documentary theater to epic performance and still others, might be the subject of another study. Meanwhile, though, contextualizing the theater of narration within a broad category of practices in Italy and elsewhere in the wide-ranging categories of theater of the real, solo performance, monologist theater, and epic performance locates its closest interlocutors and points to its underrepresentation in discussions of these practices.

Laboratorio Teatro Settimo

As with many political and artistic groups during the long 1970s, Teatro Settimo's work was in part a response to the postwar climate in Italy that aggressively pursued manufacturing development. In those formative years—from the very first production in the spring of 1974, *Non ci piace questa storia: Buchiamola!* (*We Don't Like This Story: Let's Punch Holes in It!*), through *Esercizi sulla tavola di Mendeleev* (1984; *Exercises on Mendeleev's Table*), their first international success—the central theme is a confrontation with the light speed of industry and all its casualties on humans and the environment. The work of Teatro Settimo underlines the conflict between individuals with the large-scale state and corporate initiatives that took place after the war, suggesting that this very simple binary opposition with extremely complex reverberations is at the heart of that painful decade in Italian history.

In the spring of 1974, Curino was in her penultimate year of high school at a *liceo classico*, in the liberal arts tradition, and was involved in several local theater groups, including one at her church in the Fiat housing projects, where she and her family lived, as well as at a school in Turin, where she was working on one of the short teaching plays in Brecht's *Lehrstücke* collection called "The Exception and the Rule." In addition to her work with these groups, on Saturday mornings Curino was also sneaking into university courses (she was too young to enroll) taught by the professors Giovanni Moretti and Gian Renzo Morteo, who wrote about animazione teatrale during its heyday. She already knew Gabriele Vacis, Adriana Zamboni, Lucio Diana, and some of the other founding members of the Teatro Settimo from around Settimo Torinese and specifically from the bus into Turin on school mornings, but that spring they shared another commonality. At the same time that Curino was working on "The Exception and the Rule," Vacis, Diana, and Mario Agostinoni were coincidentally involved with another one of Brecht's *Lehrstücke*, "The Yes Sayer, The No Sayer," with a church group in Settimo.

That spring Curino, Diana, Vacis, and Zamboni, along with more than twenty others, followed a theater workshop called "Animazione teatrale del Teatro dell'Angolo" at the Biblioteca Civica di Settimo Torinese (their local public library). Following this, the group's first project was to create a play about the history of Settimo as "an alternative version of historical facts that signal the passage of an agricultural Settimo to the industrial boom Settimo."[30] This project would become "Non ci piace questa storia: Buchiamola!" They decided not to write a script but instead to improvise *canovacci*, the commedia dell'arte style of short scene work. It was also in these first encounters that they decided to use minimal technology—lights, sound equipment, microphones—quipping that they did not have the money then, nor would they ever, to pay for that. Among other aspects, this minimalist mise-en-scène transferred to the theater of narration.

Because the library wanted to promote the play to the public, the librarians asked the young artists what they called themselves. So began the negotiations for a name. As Vacis recalls, everyone had ideas and opinions that reflected their own backgrounds, which included everything from the local parish to the Communist Federation for young Italians. Some wanted to emphasize these different perspectives and call the group the Ecumenical Theater. Others were more direct and suggested the Proletariat Theater. In the end, as time was running out and no one put forth a name that a majority could agree upon, the library printed flyers with everyone's name under the title Laboratorio Teatrale di Settimo Torinese.[31] Though it was a simple and descriptive title, the group embraced it, trimming it to Laboratorio Teatro Settimo, with its hint of a reference to Jerzy Grotowski's Laboratory Theater. Eventually they further simplified the name, calling themselves Teatro Settimo.

Broadly, the many plays that constitute the theater of narration reflect the story that the naming of the company tells, in which the members deny an overt reference to the many divergent political opinions from Christian Democratic to Communist, in favor of a subtle yet still political nod to the founder of the Poor Theater. The connection to the location, Settimo Torinese, and how it celebrates that locality also became a notable characteristic in the theater of narration. Finally, the presence of the library in this initial moment symbolizes the energy of collectives that were prominent in the 1970s. Vacis praises the director of the library, who created something of an amusement park out of its books and collections, where the people of Settimo could take classes on yoga or macrobiotic cooking. For him, she became an angel of sorts, a savior, and he recalls her enchantment by referring to her as the famous French actress Dominique Sanda, who starred in Bernardo Bertolucci's masterpiece *Il conformista* (1970). Thanks to the vision of "Sanda," the citizens of Settimo Torinese had a refuge where they could listen to *cantautori* (singer-storytellers) who played instruments made out of hair combs and workers' tools (since the guitar was already an instrument of the bourgeoisie). They could also participate in conferences on contraceptives, join feminist groups, and, of course, take theater workshops.[32] The library was a refuge for the people in a city that was created for industry. Thanks to this space that the director created, the members of the future Teatro Settimo found each other and a way to work together.

Remarkably, even this first project winks at the theater of narration from the distance of twenty, thirty, forty years and counting. Beginning with the title, the Italian capitalizes on the dual meaning of *storia*. "We don't like this *storia*." Instead of following with the imperative, "Let's throw it out," which would be *buttiamola*, a subtle change of two letters to *buchiamola* implores a pointed investigation of a *storia* that might result in reshaping its perception. To throw it out would be dismissive, as if to say, "There is nothing here worth remembering." In suggesting, "Let's poke holes in it!" the young company exhibits an innovative approach by exclaiming, rather, that they will work with it, examine it, pierce parts of it. They will engage with and interrogate this *storia*.

The premiere was April 10, 1974, and as Vacis recalls, it was a turbulent time. He notes that eight days later, the violent leftist group, the Brigate Rosse (Red Brigades), who would rise to international infamy after kidnapping and killing former prime minister Aldo Moro in 1978, achieved one of their first serious acts of terror by abducting the judge Mario Sossi, whom they later released on ransom. A month after the premiere, Italy voted to maintain the right to divorce, which had only become law in 1970 and was threatened again with a referendum vote in 1974. Less than two months later there was a massacre during an antifascist protest at the central Piazza della Loggia in the northern town for Brescia, in which eight people were killed and over one hundred injured. These were the 1970s, the years of lead.

Perhaps too close to this present, the young group looked to a much smaller *storia*, less well-known and more local: conflicts between the farmers and clothing launderers in the mid-nineteenth century outside Turin.[33] Though little remains of this production besides what Vacis recounts, it is clear that the group used this conflict, which they could research in the library, to explore the intricacies of southern-to-northern Italian migration, a theme close to their hearts, as many of their parents were migrants from the South who had come to find work in the wave of industrial development. The choice to focus on a small-scale story with large-scale relevance became a primary characteristic of the theater of narration, but it had been an interest in the minds of Teatro Settimo artists since the very beginning. Though the chaos of the long 1970s brought continual drama to the everyday lives of Italians, Teatro Settimo veered away from that to reflect on what they could learn from unpacking other conflicts from other times.

Teatro Settimo is the prototype for the theater of narration because of the way these ideas and values were furthered in future productions, but also because the company was a gateway for many principal narrators. As the academic year started up again in the fall of 1974, members of the group stayed in touch under the new possibilities of the theater company, and though most of them attended university in Turin the following year (Vacis studied architecture and Curino literature), they arranged regular gatherings to discuss and debate theater. While Curino and Vacis were among the initial

Fig. 1. Teatro Settimo's *La storia di Romeo e Giulietta* (Taormina, 1991) with Laura Curino and Marco Paolini (center) facing forward as the Nurse and the Friar. Photograph by Maurizio Buscarino. Courtesy of Laura Curino and Federico Negro.

group of students who met at the Settimo library, Marco Paolini performed and wrote with Teatro Settimo from 1986 to 1992. He also consulted several of his colleagues in the company as he was devising his first solo show, *Adriatico* (1987), which he debuted in Settimo Torinese. This production became a part of a series he called *Gli album* (*Photo Albums*), to which he added other vignettes until 1999. His time with Teatro Settimo forged an important professional relationship with Vacis, with whom he has continued to work and with whom he coauthored the pivotal narrative theater piece *Il racconto del Vajont* (1994; *The Story of Vajont*), which Vacis directed. Other Teatro Settimo artists who later practiced narrative theater, and some of their most celebrated productions, include Mariella Fabbris (*Il mestiere dell'attrice* [1993]), Lucia Giagnoni (*Modelli* [1992], from poems by Amy Lowell), Beppe Rosso (*Dei liquori fatti in casa* [1993], coauthored with Vacis and Remo Rostagno, who also worked with Baliani on *Kohlhass*), and Eugenio Allegri (*Novecento*, from Alessandro Baricco's 1994 novel). Lucio Diana from Teatro Settimo also designed the sets for many of these artists and continues to work closely with Vacis, as does original Teatro Settimo member Roberto Tarasco, an expert in lighting design.

As the company continued to create theater together, their plays loosely fell into two categories, the first of which initially appears to have little in common with the theater of narration: (1) adaptations of classical or canonical literary texts from authors as diverse as Aeschylus (*Seven against Thebes*, 1992) and Aristophanes (*The Birds*, 1996) to Shakespeare (*Romeo and Juliet*, 1991; fig. 1), Molière (*Tartuffe*, 1995), and Goethe (*Elective Affinities*, 1985); and (2) plays that the group collectively composed based on interviews and historical research. These plays emphasize storytelling through minor characters and aim to engage local community as the theater of narration would later. In addition to creating and producing plays, Teatro Settimo also developed cultural initiatives for Settimo Torinese, including theater activities for youth and the elderly.

Much like microhistorians and oral historians, the artists of Teatro Settimo understood storytelling in continual relation to historical perspective. As early as 1982, seven years after their first serendipitous encounters at the public library, and after having created several shows for children and street theater pieces, Teatro Settimo premiered *Signorine* (*Young Women*). Although there is no extant script, one can still glean various details about the piece thanks to secondary sources left by Curino, Vacis, and Guccini. In a 1982 document by Teatro Settimo members, the authors state that starting with the town Settimo Torinese, the company sought to unravel the discrepancies between "the history books and the stories that people live."[34] In a similar vein, specifically reflecting on *Signorine*, Vacis recalls that the company wanted to reconstruct the memory of the city where they were born and in which they continued to live. For them, it was a city with no memory.[35] He continues by explaining that there was a loss of a unified collective history, since those industrial towns (not just Settimo) could not produce a synthesis of memories.[36] Starting with *Signorine*, one of their main goals was to offer a coherent narrative that would give their town a life beyond its work life, beyond its industrial productivities.

Inherent in these reflections lingers a question: Which stories get told? Which stories become History? Which stories will come to define a person or a place or an event? Through their very narratives, Teatro Settimo meditates on how everyone not only has the ability to change history but already does in fact change history. Ordinary people change history both by their own actions and by how they remember the past, influencing how they pass it forward through oral tradition. Just as historians realized that narratives were useful to understand history, the members of Teatro Settimo discovered that historical reflection was crucial to their stories. In the words of the celebrated oral historian Alessandro Portelli, "The historian must work on both the factual and the narrative planes, the referent and the signifier, the past and the present, and, most of all, on the space between all of them."[37] For the young Teatro Settimo artists devising one of their first shows, that space between the past and the present, between a story and what actually transpired, is memory. This is the space where they worked as they began to define the objectives of their projects.

In *Signorine*, debuting in 1982, the primacy of memory was conveyed through a strong sense of nostalgia for postwar 1940s and 1950s. In a published letter that Guccini wrote to Teatro Settimo, he summarizes the play as a mosaic of short private stories collected from people around Settimo deriving from an animazione exercise at a center for the elderly. With minimal set design and lighting, Guccini concluded that it was obvious that the artists wanted to connect with the public by telling them their own stories in a direct mode of address, free from distractions.[38] The theater critic Roberto Canziani interpreted the play as a more personal exercise in which the artists were trying to connect their own experiences to the lives of their parents when the latter were in their twenties. In addition to the stories from the elderly home, they built on memories that their parents had shared of themselves as young adults and created a play that integrated some of the central struggles of those times.[39]

That first play already approached major themes in the theater of narration: it recovered forgotten or dismissed histories and demonstrated the suppleness of history. As a result of these interviews, one of the main leitmotifs in the piece is the act of remembering, and how that process inevitably privileges certain stories over others. It also begins the dialogic form of historical recuperation so prevalent in the theater of narration, not just in the way it builds its narratives on oral accounts but also in how these stories are presented back to those who first shared them. In performing the piece locally, they showed their parents' and grandparents' generations how their stories were part of a larger history and how the act of retelling their private histories helped to construct this larger shared history.

This idea of repetition and retelling, and its relationship to historical praxis, is one of the first theoretical considerations that Teatro Settimo explored. To investigate the relationship between performance and what remains, Rebecca Schneider states her fundamental interest in a "porous approach to time and to art—time as full of holes or gaps and art as capable of falling or crossing in and out of the spaces between live iterations . . . the warp and draw of one time in another time—the *theatricality* of time."[40] In contemplating some of the effects of such an approach, she invokes Toni Morrison's powerful idea (featured in the novel *Beloved*) of "rememory," and specifically the "irruptive experience" of remembering someone else's forgotten memory. She also turns to Adrienne Rich's seminal essay "When We Dead Awaken," specifically the connection to survival that, Rich insists, benefits women who critically confront the past.[41] There are several elements in these observations that illuminate *Signorine* (and the theater of narration): first, the play takes its own "porous approach" to its recuperation of history by creating a past out of the personal memories of a handful of ordinary individuals. Second, the artists themselves enact a "rememory" of sorts when they embody the memories of their parents and those at the senior center. Finally, the emphasis on the critical is the key idea from Rich that is useful here. The layers of nonlinear time, the experiences of others, and a critical engagement with both are the foundational gestures of this form of theater, in conversation with more specifically historical methods of inquiry.

This type of metadialogue in which the narrators include themselves, their city, and their parents mirrors the personal involvement of the microhistorian. Ginzburg described the dawning of the relationship to his archival work while reading what others wrote of his main figure, Menocchio, in *The Cheese and the Worms*. During his research, he realized that his perspective was handicapped irrevocably by subjectivities that included not only those who were judging Menocchio, but also his own. As a historian, he was reading the notes of Menocchio's inquisitors and noticed that the questions about this person they had asked were similar to those he was asking. Suddenly he was identifying with their positionality.[42] In a separate reflection, fellow microhistorian Carlo Levi also explains that "the researcher's point of view becomes an intrinsic part of the account . . . involved in a sort of dialogue and participates in the whole process of constructing the historical argument."[43]

Narrators have translated this researcher's point of view for the stage through the use of autobiography. Vacis's description of *Signorine* as an effort to construct a collective memory for the company's hometown also suggests an attempt to decipher how their own stories fold into those of previous generations. He explained that little by little the company understood that to create a reason for living in a place like Settimo was to create the place itself.[44] Ultimately, to construct history, to furnish memories for a city, is to become intertwined in those memories, since, like Ginzburg, who ultimately had to select which texts would tell the story of Menocchio, the narrators must choose which stories will be the blocks that build their city. Rebuilding Teatro Settimo with the stories of ordinary people is the act of creating a people's history. This might have been Ginzburg's goal as well.

Resonating with Schneider's porous approach to time, another key dynamic to microhistory is what historian Matti Peltonen considers Ginzburg's and Levi's most important contribution: the "method of clues" (*paradigma indiziario*), an investigation based on an element that does not seem to fit or seems odd, causing the researcher to take it as a sign of a larger unknown structure.[45] Peltonen refers to a 1978 article in which Ginzburg argued that as a result of this "method of clues," which required a catholic assessment of texts and methods ranging across centuries, "reality is opaque; but there are certain points—clues, signs—which allow us to decipher it." Ginzburg acknowledges that this is not a new idea, since psychoanalysis is "based on the hypothesis that apparently negligible details can reveal deep and significant phenomena."[46] Nonetheless, he views it as crucial to microhistory.

In 1993, fifteen years after his first considerations on the method of clues, Ginzburg refers to it again, noting that the lacunas that had led him to focus on a particular area would become a part of the story he wove together. The clues themselves were an important aspect of the research and add meaningful layers to the narrative. Ginzburg hypothesizes that the more improbable the documentation, the richer the yield, allowing any hidden social structures to emerge from the interaction of numerous individual strategies.[47] This method of clues brings together several other features of microhistory. It is the reasoning behind the wager that smaller units can inspire large questions, and it also implicates the researchers themselves in their investigative approaches. Further, Ginzburg's reference to social structures underlines the importance that these discoveries can have in the emergence of more heterogeneous communities.

Returning to *Signorine*, Vacis echoes the "method of clues" in his description of how the company researched the play. In order to create a historical narrative, they began by talking with older residents about their experiences of living in one of Italy's most important industrial peripheral towns. Suddenly, he recalls, he and his company members found themselves contemplating the hydrogeological arrangements of the country, the huge events in postwar Italy, and the "biblical migration" from the South to the North. "What was surprising, however, was that the epic scales were not in opposition to the smallest details of private memories, but coexisted peacefully, even proudly, thanks to the strong network of relationships that we wove."[48] Vacis defines the creation of this early play through a search for something that was missing and even acknowledges "the strong network of relationships" that emerged from their efforts. As the young company members listened to individual stories, they began to notice that these personal accounts represented much larger circumstances that could describe a collective *storia* of postwar Italy.

Circa 1981, in preparation for the creation of the play, the company members submitted a research proposal to Settimo municipal's Department of Culture that reads like a methodological blueprint for what would later become *Signorine*. They describe Settimo Torinese as a place where its habitants were violently subjected to economic boom and bust. Though they never mention the play by name, they articulate their intention to create a theatrical production that revisits the history of Settimo based on research that would include an analysis of publications, photographs, and, above all, oral testimony from the 1950s and 1960s from interviewees categorized by age.[49] One of the more important findings this document reveals is the depth and the longevity of the group's engagement with Settimo's community. In the four or five years between those early articulations of how the rhetoric of the economic boom promoted a false identity of their town and its inhabitants, through the creation of *Signorine*, and finally Vacis's own recollections nearly fifteen years later in 1996, the core values of the company remained the same.

That so many of the artists were students and that the 1970s was such an intellectually prolific period are fundamental to the company's formation. In terms of their schooling, Teatro Settimo members display a diverse range of disciplines. With company members trained in architecture (Vacis, Zamboni, Diana), economics and business (Agostinoni), philosophy (Federico Negro), and modern literature (Curino), it is perhaps unsurprising that prominent historians who favored interdisciplinary approaches influenced the group. Throughout Teatro Settimo's 1981 eight-page research statement, the authors reference novels by Umberto Eco and Heinrich Böll, as well as scholarly works by Bloch, Foucault, Céline, Baudrillard, and of course Ginzburg.

When the group cites Ginzburg's *The Cheese and the Worms* (1976) in their bibliography, they proclaim his superior articulation (over Bloch) of "signs" (*spie*) quoting the same passage from his 1978 essay that he revised in 1993: "Reality is opaque; but there are certain points—clues, signs—which allow us to decipher it." In their statement, they acknowledge that the "method of clues" serves as a key concept in their research and express their hope that it will uncover complex social structures. They explain how they develop and adapt the method for the stage so that "micro-news," which is seemingly insignificant but in reality can reveal profound phenomena of considerable importance, is central in their productions.[50] These habits and practices that began in the company's earliest stages became the fundamental practices in the theater of narration, but not before Teatro Settimo rehearsed them in several projects throughout the 1980s.

In the three plays that followed *Signorine*, the company continued to develop these methods, interpreting other materials through the lens of Ginzburg's ideas. What eventually turned into a trilogy first began as *Exercises in Mendeleev's Table* (1984), followed by *Elementi di struttura del sentimento* (1985; *Structural Elements of Feeling*), in which the actors give voice to the servants of Goethe's *Elective Affinities*, and which the company redeveloped seven years later using Goethe's title (fig. 2); and finally *Riso amaro* (1986; *Bitter Rice*). In an interview in 1996, over a decade since the first production of the trilogy, Curino recalled that the company was attempting to create a play in the same way that Mendeleev conceived his periodic table.[51] She explains how the nineteenth-century Russian scientist risked his reputation by asserting that certain aspects of his table did not yet make sense, not because the table was flawed but because science had yet to fulfill the discoveries he hypothesized. The company members imagined a table partially completed with empty squares that only twentieth-century scientists would be able to finish. Mendeleev's technique recalls the same spirit of research as in Ginzburg's "method of clues," led by that which was *not* apparent. Rather than scrapping the idea for the table of elements, Mendeleev embraced the lacunas, which is what attracted Teatro Settimo. The empty spaces intrigue. The barely existent voices—like the servants in Goethe's tale, who manage to leave an echo—are the true engines of history in the practice of Teatro Settimo.

To return to the emphasis on dialogue in the theater of narration, Curino's (and her company's) understanding of Mendeleev's efforts depict an individual in conversation with future colleagues whom he would never know, but who would take up his work and respond to it by completing (or debunking)

Fig. 2. Teatro Settimo's *Le affinità elettive* (Palazzolo Acreide, 1992) with (*left to right*) Mariella Fabbris, Lucilla Giagnoni (both of whom later joined Curino in *Adriano Olivetti*), Anna Coppola, Laura Curino, Paola Rota, and Benedetta Francardo. Photograph by Maurizio Buscarino. Courtesy of Laura Curino and Federico Negro.

his postulations. In that spirit, returning briefly to Hayden White and placing his respect for fiction in dialogue with Ginzburg's method of clues and Mendeleev's reverence for hypothesis, what begins to emerge is a technique in historical recuperation that relies on the creative thinking of artists. In his examinations of underlying structures of historical discourse, White argues that elements of literary technique, including metaphor and plot, are crucial to historiography and that historians should engage critically with these elements. As part of this process, "the historian must 'interpret' [their] materials by filling in the gaps in [their] information on inferential or speculative grounds."[52] The integration of documented past with imagined past is a conversation along what White calls "the truth-reality distinction," since "the conjuring up of the past requires art as well as information."[53] When narrators take liberties to fill the gaps in the historical record, they enact what White lamented the practice of history had lost: the creative courage to openly embrace hypothesis, which is essential for rigorous, scientifically minded inquiry.[54] White, Ginzburg, Mendeleev, and the members of Teatro Settimo were motivated by this idea that the empty spaces were opportunities to further enrich what the documented facts could only outline. An awareness of one's subjectivity and confidence in hypothesis opened up a space that allowed for a reassessment of history and its protagonists.

Teatro Settimo's Lingering Influence: Celestini's *Radio clandestina* (2000)

While many of the narrators that this book features worked with each other at various points in their career, including cross-generationally, Ascanio Celestini, a principal of the second generation of narrators, developed his poetics independently from any consultation or collaboration with Teatro Settimo artists. Yet his work shares remarkably similar choices. During the early 1980s when Teatro Settimo was just beginning to hit its stride, the theater of narration had not yet come to be, but by the time Celestini emerged on the scene in 1998, Curino, Paolini, and Baliani had already begun to refine this rendering of solo performance, a decade into it. While Celestini contributes his own poetics with his highly stylized, fast-paced, often deadpan delivery, both the aesthetic storytelling core and the methodological choices that share so many commonalities with the practice of microhistory are still key components in his work. Celestini only makes it clearer that the theater of narration is both a practice and performance of microhistory, taking its cues from the work of Teatro Settimo.

After several years in street theater and with four full-length plays behind him, Ascanio Celestini premiered *Radio clandestina* (*Clandestine Radio*), adapting Alessandro Portelli's oral history book *L'ordine è già stato eseguito* (1999; *The Order Has Been Carried Out*), in 2000.[55] As in several other narrative theater pieces, World War II is the overarching event. Consistent with the genre, the contemplation of history is a continuing force. The central dilemma of *Radio clandestina*, as with Portelli's book, is the way people have remembered the Nazi massacre of 335 Italians at the Ardeatine caves in southern Rome on March 24, 1944. It was an act of retaliation from the day before, when partisans attacked an SS battalion marching toward the Piazza di Spagna, killing thirty-three soldiers. In the days after the partisan attack, Nazis posted signs around the city informing people that the consequences of the attack would be the deaths of ten Italians for every German soldier. Portelli's book takes its name from the last line in the communiqué: "This order has already been carried out." Popular belief, however, holds that there was a different ending to the bulletin, one that would have turned the message into a warning rather than a fait accompli: this alternative bulletin read that if the partisan attackers came forward, then the Nazis would not carry out this threat. Both the scholarly text and the artistic performance explore the consequences of altering the historical record through the stories of ordinary citizens. While Portelli is more interested in uncovering how this myth came to be, Celestini concerns himself not only with the responsibility of revealing the truth during his performances, but also with his audiences' ability to both consider the version that he tells and think about their own relationship to storytelling and truth.

Here as in *Signorine*, historical reflection propels the narrator to ask questions about memory, which serve as an impulse to narrative. In reflecting on

Fig. 3. Ascanio Celestini in *Radio clandestina* in a performance on the twentieth anniversary of the show. Auditorium Parco della Musica, Rome, 2020. Photograph by Musacchio, Ianniello & Pasqualini. Courtesy of Fondazione Musica per Roma.

Portelli's book, Celestini writes that what struck him was not so much the history that it told, but the histories that it told about ordinary people and the intimacy with which it presents historical events.[56] Similar to how *Signorine* was as much a play about the nature of memory as one about specific memories, *Radio clandestina* (fig. 3) is as much a play about the telling of history as one about a specific history. Celestini provides the narrative framework through the invention of a fictitious character, *una bassetta*, or a little old lady, who is in search of a home and asks him to read the posted rentals every day. When it dawns on him that she cannot read, it fascinates him. She is from another time—a time when his grandfather, who owned a cinema house in Rome, used to read the instructional posters of the occupied city to his fellow neighbors, some of whom were illiterate and would ask him to interpret the directives.

From here, Celestini recalls the one strange poster informing the people that 335 Italians would be killed. He continues his story to the audience as though he were telling the story to the bassetta. In his preface to the play, Portelli highlights Celestini's fictitious framework with the invention of the bassetta, praising her both as a concentrated metaphor of a wartime Roman populace and as serving a narrative function, since her presence puts the very act of storytelling onstage.[57] More than that, however, by highlighting oral traditions, Celestini also raises important questions about their place today. He uses the construction of the bassetta to reflect on the function of narrative in contemporary Italy in a number of ways. Her lonely search for a home symbolizes the scarcity of oral traditions in the present. The opening scenes with Celestini reading the rental advertisements is also about reading aloud and the spoken word, and the fact that the bassetta never finds a home prompts the question, What place do oral traditions have in today's technologically paced cities? That, of course, is a rhetorical question that Celestini and others answer with their very performances.

Throughout the piece, he explores the relationship between narrative and history, a dynamic he shares with other narrators and with microhistorians, who, according to Levi, were first and foremost concerned with the historian's procedures, not with the scale of their subject matter.[58] As Celestini arrives at the point in his tale where he must directly address the Fosse Ardeatine massacre, he pauses, reflecting on how to tell this part. It is one of those stories, he says to the bassetta, that people think they know, that they only take a minute to recount, but to really tell it would take a week. He decides to start with the one-minute version:

> March 23, 1944, at four in the afternoon the bomb that the Roman partisans put in via Rasella explodes, and the next day in retaliation the Germans kill 335 people and this is known as the Fosse Ardeatine massacre. Period. End of story.[59]

This version demonstrates, indeed performs, how brisk history can be, glossing over a huge event without ever stopping to really listen to the voices of those times. In performance, it takes him approximately one hundred minutes to share a fuller account of those events, insisting that one must begin not with the war but almost seventy years prior, with the situating of Rome as the capital city in the recently unified nation of Italy, since that was when those caves were mined. Some of the structural splendors of the new capital were built with the materials from what would become a mass grave in World War II. He dramatizes temporal distance, playing with intimacy and apathy by sharing conversations that he remembers with his grandfather and then shifting to a textbook tone to remind his audience of the nation's official past when he cites numbers and milestones and other seemingly irrelevant information. This pattern of delivery begins to raise questions about historical construction, specifically how to incorporate personal accounts into public narratives.

Celestini more explicitly asks some of those questions about histories that are told and histories that are kept secret when he spends a moment reflecting on Italian colonialist interests in East Africa. This sequence is noteworthy not only for its historiographical point but also because it marks one of the few moments when the theater of narration, or even Italian theater more generally, openly discusses the country's colonial past. While this practice is not shy to criticize the state—quite the opposite; it very much asks for accountability from the state—it has yet to richly confront both colonialism and the current migrant crisis, which are connected insofar as they share histories in which governments aggressively destabilized foreign lands to reap their material benefits. Briefly but pointedly, Celestini likens the Nazis' brutalism in Italy to that of the Italians in Ethiopia, though he does not go far enough in educating his audience members about how violent the Italian fascist colonizers actually were.

During a sequence when Celestini details the mounting state-sanctioned prejudices as early as 1938 against Jewish Italians, from where they could work to whom they could marry, he takes a surprising turn when he recalls this same year as one in which Italians were already involved in war. Though at first he mocks Italians' own mockery of their inept colonizing, as they generally brush off the violence of their presence in Eritrea, Ethiopia, and Somalia under the fascist regime, he takes a more somber turn when he draws a parallel to this dismissive pattern in noting the ways Viceroy Marshal Rodolfo Graziani and General Pietro Maletti easily avoided accountability. Celestini states that on returning to Italy, Graziani testified that "a hundred or so" "Africans" died in the massacre at Debre Libanos, when in fact, Celestini goes on to specify, "To be precise, there were 349, in other words 14 more with respect to the Nazi slaughter in the Fosse Ardeatine." He then adds that with the retaliations there were more than a thousand civilians who died.[60] After this he quickly switches back to Italians, this time the soldiers who were unqualified to question the orders of their fascist superiors and who suffered dire consequences as a result, slowly making his way back to occupied Rome and the story of the Fosse Ardeatine.

His points about selective memory, the fleeting whisper of the still-current inability of many Europeans to actively comprehend and reflect on their colonial aggressions, and the reality that Italians were also subject to the violence of fascism resonate clearly enough, yet the brevity of the sequence on Ethiopian history is regrettable. The massacre in Debre Libanos occurred in May 1937, when Graziani ordered Maletti to execute all of the occupants (monks and deacons) of the ancient monastery there because he believed they were hiding two men who were partially responsible for organizing an attempted assassination of him in February of that year. As Celestini notes, in connection with the assassination many more than the monks died, though they were rounded up and slaughtered in a way similar to the Italians by the Nazis at the Fosse Ardeatine, which was what drew Celestini's attention.

May, however, was only the ending to a story that began in February after nine hand grenades were thrown in the way of Graziani during a large assembly. His guards opened fire on a crowd of an estimated three thousand poor, elderly, and disabled Ethiopian civilians who had gathered for an almsgiving ceremony in the now-occupied courtyard of a palace built for Emperor Haile Selassie. This retaliatory killing, which lasted three hours, resulted in the deaths of the vast majority of those civilians, but it did not stop there. In the most grotesque of ways, Italian soldiers waited till nightfall to move into the residential areas of Addis Ababa, where they brutally killed thousands more over the next forty hours.[61] So while it is laudable that Celestini invites comparison to the Debre Libanos massacre, he falls well short of really facing it, and incorporating it into his philosophical musings on the nature of historical thinking.

Celestini has shared that he has come to believe that in Italy, "we've passed from a nostalgic view of history to a comforting view of the past," ignoring the horrors that persist today. "It's become the new rhetoric . . . [since Italy] has been anesthetized by years of misrepresentation and disenchantment."[62] In *Radio clandestina*, he dramatizes this effort to mollify history when he speaks of how people change their memories to mask the harsher realities. With respect to both the atrocities of colonialism and those of the Nazis, people do not want to do the hard work of confronting the factors that resulted in specific realities. In the climactic moment of the play, he finally unravels the myth that there were warnings about the massacre by turning to archival evidence. Celestini summarily dismantles the invented memory of posters stating that if only the partisans come forward then the Nazis would not kill ten Italians for every German soldier, by quoting from court proceedings after the war in which a judge asked a Nazi defendant if they had printed any such warning. The defendant stated that they had not. Celestini works through this realization: "And yet still today many people say, 'my grandfather, he saw the posters . . . my uncle saw them . . . there were posters . . .' because people saw the posters even if no one had ever printed them . . . because in this lie that people have carried forward for more than fifty years, there was hope for those 335."[63] But the truth is that there was no hope. This moment performs the link between narrative and history, and the risks in constructing false histories, since the idea that all these deaths could have been prevented puts the blame squarely on the seemingly cowardly partisans.

Portelli has also reflected on misremembering and fantasy in recalling the past. With respect to oral history, he has written how the role of the imagination in the construction of history might be as important as what one considers fact. Taking a different approach than White, who focuses on the benefits of narrative construction, Portelli argues that even if a statement such as the one about the existence of the posters is empirically incorrect, it is still psychologically true for the people who share it. Accordingly, that belief, albeit fallible, might still lead to important historical insights.[64] Celestini works through the psychological truth that Portelli emphasizes. The misremembered posters are appealing because they make it easier to blame someone for the murders. In occupying that space of tension between historical myth (accounts of the posters) and historical fact (Nazi testimony that they did not exist), Celestini compassionately highlights the inherent problem in holding on to the idea that any of the 335 people who died at the Fosse

Ardeatine had any hope of a different outcome. Without condoning the partisan bombing on Via Rasella, he defends the partisans by underlining that they never actually had an opportunity to come forward.

For several minutes toward the end of the play, Celestini keeps coming back to the same question: "How is one supposed to tell this type of story?"[65] Most people do not want to hear it. People go out of their way to make sure that they do not, he explains, as when owners of a local bakery let relatives of those who died in the massacre pass ahead of others. It is not because they are being honored in some special way, but because people want them to buy their bread quickly and leave so that they do not have to hear their stories.[66] Yet Celestini is there trying to tell the bassetta, and his audience, about these pasts. He invites the audience to contemplate how narration affects history, and how those versions of history affect the present.

Although each narrator has carved out and defined their own poetics, the core of their work—of the theater of narration—embraces the overarching poetics that Teatro Settimo devised in their early years: a commitment to local stories, plurality of voices, and the personal stakes for the narrator as an analogy of the personal stakes for the ordinary citizen. In this practice, the audience learns how a Roman whose grandfather lived in the occupied capital during World War II, or young kids growing up in a factory town seven kilometers north of Italy's first capital, reshape collective understandings of past events. In their peripheral stories linger the major events that societies pass down as official histories. On the human scale, the official history is actually the one that is peripheral.

Chapter 2

✦

The Cultural Laborer

The figure of the narrator alone on a bare stage commands the audience's focus. This person is first a talented raconteur who enraptures the public with well-honed acting and skill of delivery. Narrators are also public intellectuals. They shade their tales in varying degrees of political intent, while they synthesize intellectual concepts in their productions. Marco Baliani's *Tracce* (1996; *Traces*), for example, is entirely a reflection on Ernst Bloch's eponymous collection and is among the most cerebral of productions. Unlike many works of the avant-garde, however, Baliani steers away from a complex formalism, and instead sits casually on a chair to address the audience directly. Finally, narrators have a sense of civic duty, which they demonstrate by guiding their audiences toward new perspectives about someone (an entrepreneur, a midwife) or something (the assassination of the prime minister, the industrial peripheral cities of the North). Taken altogether, they position themselves to construct dialectically a persona that converges the skills of the creative performer, the public intellectual, and the civil servant. While each narrator has a different performance style, they all nonetheless demonstrate a unique balance between these three identities. The resulting figure is a cultural laborer, a term I adapt from the animazione teatrale practices of the mid-1970s.

At the heart of the theater of narration is a sense of responsibility to converse in a productive way. Narrators produce knowledge, new histories, and the experiences of others. They create projects from this impulse, which leads them to engage diverse communities, social issues, and historical events. In founding a new dramaturgical language, the first generation of narrators devised a practice of listening and moved away from the visual stimulus of the physical theater that was so much a part of Teatro Settimo's oeuvre. Hinting at the oratorical dimension of a soloist speaking directly to the audience, the term "cultural laborer" underlines both public service and pedagogy in the narrators' practice. This concept acknowledges the work, the labor of their jobs, and the urgency and necessity of reconciling the past in terms of individual experience.

Ethnography is an important component of cultural labor, in part because narrators adjust the practice to contain more overt didactic implications, and in part because of its basis in empathy. When narrators perform, they hold a mirror in front of their publics not just to beg their gaze, but to beg their critical, self-aware gaze: Where is your reflection? Where are *you* in this history? As cultural laborers, they first conduct an ethnography of themselves as a way of centering their personal stakes against larger sociocultural events, communities, or individuals. Their second use for ethnography is a more traditional investigation of individuals from within their communities. Performance scholars Suzanne MacAulay and Kevin Landis define the practice of ethnography as simply the practice of getting to know other human beings intimately and well, especially through their everyday experiences.[1] For narrators, this process leads to a historical praxis in which they put their own critically examined private histories in conversation with other microhistories, and then reassemble the greater historical narrative to include those two parts.

Taking inspiration from the animazione movement's collaborative spirit, while also acknowledging the inherent power structures between themselves and their publics, narrators cultivate a rapport with the audience in which they are several steps ahead—Virgilian guides—as the audience follows along a journey that is often intensely personal and eminently public. As they reconsider the past through a people-empowered lens, they work in a reflexive, methodologically transparent, Brechtian pattern so that audiences can embrace these tools for their own purposes. A better understanding of narrators' personas reveals not only the practice's revolutionary potential, but also its dependence on this single individual and their ability to convey the relationship between ordinary people and extraordinary events.

The long 1970s in Italy were also influential in shaping the concept of the cultural laborer as intellectual discussions from the period confronted the prospects of an artistic and politically engaged life. An investigation of the contextual influences uncovers some of the cultural sparks that inspired the founding narrators' self-conceptions. As narrators begin to understand their relationships to surrounding environments through a practice and eventually performance of autoethnography, they reveal the influence of cultural anthropology on the theater of narration. The oft-referenced writings of Victor Turner and others concerning the "anthropology of experience" in conversation with D. Soyini Madison's notions of critical ethnography and the positionality of the researcher illuminate the delicate balance of self-awareness and full immersion that narrators negotiate. In examining themselves and their environments, albeit retrospectively, they also perform for the audience a method of examination. They suggest that an attentiveness to one's surroundings and one's relationship to their surroundings will inform and influence the ability to read historical events more generously, more compassionately, and with greater depth.

Finally, the last major characteristic of the cultural laborer is the desire to obtain a dynamic understanding of others. The ways in which narrators turn the mirror of an autoethnography outward to conduct a traditional ethnography composed of oral histories completes their tapestries of ordinary people, which ultimately depict a large-scale, widely recognizable moment in the national history. Studies by the oral historians Alessandro Portelli and Luisa Passerini, along with performance studies scholar Della Pollock, help to articulate the potentials of oral history, particularly in the theater. Together, these three components—an intellectual breadth, an ethnography of oneself, and an oral history–driven classical ethnography—articulate the core of the narrator as a cultural laborer: someone whose trade is art but who works from the perspective of a public servant.

The early work of Teatro Settimo beginning in 1974 that was heavily influenced by the popularity of animazione exhibits the most conscious intentions toward creating a theater in the vein of cultural labor that the narrators refined in their practices. Laura Curino first demonstrates the dialectic of self-awareness and activism in her 1987 *Passione*. Similarly, Marco Baliani's involvement in student-led activism in Rome during the 1970s inspired an ethnography of himself, which he so pointedly shares in *Corpo di stato* (*Body of State*). Debuting in 1998, this production demonstrates how the auto-ethnographic technique became a hallmark of the narrator's work, even for someone who did not study directly with Teatro Settimo. More than ten years later, when the second-generation narrator Giuliana Musso premiered *Nati in casa* (2001; *Born at Home*), she demonstrated an energetic engagement with cultural labor, also proving how this concept continues to follow narrators who came of age during different periods and in different parts of the country. This particular piece focuses on issues of modern obstetrics practices, basing her play on ethnographic research of midwives and obstetricians near her home region in the Northeast.

Baliani, Curino, and Musso continue to perform all of these plays at theaters and festivals all around Italy and occasionally abroad into the 2020s indicating their continued relevance and popularity even thirty-plus years after the debuts of some. *Passione* and *Corpo di stato* exhibit in especially clear terms the ways in which narrators engage an ethnography of oneself, but they are also two very different pieces offering distinct ways in which the narrators interpret public memories through private experiences. *Nati in casa*, meanwhile, is exemplary in its dexterous melding of oral history and creative imagination to build an argument. While these artists have worked with various degrees of intention toward a concept of cultural labor, they open up the work of other artists—and not just theater artists—to reconsider their product in economic terms with a specific value for the well-being of societies.

Impegno and the Intellectual

The animazione movement popular during the 1960s and 1970s demonstrates how members of Teatro Settimo understood its practice of pedagogical theater in relation to their responsibilities as theater artists invested in their community. A closer investigation of its main principles in communion with the theater of narration reveals its profound influence in the concept of the narrator and in how narrators crafted the persona of the cultural laborer. The movement created a path that led students on a journey to create lives as artists, intellectuals, and active members of society. Particularly insightful is Curino's copy of Morteo's manual for animazione from her private archives, which she first read around 1978 during the dawn of Teatro Settimo. In its introduction she underlined a paragraph in which Morteo explains that the animator is not someone who executes a project, but a laborer or worker (*operatore*) who, in consultation with collaborators, produces interventions suitable to particular situations.[2] With the choice of "laborer" instead of "artist," Morteo implies that the animator provides a service to the public, offering a utilitarian conception of the theater artist.

Returning to the opening of her most successful solo show, *Camillo Olivetti*, which debuted in 1996 almost twenty years after she studied Morteo's book, Curino shares a similar thought: "This work is dedicated to Adriano Olivetti. I say *work* and not *play* in the memory of an expression that my parents used. . . . They would talk about going to the theater to see this or that particular artist because . . . the actor works well. Works, they said, not *performs*."[3] Her show, about one of the most famous entrepreneurs in modern Italy, is for ordinary people like her parents who recognized work when they saw it. Referring to herself, she makes it clear every night to a new audience that the performance they are about to witness is an act of labor. Rather than Morteo, she credits her parents, a seamstress and a Fiat worker, with this notion that art and work had something in common, but such an idea was also all around her, in her coming of age during the 1970s with ubiquitous discourses about the concept of labor, and in her own introduction to animazione, where she had underlined Morteo's use of *operatore* to describe performers.

Returning to Morteo's manual, a little farther down the page from where he first introduces the concept of the laborer, Curino had starred a paragraph in the margins and underlined specific phrases. Morteo explains that one goal of animazione teatrale is "to design a way to live the cultural experience, or perhaps more precisely, if limiting, to make one live, to help one live the cultural experience, someone who has not or has not yet gained familiarity with such an experience"—a passage Curino underlined.[4] Morteo clarifies the term "cultural experience" as the "incorporation of an indeterminate plurality of attitudes and operations," which Curino underlined in squiggles, and goes on to emphasize that "it is a functional imprecision that relates to a plurality of attitudes and operations."[5] Culture, then, is something messy for Morteo, something imprecise because it encompasses many voices. To experience this plurality, especially for those who never have, is also the main objective of animazione, and struck Curino as a key point. The implications in this work for theater as an act and spectatorship as a mode of witnessing constitute an ethos of service. Morteo implores the artist to practice sharing a multitude, and invites the public to live this new experience. As explored below, the idea of many voices resurfaces in the theater of narration, as does a similar appeal for the audience to embrace these many perspectives.

For the next several pages, Morteo stresses the importance of group work, and he concludes that "collective behavior is a hallmark of animazione, one of the main elements that juxtaposes it to how one generally understands what it means to participate in an artistic (and in a broad sense cultural) event that is prevalent today."[6] At the time she was studying this text, Curino was in the midst of founding Teatro Settimo, with whom she devised and performed dozens of plays for the next decade before creating *Passione*. She took Morteo's advice literally by collaboratively creating theater with a company of artists whose plays were frenetic and physical, often involving large casts who could follow their impulses and improvise movements and gestures in the direction of a collective goal. A decade later, as Curino tells the story of her youth in *Passione*, reflecting on what it meant to grow up in the industrial North and more specifically in the town of Settimo Torinese, she operates as a soloist, developing these concepts of plurality into a more sophisticated dramaturgy that functions less literally.

For narrators, the use of autobiography—which they push into the realm of an autoethnography, as the following section explores—becomes a way to dialogue with others in imaginative interactions and explore the spirit of the plural. It also combines the civic responsibility of the intellectual with the dramatic imperatives of a storyteller. The narrators use their own subjectivity to balance a delicate neutrality in their work with the implicit decision to disseminate new perspectives, but they refrain from condoning any outright political position. Such restraint defines the terms of their cultural labor, putting the service back into civic responsibility. They do not proselytize. If the cultural experience is one that is meant to incorporate a cacophonous symphony of perspectives, as Morteo described it, then it is also one in which there is no single better experience.

On some occasions, narrators blur the boundaries of the genre by performing works by other authors, but in a style of solo performance that is suggestive of the theater of narration. Lella Costa fascinatingly draws attention to constructions of gender in her performance of the great Italian comic actor Franca Valeri's play *La vedova Socrate* (*Socrates's Widow*, first written and performed by Valeri in 2003, in her early eighties, and debuting with Costa in July 2020, just before Valeri's hundredth birthday; fig. 4). Costa, this time through Valeri, portrays the infamously cantankerous wife of Socrates, Xanthippe, with compassion and intelligence, suggesting that such a reputation was unfounded and unfair, and inherently questioning the way women are judged, especially in relation to their husbands.

Fig. 4. Lella Costa in *La vedova Socrate* (Teatro romano di Fiesole, 2020). Photograph by and courtesy of Bernardo Baluganti.

Narrators are not completely impartial because they are aware of the ways in which their stories are relevant today. They are not simply recounting facts but also relaying their persistent significance through a critical perspective.[7] As they highlight events that official history has repressed, helping to contextualize their importance for the audience, there is an implicit judgment that society would be bettered by listening to these other voices. Some critics have explicitly referred to several productions that have more of an investigative journalist tone as civic theater, such as Paolini's *Vajont*, but all theater of narration is civic theater because it asks its spectators to actively engage with society by forming its composition from as many perspectives as possible, and not just an elite few.

This notion of civic theater surfaces in other theaters of the real and performances that wrestle with the past. In his preface to the English edition of *Corpo di stato*, theater scholar Ron Jenkins compares Baliani's work to that of Spalding Gray, particularly Gray's *Swimming to Cambodia*, about his experiences filming *The Killing Fields* (1984). Especially resonant for Jenkins is when Gray refers to himself as a "poetic reporter," meaning that he places the emphasis not on facts but rather on how to process them once they have settled with time.[8] Similarly, Rokem conceives of actors who perform historical figures or events as "hyper-historians" who physically embody both the past and the creative process of the present.[9] These descriptions also suit the work of narrators who similarly negotiate tensions between documented historical events, memory, and invention, but the work of the cultural laborer is more far-reaching.

One important task for a cultural laborer is to serve as a liaison to some of the leading arguments with which societies grapple. Intellectual concepts that were in conversation with protesting populations are present in the theater of narration, both formally and thematically. Decentralization and redistribution of authority, for example, became central tenants of worker revolts that took shape as early as 1962 with violent protests in one of Turin's main squares, Piazza Statuto.[10] Curino's *Olivetti* plays might be the most apparent example, since the two plays discuss factory labor and industrialists, interrogating the possibility of a factory that was largely in the hands of its workers. While she does not critique the Olivetti family, she subversively narrates their story largely through the two matriarchs, Elvira Sacerdoti, the mother of engineer Camillo Olivetti, who founded the company, and Luisa Revel, his wife and the mother of Adriano Olivetti, who further developed the company. Sacerdoti and Revel were so unknown that Curino herself conducted the research that finally settled the correct spelling of Sacerdoti (and not Sacerdot*e*).

Embodying these two women and hearing the fabled Olivetti history from them is an example of the ways in which narrators incorporate the positions of ordinary people in their productions. It is also a formal choice that performs the ideas of decentering (in this case Camillo and Adriano Olivetti) and redistributing authority (to Sacerdoti and Revel). The *Olivetti* plays exemplify the sophisticated and subtly crafted methods with which the theater of narration engages themes that were vital in the long 1970s, but in earlier works there are more overt demonstrations of activism. In Curino's first years with Teatro Settimo, the group occupied public spaces turning them into performance spaces and engaged in acts that mirrored the violence they witnessed, such as smashing and setting fire to a car, as in their show *Esercizi sulla tavola di Mendeleev* (1984).

This broad conception of the narrator who engages in acts of social justice not only pursues the areas of overlap between theater and activism from the stage, but also conveys the theatricality of protests, ubiquitous in 1970s Italian society. One of the main oppositional forces during the 1970s was the development of countercultures, such as radical groups that decentralized power.[11] Activists employed theatrical behaviors in complex ways, as the relationship between students and workers demonstrates: rather than staging forms of protest that would signal theatricality (e.g., with costumes, props, and scripts), students and factory workers were attracted to the characters that each represented, beyond the social issues. Both groups began to transfer their identities onto the other, attempting to alter some of the ways in which society viewed them. Generalizing, students held utopian ideas of community environments in factories with Maoist Chinese models in mind, which, for some, led to Marxist fantasies of revolt.[12] The performative implications of this Maoist ideal, where students live out a fantasy of worker revolt, point to theatricality as a practice of existence during these years.

Jean Baudrillard suggests a separate angle when he considers the exhibitionist temptations of terrorists surrounding the Moro capture as not so unlike those of establishment politicians.[13] For him, those elected officials and those extraparliamentary revolutionaries were all involved in a practice of performance in order to influence the general public. The literary scholar Jennifer Burns has argued that several major writers and intellectuals in the twentieth century responded to the terrorism of the 1970s as a fantastical larger-than-life occurrence, as though it were fiction.[14] These years, which were so fraught with struggle for social progress, curiously blurred the creative with the political as a way not only to interpret social movements but also to practice and exist in them.

Returning to students and workers, from his personal involvement with Marxist-oriented collectives, Portelli observed that while the radical youth movements of that decade helped in changing the perception of working-class culture, most educated youth still rejected identification with working classes. Many university students preferred to identify with and meet in groups of "young people" rather than with groups of workers.[15] On the one hand, the students and workers were united, but on the other, they were oppositional. These two very different observations about the behaviors of these groups speak to the intensely variegated directions of the 1970s. These extremes demonstrate the need for a dialectic result to harmonize the polarities and create something out of their mutual attraction, which is precisely what the narrators found in their conception of a cultural laborer.

The concept of political engagement, or impegno, is fundamental to the definition of an Italian intellectual, particularly from the 1960s through the 1980s. Certainly many Italian theorists, philosophers, and artists have considered what it means to be an intellectual, as is easily visible from the writings of Antonio Gramsci and Norberto Bobbio to Italo Calvino and Pier Paolo Pasolini. As literary scholar Vincenzo Binetti notes, after fascism and the war, it seemed likely that leftist intellectuals would emerge to publicly reevaluate society via culture. Being an intellectual in the postwar climate meant being a cultural ambassador or interpreter rather than an ideologue.[16] Yet the role of the intellectual became more fraught in the latter half of the century. Binetti argues that the mass-mediated system and the continued growth of technology imposed an irreversible process of alienation that problematizes the role of the intellectual in society. Gone are the postwar intellectuals who served as the moral conscience of a nation, supreme judges of historical developments, and passionate guardians of civil rights.[17] Binetti's tone is elegiac, yet this might be a positive development insofar as it suggests a democratic dispersing of intellectual potential. Many people invested in social movements reflected on them, commented on them, and ultimately shaped the role of the intellectual in Italian society.

The rapport between students and noted intellectuals, which was often contradictory and conflicted, also reflects the shift that Binetti elucidates. There was tension, since the students viewed intellectuals as living complacently within the bourgeois system. Many intellectuals, however, aimed to support students, persuaded by their calls to alter aspects of the university experience, and joined their causes through various facets of artistic production and propaganda.[18] One of the main tenets of the 1970s-era student revolts was based on the desire for a system that was more responsive to their social needs and experiences instead of an institution in which they attended school and "received" knowledge through grandiose lecturing.[19] Students, and eventually narrators, wanted to change a system that presumed mere compliance with authority. They wanted more control over the practice of acquiring knowledge, which would have distributed power more equitably within the educational system.

Though it was a score and some years later since the height of student uprisings and occupied universities, Baliani's 1996 *Tracce* is a provocative undertaking that offers an example of both the expansive creativity with which the theater of narration can operate, and how narrators can repurpose complex intellectual concepts, or in this case a philosophical text itself, and render it accessible on a large scale. Taking inspiration from the passage in *Traces* in which Ernst Bloch suggests that "in short, it's good to think in stories too" Baliani devised an entire production that mimics Bloch's associative style, which is its own performance of thinking rendered textual and performative.[20] In Baliani's three-dimensional free-form narrative, which changes dramatically between performances, he works to privilege the mere idea of narration, of speaking and listening, by musing in a Joycean train of thought about the power of stories. At times he recites poetry, as if to perform the beauty that a vocalized poem can transmit. In a Brechtian fashion, but also in a way that involves the spectators, he opens his show not just narrating content but describing what is occurring onstage. In the first lines he offers, "I like to begin allowing my voice to resonate in the darkness as I recite a poem." He ends the play the same way, with both a description of his actions and a poem. "Now I leave you . . . and as I recite the poem, the lights dim little by little until it is only darkness around us." And so begins his excerpt from Rilke. (He opens with Dylan Thomas.)[21] This play represents the theater of narration in one of its most experimental forms and demonstrates how narrators are attracted to intellectual material and rendering it accessible on a large scale.

An Ethnography of Oneself: The Personal Terrain of Public Events

The political and intellectual environment that surrounded first-generation narrators in their early years stimulated community-creating and the exchange of ideas, but the theatrical framework to which they were drawn, which offered an embodied experience for both the performer and the audience, required the narrator to find a method with a physical-awareness that could complement the intellectual and argumentative aspect of their practice. From this need for a physical center-point emerges a practice of autoethnography. The origin for this term as it relates to the theater of narration lies in some of the last writings of anthropologist Victor Turner, regarding notions of experience. In a volume coedited with Turner, Edward M. Bruner credits late nineteenth-century sociologist Wilhelm Dilthey's concept of experience (*Erlebnis*, or what has been lived through) as having inspired Turner's notion of an anthropology of experience.[22] Clarifying the relationship between anthropology and experience, Bruner asserts that anthropologists attempt to understand the world through the "experiencing subject," striving for an inner perspective.[23] For many narrators, the effort to share the world of those subjects, to tell their stories, first begins with themselves as they reflect on what they have lived through, and how they use their own experiences to navigate a shared journey with their subjects.

Narrators promote the idea that historical recuperation is ultimately an interactive process. As such, one of the closest ways in which they can experience the world of their subjects is through a method of immersion, like an ethnographer. They adjust the focus of their investigation to first examine themselves, rather than others, in a specific environment. When Paolini, for example, begins his tale of the dam construction and landslide in *Vajont*, he opens with an analysis of what the dam meant to *him* as a young boy in the Northeast. When Curino tells her story of Camillo Olivetti, the first section recalls what the Olivetti factory meant to *her* growing up in the industrial North. When Davide Enia recounts the murder of two Sicilian judges trying to stop the Mafia, he sets the scene at the kitchen table with his parents in his home in Palermo having just heard the news.

Related to autobiography, an autoethnography signals a deeper critical rigor and contextualization of cultural surroundings. Autoethnographic texts include "cultural reflection" as opposed to the "merely personal."[24] The practice offers a broad sociocultural analysis through personal narrative.[25] In the theater of narration, the autoethnographic aspect also motions toward the ways in which narrators perform a pedagogy. This technique concerns a process of thinking. The anthropologist Barbara Myerhoff explains how self-reflection is useful for people to have a better understanding of themselves:

> One of the most persistent but elusive ways that people make sense of themselves is to show themselves to themselves, through multiple forms: by telling themselves stories; by dramatizing claims in rituals and other collective enactments; by rendering visible actual and desired truths about themselves and the significance of their existence in imaginative and performative productions.[26]

The narrator takes these same techniques and uses them as a way not just to know themselves but also to know intimately a public event in terms of others. Through their stories, and the retelling of them, they guide their publics to search for better understandings of themselves in relation to each other and their shared histories.

Baliani's *Corpo di stato* and Curino's *Passione* demonstrate two distinct ways to perform autoethnographies. Baliani negotiates his role as a student during a time with violent student protests and presents a way of thinking that the audience members themselves can mimic. He revisits his late teens and early twenties in the 1970s, when he was an active protestor in the many movements that challenged the status quo, showing how he, as a left-leaning student, emotionally processed two climatic events of the decade: the kidnapping and assassination of Prime Minister Aldo Moro and the Mafia-led murder of Peppino Impastato.[27] Baliani stands downstage for most of the performance addressing the audience directly, occasionally sitting on a bench during moments of silence when he screens black-and-white photographs depicting several protests and clashes with the police. Baliani's text is a visual arrangement reminiscent of cinematic montage in that he weaves together different memories from his more revolutionary past in a charged and emotional register.

Passione is Curino's great homage to her hometown of Settimo Torinese, which she introduces through her eyes as a young child having just moved there from Turin on account of her father's work as a Fiat employee. Largely in first person—though also portraying many characters, including the curious women in her town who both intimidated and intrigued her as a young girl, and other women she had invented in plays she wrote with Teatro Settimo—she recalls her own personal history as a conduit through which to explore and better make sense of a national identity in a quickly industrializing society and amid a growingly diverse constellation of regional cultures. *Passione* embodies the complex layering of many influences as Curino compresses time through her memory in a long-view examination of her past. She offers a varied performance haunted with many people of her life, real and imagined, and with references to the literature of Pasolini, Goethe, and Allende, setting the tone for a complex interweaving of not only a private past, but also a cultural past shared by many.

Victor Turner's conception of culture as an uncontrollable plurality incapable of containing meaning mirrors Morteo's explanation, yet Turner also added that people were active agents in the historical process.[28] One of the benefits of the narrators' ethnographies of themselves is how the method requires them to acknowledge the inherent tensions in their attempts to provide a more authentic people's account of particular moments or places. Baliani confesses that one of his many initial reactions to Moro's kidnapping was not anger or sadness but exhilaration. Curino laughs at the squalid environments that characterize parts of her childhood as she also looks back with remorse. The fact that they incorporate personal experiences underscores the reflexivity in being subject *and* object, interviewee *and* interviewer, in dialogue with themselves as much as with others.

Baliani's Corpo di stato

Baliani's play frames the deaths of Impastato and Moro as well as the social and political unrest of the later 1970s from the perspective of the student movements that occupied Italian universities, particularly La Sapienza in Rome. He depicts the main events that defined his early adult life, as they defined many at that time. Amid the myriad of conspiracy theories and mysteries surrounding Moro's death, Baliani admits plainly that he is not concerned with discovering what actually happened. Rather, he wants to confront what was happening to him emotionally during these times.[29] Once he understands his interior state, he will be able to more deeply understand the exterior events. He quickly switches registers to a private, even confessional tone in which he shares with the audience the inner conflicts these traumatic events brought forth. He cues the audience that he is about to reveal something very delicate:

> I know, I could tell you something completely different, it wouldn't take much, with the wisdom of hindsight I could tell you I got angry when I heard the announcement on the radio [that Moro had been kidnapped and five of his guards murdered], that I immediately condemned the action of the Red Brigades. No, that's not true, it didn't go like that.[30]

Baliani is showing his audience that he has a choice in what to say, in how to construct that narrative of his innermost feelings. He could pretend to the audience, and maybe even to himself, that he felt a certain way, a way the audience would readily consider honorable, but instead he chooses to acknowledge something closer to the truth, however unglamorous it might be. He admits plainly that when news reached him of the kidnapping he "felt a sense of exhilaration." Although he defends himself by saying that he had never endorsed the extreme measures of the Red Brigades, he still bravely acknowledges this initial reaction, wondering how and why he felt a sense of euphoria over the kidnapping as though he belonged to the cause.

In a way, he *did* belong to the cause, and the piece is largely about figuring out what that "belonging" means. This act of self-locating demonstrates how the narrator works with the audience to provoke questions about where they and their stories belong within other stories and the stories of others. Baliani wondered how he could participate in the energized protests of those days, while also opposing this act against Moro, a symbol of negotiation and compromise. How can he participate in violence without acknowledging

Fig. 5. Marco Baliani in *Corpo di stato* (Rome, 1998). Photograph by Maurizio Agostinetto. Courtesy of Marco Baliani. The expressionistic image, which was also used for the program, emphasizes the emotional stress and confusion that Baliani dramatizes in his performance.

his complicity when that violence escalates? Baliani cannot answer these questions, but by asking them he shows how one person, in their lonely singularity, can confront events that affected many.

In performing an ethnography of himself, Baliani (fig. 5) slowly unfurls his story into a sequence of broad reflections in which he asks a series of questions that then inspire him to make connections with more public names. This is his transition from the questions in his own mind and how they lead to the more familiar situations of the time.

> How had it come to this? How did it happen that friends, comrades from my own political group, from the marches, had suddenly started talking about weapons . . . ? But what could you do, if the police went around dressed as students during the protests, holding pistols in their hands to provoke the crowds? What could you do if they shot tear gas canisters at your head during the marches? Isn't that how they killed Francesco Lorusso in Bologna? And Giorgiana Masi in Rome, on the Garibaldi bridge. . . . What were we supposed to do? When did the clash turn so harsh, when did it get out of control, when?[31]

The naming of Lorusso and Masi calls forth the memory of two protestors who were killed during demonstrations. In a bold suggestion, Baliani references the "strategy of tension" when he recalls undercover police provoking crowds so that they could use force in suppressing them.[32] Amid this confusion, chaos, and ultimately tension in the atmosphere, he insinuates that the police themselves created a situation in which they would be pardoned for the deaths of protesters. The stories of Lorusso and Masi evolve from two protesters who were killed to two protesters who were lured into a dangerous atmosphere by police, who then killed them.

Such an important shift in perspective is possible only because of the ethnographic techniques that Baliani employs. This moment shares methodological similarities with what cultural anthropologists and ethnographers call "participant observation," in which they take part in the experience they are studying at the same time that they are observing it. Here Baliani's entryway into a reflection on Lorusso and Masi is through his own experiences of being in the middle of a protest. As Bruner explains, "The anthropology of experience deals with how individuals actually experience their culture, that is, how events are received by consciousness," including one's feelings and expectations toward these events.[33] For narrators, their method is reflective, while the anthropologist takes notes in the present. Though the reliance on memory might seem problematic, as it could signal inaccuracies and fictions, Turner notes that "it is structurally unimportant whether the past is 'real' or 'mythical,' 'moral' or 'amoral.' The point is whether meaningful guidelines emerge from the existential encounter within a subjectivity of what we have derived from previous structures or units of experience in living relation with the new experience."[34] These ideas are in communion with Certeau, White, Jenkins, and other historians who have theorized the vitality that occurs between history and fiction. Bruner also endorses this perspective, noting that "there is no fixed meaning in the past, for with each new telling the context varies, the audience differs, the story is modified."[35] This is ever more true in the theater of narration, in which narrators are constantly retelling stories from one night to the next with different audiences, yet their personal histories, even if they might differ slightly between performances, serve to ground them.

The method of allowing an ethnography of oneself to lead to an ethnography of others is problematized not only by memory but also by the fact that representing the experiences of others is a complicated and even controversial undertaking that has consequences. In her work on performance ethnography, D. Soyini Madison stresses the need to discuss the positionality of those who represent others and to be attentive to slippage with subjectivity:

> Ethnographic positionality is not identical to subjectivity. Subjectivity is certainly within the domain of positionality, but positionality requires that we direct our attention beyond our individual or *subjective* selves. Instead, we attend to how our subjectivity *in relation to*

> *others* informs and is informed by our engagement and representation of others. We are not simply subjects, we are subjects in dialogue with others.[36]

In the spirit of the cultural laborer, narrators ultimately want to shift the story from their own to that of others, but by starting with their own, they position themselves as insiders. They are not researchers from faraway universities coming in to study small populations and then leaving. Narrators work from home.

In *Corpo di stato*, Baliani spends more than a third of the entire show speaking about three characters inspired by people he knew to varying degrees of closeness. In many ways they were just average citizens, but they had strong beliefs and suffered consequences for their political commitments and decisive actions during the late 1970s. Their actions were not extraordinary, yet they paid dearly for them. The three men, each given their own sequences in the show, were named Giorgio, Riccardo, and Armando. Giorgio was a few years younger than Baliani and many of the other seasoned protestors, who were in their twenties. As some of these groups began to steer toward more hostile and violent action, the younger ones, Baliani says, often felt that they needed to prove something. In 1977, Giorgio and some others were caught by the police after an attempted bank robbery. Though he was unarmed, he reached into his pocket for an ID card, and one of the cops—probably as young as Giorgio, Baliani offers—shot and killed him. While Baliani explains what happened to Giorgio, he also shares more intimate moments, such as looking at a photograph of Giorgio where someone snuck his hand behind his head, giving him bunny ears. His aim is always to humanize the people in his memories, including himself, into ordinary individuals to whom many can relate.

Armando's situation is particularly provocative for Baliani, and he uses it to construct a reflexive world of what-ifs: What would he have done if he had been in a similar situation? After giving up much of his political affiliations with groups who had grown more and more violent, Armando had a wife and young daughter by 1978 and spent much of his time working in the hospital. One evening an old friend rang his doorbell and begged him to hide a package that he was carrying. Armando's wife was not home, and eventually he conceded to his friend's pleas, never telling his wife what occurred. After two days passed during which the friend was supposed to return for the package, finally, on the third, the building was surrounded by police who found it: a gun. Armando ended up with a three-year prison sentence. His wife, who Baliani says has never forgiven him, also spent three months in jail trying to prove that she knew nothing about it.

These memories of visiting Armando in jail, of his unfortunate story, stir in Baliani many mixed emotions from guilt to gratefulness and even paranoia. He wonders what he would do if an old beauty from his youth who was prominent in the revolutionary groups, and whom he always tried (and failed) to impress, showed up at his home one day asking for the same favor. Baliani depicts Armando as a good person, fighting "the good fight," who turned his back on it when it grew too violent, became a family man and then, maybe out of nostalgia, or maybe without any real reason, made a bad decision for which he suffered the consequences. In part Baliani is asking the audience, How do you step back and realize things have gone too far when you are in the middle of something? The use of his own emotional conflicts in connection with stories about his friends reduces the distance between the audience and himself, since reflexive questioning and role-playing are familiar acts.

By performing those behaviors as part of his show, Baliani nudges the spectator to do the same and, in doing so, share the experiences of Armando. As Richard Schechner has specified, "Everything imaginable has been, or can be, experienced as actual by means of performance. And that, as Turner said, it is by imagining—by playing and performing—that new actualities are brought into existence. Which is to say, there is no fiction, only unrealized actuality."[37] This hypothetical realm of the imagination affects not just the way in which Baliani or audience members tell stories of events that they lived through, but also the way they tell those stories that then become histories. The ability to intimately connect with the experience of others, to see those experiences from one's own perspective and wonder what one would do, demonstrates a rich empathy that guides the historiography of the specific events that these plays discuss.

Curino's Passione

In her critique of small towns in the industrial North, Curino offers a multidimensional example of the participant observer in which one must have a particularly heightened awareness of positionality. Toward the end of her play, Curino recalls the evening when a neighbor brought her to see Dario Fo and Franca Rame's *Mistero buffo* (1968). The penultimate scene of *Passione* is of a young Curino as a spectator in the audience just before this particular performance begins. It is a virtuoso moment including southern dialects, colloquial expressions, and touches of Spanish. Curino reminisces about the local people of Settimo Torinese completely filling the piazza, full of joyous energy, where husbands, wives, and lovers alike merrily awaited the event. "And you laugh, laugh so hard that your heart takes off, it flies, until you don't know where your heart is anymore," she recounts.[38] With her own memory as the base, she portrays the small-town local production as a liberating moment for many in Settimo.[39]

Looking out into her audience as she performs *Passione* (fig. 6), she reconstructs a moment when she was looking at another audience, that time as an audience member herself, when she was a young woman attending Fo and

Fig. 6. Laura Curino in *Passione* (Dro, Trentino-Alto Adige, ca. 1995). Photograph by Paolo Rapalino. Courtesy of Laura Curino and Federico Negro.

Rame's show. Of all the details that she could have gathered, she assembles the joyous laughter that she shares both with that earlier audience and with the audience presently before her in a layered participant observation. Straddling time, she addresses both these groups directly with *you* ("you laugh," *tu ridi*), purposefully confounding them; one as she remembers them, the other as they are before her. Then she breaks away from her memory to address the audience in front of her to say that she wishes they could have been there. In that hope, there is the reminder that the audience will never know for themselves, only through her guidance, what being a part of that play in *that* audience of locals from Settimo Torinese in the early 1970s was like, yet the present audience is also a part of her play in the present moment as its members listen to her.

Curino further complicates her positionality when she follows her recollection of Fo and Rame's visit with an actual portrayal of Rame's monologue from *Mistero buffo* of the Passion of Mary before the Cross. Curino's play articulates an ability to be fractured across time and place in the same way that sociologist Erving Goffman theorizes frames as boundaries that orient people to a collective understanding of behavioral norms.[40] Goffman points toward a self that adjusts according to the framework in which one exists, but Curino demonstrates how the dynamics of the self can exist in a single framework in these last scenes. There are several subversive strands among the dexterous shifting of frames that Curino creates, from layering the performance space of postwar suburban Turin over the one she is currently in, to challenging not only the traditional practice of theater but also that of storytelling in her vacillation between her characters and herself. Further, the very subject material of the Mary scene dramatically shifts attention from Jesus to his mother. Curino's practice plays with constructions of memory (what she remembered of Rame's performance) and challenges what in history should be remembered (what she, Curino, decided was worth relating to the audience). In the case of Rame, Curino rewrites a performance history that includes a diverse working-class audience but also, and finally, one that allows Rame to share a spotlight that is almost always aimed at Fo.

Curino credits Rame's monologue from *Mistero buffo*, which offers a feminist perspective of the Catholic ritual of the Passion that borders on the sacrilegious (and was most certainly according to the Church), with making her want to pursue theater. As Mary watches Jesus slowly die, she viciously curses and swears at the Roman guards, eventually trying to bribe them to let her dab her son's bleeding skin. A nod to the groundbreaking feminist theory of the 1970s that considers language and *écriture féminine*, Rame's monologue is notably in an archaic tongue somewhere between Latin and a southern dialect, requiring her to rely on an experiential language of communication. After the guards refuse, she condemns the archangel Gabriel for having visited her in the first place. In the horrific suffering of witnessing her son's grisly death, she wishes that he had never been born. This portrayal of Mary is hardly the patient and understanding saint who accepted her fate and recognized the honor of her role in Jesus's life. She is a weeping human, a helpless parent, a fighter with agency to protest until the bitter end.

Both Rame's and Curino's very presence as female artists alone onstage introduces an implicit story of resistance in this version of Mary. As the scholar-performers Lynn C. Miller and Jacqueline Taylor have written, women's autobiography in performance must confront the disembodied, traditionally masculine, "universal subject" that constrains so many as "others" bereft of voices or physicality.[41] Layered over the public performance of Rame's Maria, Curino's private recollections show both the importance of her own memory and the continuing political relevance of giving Mary the powerful voice that Rame did. Ryan Claycomb argues for the inherent reciprocity in feminist theater, in which performing real life demonstrates the extent to which real life is performative. He adds that this autobiographical action then challenges cultural structures that define and continue to enforce gender norms.[42] Curino honors Rame's Mary as a representative figure of women's courage and resistance under extreme duress and physical threat (here by the Roman soldiers). At the same time, she also embodies the intellectual and creative passions of a female artist whose project is largely independent, presenting her work in a traditionally unwelcoming space to such individuals.

Curino and Baliani embrace a positionality of vulnerability in presenting different aspects of themselves. What Miller and Taylor, Claycomb, and

Heddon have flagged as techniques for a feminist theater are applicable to the whole of theater of narration, which adheres to their definition of a feminist methodology. To borrow again from Miller and Taylor, autobiography "reclaims, celebrates, and complicates the construction of the female self."[43] In the case of Curino, she revises the past by creating a space for female stage artists when she recalls Rame's performance and offers her own rendition of it. Meanwhile, Baliani creates a space of remembrance for ordinary people, in which he "reclaims, celebrates, and complicates" those individuals who sacrificed their lives to effect societal change. As Curino and Baliani dance between storytelling, acting, private remembrance, and shared histories, they reinvent the Goffmanian frame into a space that can hold many selves. For Curino, this choice is gendered, but this technique also suggests a rebellious positionality, which points to how the theater of narration can be a vehicle for ideological dispute.

The risk in being the solitary voice onstage, tasked with the responsibility of offering a more dynamic historical record through specific viewpoints, is that a power dynamic develops in concert with the more magnanimous gesture of giving voice to others. The ability to shift perspectives that emerges from an impulse of contextualized self-reflection along with the pluralistic spirit of the theater of narration is at odds with the authoritative associations of a single individual onstage. Narrators might strive to promote ordinary people and the value of a critical narrative, but they are in a position of power as the author and actor. This is a fact of their genre and relates to similar conundrums that ethnographers confront.

One way that narrators correct or at least check their authority is simply with this self-awareness in the spirit of Ginzburg, who acknowledged his subjectivity as he conducted research. Practicing an autoethnography in concert with ethnographic research is another way to work through this dynamic. Madison contends that "the critical ethnographer also takes us beneath surface appearances, disrupts the *status quo*, and unsettles both neutrality and taken-for-granted assumptions by bringing to light underlying and obscure operations of power and control."[44] Craig Gingrich-Philbrook agrees, reframing autoethnography from a method to an orientation. He understands autoethnography as having developed from the need "to signal when ethnographers questioned their participation in the domination of the other through their own cultural regime of truth."[45] The idea to include oneself as a way to check one's authority acknowledges an unequal dynamic, helping narrators to call attention to that reality rather than pretending it does not exist.

In *Corpo di stato*, the smaller everyday events that Baliani recounts, such as driving in the car with his partner and their baby or enjoying a day at the beach with friends, signal an epistemological shift in perspective because they address material which hitherto had no pertinence for bourgeois-made history and which would not have been recognized as having any moral, aesthetic, political, or historical value. Paying attention to the micro level of the everyday enacts a process of rediscovery not only of the previously overlooked histories, but also of the ruptured outcomes of conflict and struggle. Local or regional knowledges are not only about the events that have been overlooked. *Corpo di stato* works to broaden knowledge of experiences in the process of uncovering these struggles, while at the same time demonstrating the broad value and greater historical implications that private colloquial instances can hold.

Narrators also exercise a specific performative agency to rectify the inherent power structures in their work. As narrators encourage spectators to think about their own memories and private struggles, they are rearranging the audience's "structures of knowledge." Guccini and Marelli have written that after every narration the story dissolves into a residue of signs made newly available for one to interpret, encouraging the individual memory to exert its own obscure power of creation.[46] In performing the process of pairing the personal with the public, and in the inherent suggestion that everyone listening to them can do the same, they point out the inherent agency of those in the audience. Here again is the face of the cultural laborer as someone who creates the potential for activism as well as its continued discourse through art and critique.

Looking Outward: Giuliana Musso's *Nati in casa*

The imbricate voices in the theater of narration originate with the narrator, but they quickly move to consider the experiences of others through interviews and documented histories, frequently engaging methods in oral history to construct pluralistic accounts of the past. The lens of postmodern theory, in which the self can be both stable and linear as well as multiple and fragmented, provides a metaphor for the narrator: in the theater of narration the self is a steady and centrifugal force from which the story strays to intermingle with the experiences of others and to which the story returns. Plays establish connections between events, people, ideas, and struggles, and they operate in several registers in order to distill a perspective that is difficult to approach through more conventional forms of reflection. If narrators begin with themselves, they eventually shift their ethnographic strategy to understand the world through the lens of their neighbors, and often this focus is the main content of a performance. Beyond the fact that these shifts move the narrative into its main sequence, they also signal essential moments in the production by performing the interconnectedness between one's private history and another's, and how together these histories form the tapestry of a public history.

This negotiation between plural histories, which are fundamentally a collection of singular ones, encourages the audience to consider the ways in which personal experience fans outward, and how reflecting on the connections in one's own experience and that of others constitutes history making. History, then, is always a multiauthored living collection of voices. As Pollock notes, "No one person 'owns' a story. Any one story is embedded with layers of remembering and storying. Remembering is necessarily a public act whose politics are bound up with the refusal to be isolated."[47] Narrators demonstrate this joint ownership when they incorporate other voices into their works, aided by practices of oral history. As narrators engage other perspectives in an effort to create a multidimensional history, it becomes clear that many stories are not only about clarifying aspects of the past from those hitherto unheard perspectives but also, importantly, about how to interpret those events in both personal and collective ways.

Giuliana Musso's *Nati in casa* (*Born at Home*, performed in repertory since 2001) exemplifies both the shaping of history through multiple voices and the act of interpreting that history and its implications in the present with the help of oral testimony from ordinary people. The piece, which is part of Musso's "investigative theater" trilogy (*teatro d'inchiesta*—how she describes her theater), weaves together stories of midwives from the early twentieth century in northeastern Italy, Musso's home region. The other two pieces include *Sexmachine* (2005), for which she researched and conducted interviews on prostitution, and *Tanti saluti* (2008; *Best Wishes*), on how society handles death and dying people. The themes of these productions travel from meditations on birth to sex to death (the fundamental processes of life, in other words), but they are often thought of as a trilogy, largely because of Musso's research methods, which rely heavily on collecting oral histories. She went on to translate poetry and prose into dramaturgical texts for her next shows, but later returned to similar research methods, in the mid-2010s with *Mio eroe* (2016; *My Hero*) based on the testimony from mothers of fallen Italian soldiers in the NATO-led war in Afghanistan against the Taliban and al-Qaida (2001–14). By 2017, when she won the prestigious Hystrio playwriting prize for over seven different plays, even while she has explored other writing methods, her rigorous research of oral histories is the area in which she receives most recognition. As the critic Roberto Canziani declared, if she were not such a talented actress, then she would have been a formidable journalist for her ability to merge rigorous investigation with pathos in everyday issues that society often overlooks.[48] This could be a mantra for all narrators.

Born in 1970 in the northeastern province of Vincenza and later relocating farther east to Udine, only thirty kilometers from the border of Slovenia, Musso's artistic style is influenced by long-standing regional traditions of physical actor-based Italian theater, similar to the traveling troupes in the commedia dell'arte style. She is a master of improvisation and technically brilliant in her precise physical gestures, which can be both big and elastic, like Dario Fo's, and subtle and small. That physical command extends to her vocal range in both tone and accent, which she uses to create many characters in her productions. Though some critics associate her with fellow northeasterner

Fig. 7. Giuliana Musso in her opening monologue of *Nati in casa* (San Daniele del Friuli, Udine, ca. 2001). Photograph by and courtesy of Elena Bazzolo.

Marco Paolini, and while she studied in guest workshops with Teatro Settimo members including Laura Curino, Mariella Fabbris, and Gabriele Vacis, her artistic lineage is grounded with those itinerant troupes that often interacted with the audience following their own sketches of scripts. *Nati in casa* debuted in 2001, but it was not until the early 2010s that critics began to celebrate Musso as a major narrator.

She takes the practice in different directions, most notably with more monologue-heavy sequences in addition to the typical one-on-one conversational style of narration that she employs in *Nati in casa* (fig. 7). In later works the presence of the narrator becomes more and more subtle, taking on different forms. The opening choreopoem set to music in *Sexmachine*, and the sunglass-wearing clowns that both represent death and are themselves a commentary on death from *Tanti saluti*, are experimental incarnations of a narrator in productions that comprehensively favor characters or representations of characters (as with the clowns). *Nati in casa* is the production most convincingly grounded in the theater of narration traditions, yet Musso still opens the show with a grand monologue, to jarring effect. Wearing a pregnant suit that she later sheds, she portrays a woman going into labor. In a comedic sequence of high-pitched fast-paced banter, this woman describes her anxieties and how she is relieved to be delivering in a hospital given all of the complications that might ensue. Picking up the pace, she describes her initial conversations as she checks in and settles in; then she slows down as the nurse that she liked leaves when her shift finishes, the doctor breaks her water, the medical staff calculatingly wrestles control from her. There are a team of people observing her, they administer an epidural ("like in America!" she exclaims with nervous laughter), and suddenly she does not know when to push, what to do, and has lost much sensation in her body.

At this point, fifteen minutes into this opening, the audience hears a calm and collected voice, somewhere between that character and Musso herself, that asks several times, "Come facevano le donne prima . . . ?" (How did women do this before . . . ?). This is the first key moment of transition between an invented contemporary character, Musso herself, and the next sequence, which answers her question. Stemming from research and interviews with midwives, she tells their stories and the stories of women in whose labors they helped. Originally the director, Massimo Somaglino, was commissioned by the Pro Loco (a regionally sponsored association to promote local culture) in the small town of San Leonardo Valcellina, outside Pordenone in the Friulli Venezia Giulia region of northeastern Italy, to devise a theatrical text that would celebrate their local obstetrician, Maria, who had helped in the births of generations of the town's children. He passed the project to Musso, who did most of the research, interviews, and writing. These practices of historical inquiry themselves constitute much of the larger meaning in this production specifically, and broadly in the theater of narration as they demonstrate the richness that microstories hold. They put the human—and in this case not the science and technology of birth—center stage, quoting actual individuals and shaping a narrative that is heavily mediated by oral histories.

The very idea of positioning the human front and center shares philosophical underpinnings with the process of oral history, which replaces documented accounts with those that are brought to fruition only through the voice of another human being. Rising in popularity during the 1960s and 1970s, oral history is a method mainly associated with social historians as they conduct "history from below," with marginalized people like working-class individuals, racial minorities, and women. While it does offer glimpses of experiences that are generally hard to locate, with the work of Luisa Passerini, Alessandro Portelli, and others the focus shifted from the actual narratives to subjectivities and cultural processes.[49] For Passerini, the inaccuracies, such as misremembering an event, read like Freudian slips that nonetheless provide key meanings. The historian Joan W. Scott describes Passerini's model:

> She uses interviews not to collect facts, not to clarify what did and did not happen in the past, but to explore the ways in which the relationship between private and public, personal and political is negotiated. It is this negotiation that produces identity, the sense of membership in a collective. . . . Memory, Passerini suggests, sustains identity through its invocation of a common history.[50]

Scott continues to explain how for Passerini, one of the most valuable aspects of oral history is what goes unsaid. She reads the pauses, hesitations, and discrepancies of her interviewees analytically, providing insight into the complexity of their subjectivity. This notion of the unsaid shares theoretical ground with the detective work of microhistorians and the *paradigma indiziario*, or method of clues, which engages with the gaps in historical records. Rather than leading the historian to new discoveries, however, in oral history the caesuras *are* the discoveries.

Musso uses interviews in the same way: not to collect facts but to create a collective memory based on an individual's personal history. How did women give birth before? Before hospitals, before paved roads, before telephones, and before an onslaught of medical intervention that removed all agency from the birth mother? From her quiet thoughtful questioning, Musso begins to shift her body gently from side to side, describing the middle of the night in a rural town, as she transforms herself into a midwife who is riding her bicycle—with the bell on the right of the handlebar and a leather bag on the left—up a steep hill before arriving at the house of Rosina, a woman in labor. As she arrives, Musso portrays both Rosina's little sister, an exuberant fourteen-year-old Rosetta (Musso asks her audience to "try not to confuse them. Once upon a time that's how it went") who will help in her sister's labor, and the midwife. She colors their exchange with Friulian dialect, which gives her story both an older and a regional flavor. Then she slips back into a narrator closer to herself, referencing the interview process in preparation for the production. Looking directly into the audience, she announces,

> One of the first things that all of the municipal's midwives from back then want to tell you when you meet them is about how they traveled to the women in labor, at all hours of the day and night, by any means necessary, but usually by foot or by bicycle, or sometimes with the bicycle on their shoulders if it was a steep climb, or maybe on their backs with their legs knee-deep in mud.[51]

Throughout the play, she conveys the physical strength of the midwives, and their physical and emotional dedication as they support other women through their own moments of intense physical and emotional strength. It is not merely an empowering piece. It rewrites both the history and the *current* story of childbirth by juxtaposing the opening scene of nervousness and ultimately impotence of today's birth mother in a hospital with several anecdotes of women-centered spaces, based on memories of women, in which they had fuller participation in the births of their children.

These dexterous shifts between characters and the narrator as researcher conducting interviews demonstrate the way in which ordinary people, herself included, have the potential to create large-scale historical narratives. The key is in the listening. First she needed to do the listening, and then it was the audience's turn. Though Musso does not acknowledge the inherent hierarchy as the beholder of these stories, choosing which ones to tell and how to share them, adding and detracting, inventing as she might, she does demonstrate how one can construct a larger historical narrative by interweaving individual ones. Pollock underscores the characteristic dramatic value in these research methods:

> That insofar as oral history is a process of *making history in dialogue*, it is performative. It is co-creative, co-embodied, specially framed, contextually and intersubjectively contingent, sensuous, vital, artful in its achievement of narrative form, meaning, and ethics, and insistent on *doing through saying*, on investing the present and future with the past, re-marking history with previously excluded subjectivities, and challenging the conventional frameworks of historical knowledge with other ways of knowing.[52]

Beyond empowering the actual subjects of *Nati in casa* (the new mothers, the midwives, and Musso herself), the presence of oral history in the theater of narration leads to an epistemology with stakes in historiography itself. Oral history may create history through dialogue, but the theater of narration demonstrates how it and the other elements that go into making it (from creative interpretation to documentary evidence) are inherently performative.

The audience, and their accountability in the history-making experience through narrative, is a vital component to the theater of narration. Pollock states that when oral histories appear onstage, they both reveal "the magnitude and inherent responsibility in beholding the story of someone else" and demonstrate how stories are embodied, lived experiences that provide "a space for the complexities of indigenous or vernacular conceptualizations of experience."[53] Musso holds what she has learned from others with an unmistakable reverence that is dramatized largely by the lighting in the piece, when she is brightly centered by a spotlight or awash in blue, associated with Mary and the miracle that birthed Catholicism. She also frequently references the Northeast as she shares these stories, in particular with accent and dialect, but also with mentions of regional landscape. Above all, Musso demonstrates that the act of performing these stories in front of an audience is part of what makes a whole story, a single narrative, a history that consists of individual histories.

If Musso's choice not to reflect on or at least acknowledge the problematics of subjectivity might seem positivist, other narrators have spoken more candidly on the matter and openly worked through their hesitations. Considering the features that can alter perspective, when Celestini has reflected on the mechanisms at play in storytelling, he has commented that oral memory occurs in a certain moment of the present, even if always linked to the past. For him, memory is so much a part of the present that recalling specific events will change or efface parts of the past.[54] This idea recognizes that the inherent problem in memory recollection is that while interviewees may be willing to share their experiences, they haphazardly censor or repress different aspects of an event because they are not fully aware of or able to articulate a vision beyond their own subjectivity.

This framework is also clear in Baliani's efforts to consider perspectives other than his own in *Corpo di stato*, including that of the kidnappers. He imagines them at the moment in which they shot and killed Moro: "Did the first one to fire squeeze hard on the trigger? Could he have stopped himself in that moment, not gone through with it? Or not, or is it always the same, that by that point in the game the hands move on their own, like machines?"[55] He reconstructs a psychological drama of an action that had huge consequences for a nation, narrowing that focus to one person, wondering if, by the time the gun was raised, Moro was as good as dead, or if there was still a glimmer of hope. What is particularly revealing about the practice of the theater of narration is what Baliani says next: "But they [the hands] tremble, they tremble! So you have to make them stronger, harder, you have to steel yourself, until you see before you not a man, but a mere figure, a function of something, a thing."[56] Baliani has shifted the point of view to the actual kidnappers as they confess what one needs to do in order to carry out this task. Even though Baliani is only imagining the scenario and not quoting from one of the kidnapper's memoirs, he is still offering some type of insight into unsympathetic people, making them weaker, trembling. He humanizes them by depicting them as ordinary people who attempt to grapple with a moral choice, rather than affectless ideologues. Baliani goes well beyond his autoethnography, yet his own witnessing of the militancy in those years when he too was a part of a struggle allows him to access an empathy that provides a window into the experiences of another.

Similar to Celestini's recognition of the present, Baliani makes the case that both subjectivity and the ability to recognize it have useful benefits in the construction of history. Celestini's argument is about the relationship between the present and one's point of view from the present. What influences memories of the past is not just the present, but the perspective that the present affords. Portelli shares this idea, taking it in a slightly different direction by introducing the possibilities of misremembering and fantasy when recalling the past; narrators engage with the latter as they construct the specifics of their scenes. Maybe the kidnappers' hands did tremble. Maybe there was a moment of hesitation, maybe not. What Baliani shows, indeed performs, is the actual mechanism that confronts these public events: empathy. Emerging from his own experiences, his empathy allows him to reflect on and understand the experience of others in a personal way. By tinkering with his subjectivity and flirting with that of another, Baliani demonstrates the proximity of the relationship between the private and the public. In this example, he is saying that perhaps, for the kidnappers to be able to kill Moro, they had to strip him of his status as a leader of the nation, even as a human being, and think of him as some worthless entity. In fact, they had to block their empathy.

Several intellectual trends from the 1970s also resurface in these multitudes composed of oral histories. Passerini intuits these associations as well. In one of her early works, she explicitly makes the connection between subjectivity, autobiography, orality, and history and then links this four-part grouping to the effect of events that occurred from 1968 through the early 1980s—the long 1970s. She credits the women's movement for making personal narratives relevant in public and on political platforms. She also acknowledges the post-1968 student movements for attempting to create a historical subject based on everyday conditions that affirmed a double right: to be in history and to have a history.[57] As she describes the process of recognizing one's own subjectivity through autobiographical narrative, she speaks to the necessity of alternating between subjective and objective positions, adding that, through these exchanges, a different type of discovery of self takes place.[58]

Passerini's thoughts share striking parallels with the theater of narration as the same elements of subjectivity, autobiography, orality, and history collide. The theater of narration, however, is concerned less with the different selves that intersubjectivity can reveal than with the actual performance of how these multiple selves are mutually reshaped through their juxtaposition and interaction. By presenting different perspectives, one of the narrator's functions is to dramatize the connection between who is remembering and what is being remembered. In *Nati in casa*, it is the layering of Musso's ethnographic experience as interviewer and as fellow northeasterner who knows the landscape well and can intimately imagine trekking up hills and around muddy spring towns with the stories of the midwives who recalled their journeys, their memories of specific birth experiences, this back-and-forth, that allows her to realize a broad vision. Musso destabilizes her account as she switches between many characters, yet it is in the accumulation of these stories, interweaving them by returning to characters, that she locates a shared history. Here she exhibits a resounding characteristic across the theater of narration: that by incorporating their experiences, narrators demonstrate how they have a right to historical existence, and this right extends to everyone in the audience, and all of those interviewed. This joint valorization of individual experiences forms the possibility of continually revised collective memories.

Narrators are playing with a system that constructs a relationship between performer and audience that either mimics the narrators' relationships to themselves or extends from their ethnographic self-awareness. In one of Erving Goffman's most celebrated theatrical metaphors, he explains the private and public self by describing one's behavior as either backstage or frontstage. The frontstage behavior concerns the various affects that one acquires in the presence of others in order to come across in a particular way, while the backstage self does not behave according to perceptions, but informally acts on its own volition.[59] His metaphor here anticipates an awareness in which one decides for oneself how to behave based on audience, but when there is no audience, one does as one pleases. Goffman never considers the self an audience. In the theater of narration, when narrators share their personal histories, when they discuss their research processes, when they invoke the stories of others, they construct pasts and their own behaviors in those pasts for themselves as much as for their audiences. Agency is a backstage performance with frontstage behavior.

Toward the end of *Nati in casa*, Musso seems to conclude by bookending the piece when Rosina gives birth in her home on top of the hill. The first midwife, whom the audience meets in the beginning of the performance on her bicycle traveling to Rosina, has labored throughout the night with her, and now the baby is ready to arrive. After the birth scene, Musso turns her back to the audience and takes a few steps upstage, prompting the audience to applaud as they expect her to turn around and take her bow. But when she does turn around, she walks downstage half-laughing and, out of character, says, "I'm sorry to disappoint you. The creature was born, but the show is not over. There are still a lot of important things to do and we have to do them together."[60] In this instance, which is staged and scripted and entirely intentional, Musso is working with a variety of relationships, including between herself and the people *about* whom she is talking, as well as *to* whom she is talking, and especially *with* whom; as she specifies, this is work that they must do together. In one instance she reminisces on a common detail that the midwives shared in her interviews—those long treks through the mountainous countryside just to arrive at the woman in labor—and at another she is telling the audience that they too are a part of this narrative, that there is still much that they need to do with her. Her laughter might seem like a flash of backstage behavior, but it is an intentional performance of this behavior, which serves to demonstrate agency—an agency that is both her own and one that she is hoping to share with the audience.

In a final scene with her characters, she returns to the birth of Rosina's child, where the starry-eyed Rosetta (the young sister) follows the midwife around and asks about her profession with great admiration. Somewhat sassily, she provokes the midwife, taunting, "But if the baby had trouble coming out, then we would have had to call a doctor." To which the midwife responds coolly, "Yes, of course, but as you see, we didn't need one."

ROSETTA: No, but how many babies have trouble coming out?
THE MIDWIFE: Rosetta, so many questions! I don't know. A few. Very few.
ROSETTA: But exactly how many few?

As the midwife, Musso contorts her face for a long pause as if to say, "I really have no idea because there are so few," but instead of responding as the midwife, she suddenly shifts nearer to herself and deadpans, "Thirty-seven point six percent. Today, in our Italian hospitals, thirty-seven point six percent of babies have trouble coming out and are born through caesarian section."[61] Here is the work left that Musso needs the audience to do with her: think about this. Compare the stories that they just heard to today's reality, recalling that first character who opened the show. Then they can decide for themselves how this story should continue.

While the entire production celebrates a woman-capable-centric world, this is the moment that rings as the most activist or openly political. Musso continues to share Rosetta's story, how she grew up to become an obstetrician and works at one of the largest hospitals in the Northeast. The character of Rosetta and her experiences is based on several midwives who shared with Musso birth stories from both home births and hospitals. In the production, Musso also uses the invention of Rosetta to shore up her arguments with statistical facts, stating that according to "Rosetta," in 1985 the World Health Organization declared that there was no valid reason in any part of the world for there to be a rate of caesarian section higher than 15 percent. In this sequence—the most naked moment in the production, the most theatrically stripped-down moment with the simplest lighting—Musso does not portray any characters, but instead looks at audience members as if in conversation, leaving them with questions to take up on their own. Yet it is very precisely rendered to look as though it offers a backstage intimacy that her frontstage monologues could never offer. Musso also speaks of Rosetta as though she were one of her interviewees, when in fact Musso created her based on a number of her interviews. This penultimate section is also paced with a quick tempo. Musso does not dwell on these soundbites of information. She credits Rosetta as having shared them with her and leaves them for the audience to mull over and decide for themselves how to deal with them.

The audience has one more task left that relates to interpreting what they have witnessed in terms of their own lives as well as broadly. Eugenio Barba complicates Goffman's ideas when he articulates how the struggle to remember can develop minor tensions into the audience members' experiences of a production. Influenced by the psychological exercises in Stanislavsky's acting technique known as "method acting," Barba notes that there is a continual conversation between the actor's outer presentation of self and the inner life and that this exchange, this anxiety, can transfer to the spectator.[62] The audience witnesses and experiences a dialogic mechanism, an inner debate, that works to move the story onstage narratively forward. Guccini has noted this feature when he distinguishes between the overt presentation as the story that in this case the narrator delivers, and an inner story that takes place simultaneously where the narrator has a particular relationship by way of autobiography.[63] This autobiographical element—which is more of an ethnography of oneself—adds to the underlying tensions as the narrator dances between private and public recollections. Mimicking this duality, audience members can both identify with the narrator's experiences and recall their own. What Musso refers to as the work that is left for her and her audience to do together is the untangling of these tensions, or at least the ability to clearly see through them.

The narrator is ultimately a dynamic figure, one that adheres to certain codes while also operating originally and independently. Narrators have enough freedom to make individual unique choices, yet they share influences in their thinking and behaviors. The role of the narrator is fundamentally to guide the audience through a journey that contemplates a variety of perspectives. Working through their own stories, and often with oral histories from interviews that they conducted, narrators perform the fragmentary ways in which the past breaks down and is imperfectly reconstructed. For narrators, remembering does not pair with forgetting; rather, it suggests that there was first an act of dismembering, disjoining, or breaking apart. A strong somatic presence by way of performance lends weight to that which is intangible, such as experience or memory. As moments decompose in the past, as time and space disrupt them, they are left there, scattered separately until someone (anyone, which is part of the point) re-members them through re-collecting and re-calling them. This is ultimately what constitutes the narrator's work as a cultural laborer. In order to remember an experience, to put it back together again, narrators must recollect it. They must also recall it, or name it, in a way that resonates with the present. Naming the memory gives it a form again, and so the past begins to resurface, though with some parts missing, and others exaggerated. Building on the idea of a cultural civic servant, these reconstructions have political implications as they find relevance in the present.

Through an intellectual breadth, an ethnography of themselves, and finally from multiple perspectives, narrators reach beyond personal experience to locate the greater stage of Italy's recent history. They enact a process of layered identification with the audience as well as a dialogic practice as though there were more people onstage than just the narrator. This dialogic dimension assumes a civic responsibility as Curino, Baliani, and Musso evoke the subaltern history of postwar Turin, 1970s Rome, and the recent history of childbirth. They hold themselves and the audience members accountable for their roles in maintaining an inclusive history by encouraging them to interweave their own personal memories and experiences within a common historical framework. They embrace the spirit of what anthropologist

Edward M. Bruner offers when he acknowledges, "Stories may have endings, but stories are never over."[64] Rather, they are told and retold, and reconfigured and rethought. When private identities surface within a context of public sharing, they can shed new light on events that had become distorted in hegemonic histories. The cultural labor of the narrator is to show audiences how to rewrite more inclusive histories that are at once wide-ranging and intensely personal.

Chapter 3

A Language of One's Own

The commedia dell'arte was the theater of skill (*arte* as in "artisanal") because in addition to their work onstage, the performers also invented their skits, directed themselves, and generally approached their shows as products to trade. They did not separate themselves into actors, writers, directors, and managers but were capable in all these roles, which resulted in having more control and freedom in both how or what story they told, and for whom. In fact, these performers had a sophisticated economic understanding of their trade as a market product, cutting out the middleperson (customarily the court), and selling their "commodities" independently.[1] While there were also plenty of playwrights who rose to fame who did not act, including the fifteenth-century Roman cardinal Bernardo Dovizi da Bibbiena or the Florentine most famous for his political theory, Niccolò Machiavelli, or even the eighteenth-century feuding Venetians Carlo Goldoni and Carlo Gozzi, there were many more itinerant troupes of artisans whose work was grounded in a particularly physical mode of performance that led them to craft their stories. (Franca Rame came from such a family of itinerant performers.) They might have written outlines, but they never wrote complete scripts. In recognizing the theater of narration in this lineage, it becomes clear that narrators have reclaimed the artisanship of drama by assuming more ownership in its creation.

Inherent in such autonomy is an experimentalism that only today seems irreverent, since postwar theater in Italy—unlike in France, Germany, and the UK—had become largely director-led.[2] This return to a holistic mode of creation allows for, and even favors, a new dramaturgical language. Dialect or regional diction; a restrained physical language that nods to classical forms of oratory; and cultural jargon that infuses the practice with impegno are primary characteristics of that language in the theater of narration. These attributes have become some of the most original, poignant, and direct expressions of the practice's ingenuity, leading to an atmosphere of inclusivity where people from many walks of life converge in the semipublic sphere of the theater. Ironically, it is these diverse distinctions in their performances—the flavors of the Venetian, Piedmontese, or Sicilian countryside—that create connections not only to their audiences through a sense of community, but also among the narrators themselves in stylistic unity.

There is a long history of local languages in Italian theater since the Renaissance, particularly in Venice and Naples, two twin capitals of powerhouse regions before the unification. In addition to preserving regional traditions within regional languages, the popular and influential literary aesthetic of *verismo* and its inherent argument for realism and authenticity encouraged the continuance of dialect through unification and into the twentieth century.[3] In addition to cultural preservation, one key insight that dialect in theater offers is its ability to highlight cultural hierarchies, a theme that is frequently prevalent in the theater of narration. Marvin Carlson stresses that the dynamics of the inferior/superior binary that the dialect/standard language ratio creates ultimately provides an opportunity for the introduction of a rich heteroglossia onstage.[4] As will become evident in an analysis of dialect in Davide Enia's *Mio padre non ha mai avuto un cane* (2010; *My Father Never Had a Dog*) and Saverio La Ruina's *La borto* (2009; *The Abortion*), regional tongues enable the expression of multiple viewpoints, particularly those that are rarely taken seriously, if heard at all. More than that, its use highlights the general absence from mainstream political discourse of certain populations, such as the Sicilians who live with the terror of the Mafia's constant presence, as Enia depicts, and poor women in the rural southern province of Calabria, who endure continuing repression, as La Ruina illustrates.

One of the most distinct traits of the theater of narration is the laconic physicality of the solitary actor. Whether sitting in a chair, standing at a podium, or simply downstage center, the narrator directly addresses the audience. This physical mode of presentation most immediately recalls classical oratory, and its modern-day incarnations through lawyers before a court, politicians before constituents, or professors before students. Surprisingly, an analysis of Ciceronian rhetorical tradition reveals a thorough system of historical consideration, argumentation, and narrative, a method that turns out to have much in common with the theater of narration and offers insight into one of the practice's hallmarks: its terse physical expression. As is common with actors, some narrators also plan each gesture with incredible exactness and specific intentions in mind. An analysis of orality, or the relationship between performance and text, in consideration with Marco Paolini's *Il racconto del Vajont*, demonstrates the connection to classical oratory, and how this rediscovered dramaturgical mode successfully captures the attention of modern publics.

Finally, one way the theater of narration endeavors to take a political stance is through diction that evokes language calling for action. This chapter ends not with a production from the 1970s, but with one that fundamentally echoes the 1970s through its rhetoric, imbued with an antiestablishment spirit. Celestini's fantastic rendering of the lives and experiences of temporary employees on short-term contracts in *Appunti per un film sulla lotta di classe* (2007; *Notes for a Film on Class Struggle*) shows how even a second-generation narrator draws on the zeitgeist of the 1970s.

Celestini's piece also demonstrates the elasticity of the theater of narration in terms of textual form. Published scripts read as prose or long-form poetry. Rarely do these texts read as traditional or even experimental scripts envisioned for performance; rather, they usually read as something between a manifesto, a public speech, and a novella. Celestini has literally turned his notes for an actual film project into a theatrical event. Linguist Giovanni Nencioni's scholarship on the gradations of written to staged text helps to demonstrate how the embodied act of performance can enhance the political intent of the project. The written form ultimately affects orality: on the page, the works read fluently, and one would not necessarily presume they are intended to be spoken. Thus, when the narrators do utter their words, the event itself produces a radical nuance. The dramaturgical languages that comprise the theater of narration rely on previous methods of verbal and physical expression, while the practice also invents its own. Narrators work outside the establishment, enabling them to communicate with groups of people who might not typically experience cultural expressions in intimate and inspiring ways.

The Audacity and Intimacy of Dialect

As the linguist Hermann Haller has noted, the musicality and expressionistic quality of Italian already makes it a strong candidate for the theater. Plays in dialect have a mimetic superiority greater than that of prose or poetry, enabling them to historically represent both the speech forms of local populations and the affected and versatile interlanguages of noble classes.[5] When Marvin Carlson discusses both Dario Fo and the celebrated twentieth-century Neopolitan Eduardo De Filippo, he identifies how Italian dramatists manipulate the linguistic flexibility of Italian so that it suits a specific historical moment as much as it might also reflect a social and artistic program or status.[6] Haller, meanwhile, specifies that the dialect play has the potential to be "an anthropological treasure trove of proverbs, idioms, local customs, and regional culture."[7] Following these observations, the theater of narration shows how dialect also has the potential to function as a historical document itself. When Davide Enia explores how even a single word in dialect can come to contain the symbolism of an entire national event, and Saverio La Ruina, whose plays are entirely in dialect, shares ordinary struggles of the rural South, these narrators demonstrate how the regional diction brings the subaltern voices of their performances center stage.

The use of dialect is a hallmark of the narrators' practice. Although it is an area in which scholars have only paid fleeting attention, several have acknowledged its importance in Paolini's work, especially the *Bestiario veneto* series (1998; *Venetian Gladiator*) calling the piece a tour of the linguistic heritage of the region.[8] Indeed, the most obvious effect of dialect is its ability to conjure a geographically, and thus culturally, specific location. Paolo Puppa declares Paolini a "Gramscian surveyor of linguistic cultural origins," emphasizing the political potential of dialect as a popular language.[9] In the theater of narration, as dialect works to enhance regional connections, it clearly contributes to the effort to rethink the national in terms of the local, but more than that, as narrators draw attention to dialect, they imbue those local individuals with the agency and authority that usually accompany an educated standard Italian. Davide Enia and Saverio La Ruina, in particular, foreground its importance with a regional language that is so challenging that when La Ruina published three of his plays in a collection, he included an accompanying translation in standard Italian.

Unsurprisingly, the two artists who most fervently employ dialect are from the South, where dialect theater flourished from the unification of the country in the 1860s until well into the twentieth century.[10] Some might associate dialect with class specificity, but in Italy it mostly concerns region. While the three crowning Tuscan poets—Dante, Petrarch, and Boccaccio—inaugurated Florentine as the most elite dialect and future base for standard Italian, it also became the butt of jokes for proud literati and intelligentsia of other cities. The royal family of Piedmont, for example, often chose to speak in their dialect rather than in Florentine, especially among themselves, asserting the valor of Piedmont.[11] Such linguistic dexterity also appears among traveling artists. In the late fifteenth and early sixteenth centuries, the *buffoni in tenda* (clowns in traveling tents) from in and around Venice offered a rich multilingualism to accommodate the cosmopolitan city-states where the buffoni performed, pointing to their own learned abilities as much as to their audience's.[12] Into the twentieth century, dialect declined swiftly first under the nationalist educational imperatives of the liberal republic, then under the fascist state, and finally with the postwar introduction of mass media. In parts of the country where cinemas and household televisions were less ubiquitous, the intimately regional locutions continued. An author choosing to write in such an inaccessible register for the majority of the public takes many risks.

Born and raised in Palermo, the Sicilian Davide Enia completed his university degree in Milan and briefly studied theater under Laura Curino. Though he found much early success writing and performing in the theater of narration, he has also had an especially versatile artistic career. In 2002 he wrote two plays for the famed (and fellow Palermitan) director Emma Dante's theater company as he devised two of his most popular solo shows, *Italia—Brasile 3 a 2* (2002), and *Maggio '43* (2004). He performs these two narrative theater pieces almost exclusively in a somewhat accessible Palermo-based Sicilian with its mellifluous rhythms that call to mind the traditional storytelling once popular in the South.[13] Later he turned to crafting novels,

Fig. 8. Davide Enia in *L'abisso* (Teatro Comunale di Siracusa, Sicily, 2018). Photograph by Sergio Bonuomo. Courtesy of Davide Enia.

and finally he even wrote the libretto for a production of Mozart's unfinished opera *The Goose of Cairo* in 2017.

Enia's *L'abisso* (2018; *The Abyss*) (fig. 8), adapted from his book *Appunti per un naufragio* (2017; *Notes on a Shipwreck*), which he has performed in theaters all across Italy, marks a return to the theater of narration as he explores the crisis of migrants pouring through Sicily against the deeply personal relationships to his father and ill uncle. His poetic story ponders the current Mediterranean, with its deaths and rescues of those migrants who risk their lives journeying across it through his own observations and those of others. Importantly, he incorporates interviews from several Italian rescue workers and doctors who have borne firsthand witness to the dangers of this journey, and even from some of the migrants themselves. Though it would constitute a different project altogether, the voices of the migrants could have been much stronger, even if they are ultimately filtered through Enia both in his writings and onstage. Of the several projects concerning migration or occupation that this book acknowledges (Baliani and Costa's *~~Human~~*; Celestini's *Radio clandestina*; La Ruina's *Italianesi*; and Vacis's *Cuore / Tenebra*), *L'abisso* is the one that most directly and intimately confronts the waves of the several hundred thousand migrants per year crossing the Mediterranean since 2014.[14] It is also the play among that group that is most formally loyal to the theater of narration, emphasizing the form's great potential to confront this urgent issue. The play and its theme were rewarded in 2019 as the winner of the important Hystrio-Twister Prize, a type of people's choice award in which the public votes for the winner. Its large success leaves room to hope that there will be an increasing amount of theatrical productions that address the narratives of migrants and that the public might hear directly from them about their experiences and perceptions of the situation.

The theme of Enia's earlier work, *Mio padre non ha mai avuto un cane* (*My Father Never Had a Dog*), remains largely in the realm of a national crisis, but one that has certainly garnered international notoriety. Reading a national tragedy against a local and autobiographical lens again involving the relationship to his father, the piece is as much about the audacity and intimacy of language, particularly dialect, as it is about organized crime.[15] In this short volume, Enia recounts his own memories when the Sicilian mafia known as Cosa Nostra assassinated the judge Giovanni Falcone. He, along with fellow judge Paolo Borsellino (killed by the Mafia less than two months later), had gained international recognition for their efforts to fight Cosa Nostra's financial and political might. Similar to the beginning of *Vajont*, where Paolini recalls watching his mother listen to news of the disaster on the radio, Enia shares the moments in which both of his parents returned home after having heard the news of Falcone's slaying. Enia recalls these scenes in various depths of further- and nearer-reaching pasts that relate to this specific incident, but in his descriptions, there is a centrifugal force that casts the entire play in orbit: a resurfacing word in Sicilian dialect, *s'asciucò*, that operates thematically and historically.

In a poetic opening that returns throughout the piece like a Greek chorus, Enia announces, "The first image is that of a dog that stares. I am the dog. I am watching my father who is a rock that cries."[16] The only word he remembers his laconic father uttering is *s'asciucò*. From here, he shares experiences that color their relationship, reminisces on his hometown of Palermo, and recalls one of his youthful infatuations with a local girl. Just as the piece seems to veer away from the ominous tones of its beginning, Enia drops the word again, *s'asciucò*, and whips his readers back around to this central point. Here, in the middle of the piece, Enia offers an etymology, and it becomes evident that even in the other memories that he shared, the word was always hovering. "From the Latin *ex-sucare*, a mix of *ex*, which indicates origin and deprivation, and *sucus*, the juice, the spirit, the life made liquid."[17] The abundant imagery of liquids, particularly those that emerge from places where they normally do not exist, like rocks that cry, now takes on a new depth. All the fluid-related verbs that Enia has been employing all along to describe Palermo and its "saturated," "oozing," or "soaked" ambience, a city scattered with "deep puddles of blood" from the violence of organized crime, are now connected back to this word.

Continuing, he explains that "*exsugere* is the act of sucking or drawing out, of extracting to a state of emptiness and aridness."[18] In western Sicilian (specifically Palermo-based) dialect, he notes, a hard "c" replaces the hard "g" from *asciugare* (standard Italian) to *asciucare* (in dialect), and the word thereby takes on another meaning, the one that his father invoked in his pale utterance of *s'asciucò* "while he was crumbling."[19] This second explanation is the key to understanding the other recurring imagery in the text that Enia beckons throughout the piece, which is that of something so dry that it "disintegrates," "crumbles," "fractures," "shatters," "cracks," breaks into "shards," or is "eviscerated." With these distinct word choices that he subtly disperses around the story, he summons a whisper of *s'asciucò*. Finally, he reveals the full sentence that his father had been trying to voice, "*La mafia* s'asciucò *a Giovanni Falcone*" (The Mafia *eviscerated* Giovanni Falcone).[20] Masterfully, Enia enables this expression to serve not only as the focal point of the story but also, in his reflective dissemination of its meaning, as the bomb itself that killed Falcone. Capitalizing on the colloquial definition of *s'asciucò* as "to kill," much of his imagery suggests a state in which both the life, the "juice" (*succo*), is sucked out of someone, in addition to the shattering explosion of an utterly desiccated substance. Enia creates an aural proximity to the events surrounding Falcone's assassination, in which members of the Mafia spectacularly detonated four hundred kilograms of explosives underneath the highway when Falcone and his escort drove by. Along with Falcone, his wife and three police agents were killed. In Enia's text, he has created his own explosive device out of *s'asciucò*, constantly released through the repetition of the actual word and its oft-invoked meaning through synonyms.

In Enia's intentional use of dialect with the story's subject of Sicily and the Mafia lingers the implicit mourning of the ways the island and its corruption hold the country back. In this text, dialect draws parallels to systems of cultural hierarchy at play in Italy. As Carlson asserts, part of the reason people see dialect as inferior is that they see it as a marker of a subordinate geographical area and social class.[21] Enia uses such presumptions to his advantage. With his thorough explanation of the origins and meaning of *s'asciucò*, Enia presumes an audience that is also outside Sicily. He makes it clear that even while the tragic murder was a national disaster making its way into many Italian households, not least when the funerals were broadcast live across the whole country suspending regular television programs, it was a local act. With his focus on this single expression in dialect, demonstrating how even a lone word can contain the symbolism of an entire national event, Enia reckons with the murders as a Sicilian event. He asserts the importance of Sicily through its dialect, as if to say that the rest of the nation needs to address the region's hardships too so as not to continue to repeat them.

Similarly, through his courageous loyalty to a challenging local dialect, the Calabrian Saverio La Ruina takes the theater of narration in some new directions, not only in his linguistic choices but also in his attraction to a more monologuist theater of characters instead of narrative, like the later work of Musso. His laconic physical language and the softness of his delivery place him in a gray territory that nonetheless points to the theater of narration, because even if he rarely speaks out of character, frequently one character narrates their story to the audience as Franca Rame's characters would (often from a chair or even the stage floor). Literary scholar Angela Albanese has argued that despite the portrayal of a number of complex characters, the most central one that stars in most of his works is the "challenging and harmonious" dialect itself.[22] In his two first major solo-theater and prize-winning successes, *Disonorata* (2006; *The Dishonored*) and *La borto* (2009; *The Abortion*), he commits to a difficult Calabrian dialect known as Calabro-Lucano, stretching over two different regions and heritages, which for the majority of his audiences, who would not be familiar with the dialect, offers particular delights and demands.

Working mnemonically (and thus triggering oral traditions) as well as rhythmically, La Ruina drives the narrative with repetition, whether of phrases, words, sounds, or melodies, thereby creating a Brechtian experience of his theater, insofar as the dialect attracts yet also estranges. To engage with different layers of comprehension is both mesmerizing and off putting as the audience slips in and out of the story. He amplifies expressivity with his dialogue, but also distances direct meaning. Rather than having the ability to follow the narrative along its plot, the audience member slowly acclimates to the rhythms, repetitions, and assonances of the language, submitting to a more expressionistic experience of the performance.

In provocative and problematic gender crossing, La Ruina portrays a southern woman in *La borto* (fig. 9) and *Disonorata*. Vittoria, the protagonist of *La borto*, shares a dreamlike spiritual experience she recently had while picking white figs, in which she encounters a discerning and judgmental Jesus. Utterly alone in her existence, she shares her story with the audience, who is as much a presence for her as Jesus is: a presence who is there, if not there, but to whom she can speak. La Ruina's portrayal is soft and understated as he creates a character that is tired and worn but also sharp, ironic, and strong. Much of the story recounts the physical and psychological oppression that Vittoria has endured as a woman in the rural South, and it is refreshing, even liberating, to lose her gender in La Ruina's portrayal. He could never know in his body the way a woman lives with the oppression of the incessant predatory male gaze that Vittoria recounts. The audiences will never look at his body onstage the way they might if Vittoria were portrayed by a female-bodied actor, and there is some relief in that.

In other ways, even if La Ruina wrote the play based on interviews of many local women (none credited), it is a missed opportunity not to include at least a coauthor who is a woman, and especially to explore what this play would be with a female-bodied actor. While these choices, particularly for the staging, raise fruitful questions about how the audience accepts the story differently from different bodies, the decision not to include and credit any women in any aspect of the production is disempowering to the very

Fig. 9. Saverio La Ruina in *La borto* with musician Gianfranco De Franco behind him (Teatro India di Roma, 2009). Photograph by Tommaso Le Pera. Courtesy of Saverio La Ruina.

population that La Ruina desires to represent. La Ruina wants both to enact alterity, yet at the same time ventriloquize it and thus assimilate it into his own male authority. Surprisingly, the Brechtian distance that La Ruina's portrayal invites, which should more readily lead to critical reactions of his choices, is largely lost in the skill of his understated narration, rendering the task of accepting Vittoria via La Ruina all too easy. A further considerable distraction is also the language who stars as the protagonist of the play, as Albanese has observed. Even while Vittoria narrates in the first person, the mesmerizing, poetic quality of the dialect lessens the problematics of La Ruina's gender choices.

The story Vittoria shares is stark and cruel: at the age of thirteen she was married to a crippled brute who impregnated her eight times before she was thirty, but it is this eighth pregnancy that ends in the title of the play. Vittoria turns to the many other young women in her town in similar positions, and together they try to invent contraceptives, first via prayer (nobody seems to answer) and then via abstinence (their husbands eventually have their way).

> E cusì, cu prigavi, nu santu, e cu n'atu, cu a jinta e cu a fora, cu chianu e cu forti, u paisu parìa n'orchestra. . . . E cusì loru anu pututu turnà a si sfucà cumi a loru parìadi e piacìadi e nùai amu vutu turnà a ni pristà cumi a loru parìadi e piacìadi.

E così chi pregava un santo e chi un altro, chi dentro e chi fuori, chi piano e chi forte, il paese pareva un'orchestra. . . . E così loro si sono potuti tornare a sfogare come a loro pareva e piaceva e noi ci siamo dovute tornare a prestare come a loro pareva e piaceva.

(And like that someone prayed to a saint and someone to another, someone inside and someone outside, someone quietly and someone loudly, the town seemed like an orchestra. . . . And so they [the husbands] were able to relieve themselves again in the ways they wanted and liked, and we had to return to lending ourselves to how they wanted and liked.)[23]

At work in the dialect are rhythmic sounds that assume emotional resonances. The constant ending of words with "u," suggests an intimacy, perhaps as it resembles the familiar form of "you," *tu*, rendering some of the more difficult moments in the play personal and intimate. La Ruina also pairs consonance with the repetition of words and expressions, even in these few examples: the hard "c" in the first excerpt with "cusì, chianu," and especially *cu* repeated several times emphasize the continual prayers, the repeated effort, to whomever (*cu*) was listening. When Vittoria turns back to the men, the repetition of "p" and "t" in "pututu, turnà, parìadi e piacìad, vutu turnà, pristà, parìadi e piacìadi" brings an abruptness as Vittoria recounts how they ultimately had their way.

Finally, Vittoria/La Ruina recounts the last-resort measure, which includes the universal methods women were and are required to employ in order to rid themselves of forced pregnancies, from throwing themselves down staircases to inserting metal instruments into their bodies to drinking boiling water. As Vittoria recalls the invasive procedure to rid herself of the embryo, she thinks of Lina, who bled to death, and another woman whose life was miraculously saved. As she recalls other women with their uteruses punctured, she begins to think that maybe she herself is dying.

Addu ti mi stai jennu, m'agghiu dittu, addù ti mi stai scifulennu, m'agghiu dittu, addù ti ni voi ji, c'un i poi lassù i figghi a cusì.

Dove te ne stai andando, mi sono detta, dove te ne stai scivolando, mi sono detta, dove te ne vuoi andare che non li puoi lasciare i figli così.

(Where are you going, I said to myself, where are you slipping away to, I said to myself, where do you want to go because you can't leave your children like this.)[24]

The long breath in the repetition of the soft "a" of "Addu, m'agghiu, addù, m'agghiu, addù" draws out and dramatizes her light-headedness as she bleeds.

While the audience will only follow the meaning to various degrees, the sounds, familiar yet foreign, convey some of the emotion behind the experiences that Vittoria recounts. That La Ruina embraces the thick Calabro-Lucano as the vehicle for such politically fraught subjects not only brings them to a different population but also highlights their relevance to that population. It draws attention to a specific region and asks the audience to consider a social issue of global importance, such as abortion, among a particular group of people.

In a 1918 review of Angelo Musco, a well-known Sicilian actor at the time for whom fellow Sicilian Luigi Pirandello wrote several comedies in dialect, Antonio Gramsci, as theater critic for important communist newspaper *Avanti!*, muses how the unification of the nation (1860) marked the beginning of the end for regional dialects. And yet, he observes, though Sicily confronted this loss with much resistance, the Sicilian theater artists found a way for their regional dialect to garner a national importance.[25] In fact, Gramsci praises the Sicilian dialect theater over the literary because he finds it alive and real and believes it captures the social activity of the times. He continues to praise both Pirandello and the writer and director Nino Martoglio for their dialect plays that offer this vitality, but turns back to the actor, to Musco, as the embodiment of simple and sincere life in these dialect performances.

Gramsci offers a connection between dialect and the everyday experiences of ordinary people, those whom he ultimately spent most of his time considering. In his "it is life" declarations, he brings to surface a subtle but bold honesty that dialect affords. These elements also surface in the many moments of dialect in the theater of narration, from the intimacy of the kitchen table where Enia recalls sitting with his father, to the reflective monologues of La Ruina's characters. Particularly for La Ruina, whose plays deal with wrought social subjects such as abortion, betrayal, and homosexuality in the rural, religious South, the rawness of dialect mirrors the confessions that his characters shyly reveal. It has both a literary and performative function in that it celebrates the mellifluous voices of the everyday, serves as a metaphor for the social issues that not everyone understands (just as not everyone will understand the words in dialect), and, finally, is itself its own quirky, sincere character.

In its playfulness, secrecy, and musicality, dialect theater also embodies a palpable energy. Adding to the element of vitality in Gramsci's praises for Sicilian theater, Haller notes that Gramsci must have seen "the spirit of independence within the framework of the new national unity."[26] Along with that rebellious spirit, he saw the potential for action in the dialect, emphasizing its liveliness and linking it expressly with possibilities for change and social activity. La Ruina's plays bring awareness to underrepresented groups and nuance to old habits of sexism and homophobia, particularly in the areas where Calabro-Lucano is spoken. The specific combination of dialects that

La Ruina uses and their idiosyncratic syntax both connect his plays indelibly to their land and the history of the land, in the ways in which language evolved and did not evolve over many centuries.[27] La Ruina's revolutionary move is to pair the traditional language of a region with his criticism of exclusionary practices in that region, giving the language itself the potential to rewrite those lived practices in a new way that can still be familiar. By uttering that language through performance, it nears the potential of a speech act in which its very vocalization demonstrates new ways of thinking in the old familiar language.

First Is the Word

One of the most significant changes in the last fifteen years of twentieth-century Italian theater was the return of the "dramaturgy of the word" brought forth by the theater of narration. Identifying the practice as logocentric, the theater scholar Paolo Puppa designated its style a "dramaturgy of the word," an idea that pairs traditional dramatic analysis based on the script along with performance theory to analyze what takes place on the stage.[28] By this term he means that the word, not the action, is the focal point of the piece. Theater scholar Pier Giorgio Nosari asserts that theater had not only estranged itself from the broader culture by the mid-1980s but also abandoned its own roots in storytelling. He goes on to say, however, that the narrators fixed this double break, in part thanks to their innovative rethinking of the possibilities of orality and narrative.[29] The form draws attention to itself precisely because the content of the stories does not hide behind the spectacle of performance. As a way of drawing the audience's focus to the spoken word, the physical language of narrators is particularly laconic even as they use precise movements to great effect. They keep their gestures, the amount of stage space they occupy, fleeting impersonations, and so on to a minimum, and mostly employ it to accommodate character portrayals. Examined closely, this performance mode reveals traces of classical oratory, both complicating the narrator's understated physical language and offering a hypothesis for the practice's continued success.[30]

In its emphasis on the word, the theater of narration highlights the complicated tension between text and spoken word, and the process of inventing and reconfiguring texts that are intended to sound spontaneous, poetic, realistic, or all of these qualities. The linguist Giovanni Nencioni distinguished written language that approached everyday speech into two main categories: colloquial conversation (*parlato-parlato*) and theatrical dialogue based on a written text (*parlato-scritto*). The latter also encompasses two subcategories that differentiate between written texts. One lies within the frame of a short story or novel, such as dialogue, and the other is a type of written text meant to be read aloud or performed (*parlato-recitato*), as with theater.[31] Nencioni works through various distinctions between conversational and written language, considering, for example, the place for the possibility of spontaneity and improvisation with all the inherent moments of self-correction, interruption, inarticulate sounds in written dialogue. These impulsive articulations that can so enrich communication but that are difficult to convey in active (as opposed to descriptive) language led him to conclude that spoken language is "dirty" whereas its written equivalent, even with the intention of vocalized utterance, is "clean."[32]

Nencioni further argues that spoken language can never really be written comprehensively because the context is constantly in flux. Context here is a variable that is always based on who is in the audience, or the location of a production, which then alters the principal characteristics of spoken language to reflect the rapport between the speaker and the listener. It is the dynamic between the two that informs the speaker of what to say next (and how to say it).[33] This thinking resonates with Erving Goffman's theory of frames, even if he used a theory of performance to interpret behaviors in everyday life. Nencioni's linguistic systems offer a formal method to consider orality in the theater of narration, pointing to the inherent performativity in the words, allowing spoken text to exist as the main theatrical event on the stage. Rather than providing a base for onstage action as in a conventional production, the spoken text is the action. This is the dramaturgy of the word, in which the text claims its space—indeed, most of the performance space. The text is the protagonist.

Classical Oration

When Paolini stands downstage center speaking directly to the audience and then casually walks to a chalkboard in *Vajont*, he could be a lecturer in a classroom. When Curino remains at a podium for most of *Santa Bàrbera*, the matter-of-factness in her tone, her focus on the audience, and her professional poise convey the formality of an important business presentation. Narrators also break away from those moments when they portray characters and employ a different physicality, but this formal delivery, recalling classical oratory, lends both a gravitas and a familiarity in terms of narrative construction. The practice's similarities to Platonic readings of epic poetry, which consist of a combination of mimesis (imitative) and diegesis (narrative), point to its complexities.[34] Epic oral poetry (often associated with Homer or Virgil) with its intersections of written and spoken narrative, along with contemporary mimetic and narrative techniques, and finally ancient traditions in orality lend this very recent practice an important depth as it signals a technical sophistication.

In the late Roman Republic, the Ciceronian rhetorical tradition conceives of oratory through a tripartite system of narration that consists of *historia*, *argumentum*, and *fabula* (history, argument, and fable). With historia Cicero means to evoke a truth, whereas an argumentum is juridical with the aim of establishing the veracity of specific claims. Fabula plays on the question of doubt, introducing an element of imagination that remains ever-hypothetical, since circumstances are presented as though they actually happened, whether or not they actually did. In addition to these three elements, there is also a poetic convention, closer in form to Horatian ars poetica and analogous to the epidictic branch of rhetoric that involves praise or blame of well-known characters. Similar to satire, this practice functioned as both rhetorical exercise and popular entertainment.[35] Indeed, such a tripartite system, complete with satirical embellishments, structures many narrative theater pieces as they adhere to the arrangement where historia and argumentum favor a presentation that tends toward the formal, while fabula and its interspersing moments of satire assume a comical tone.

In classical oratory, the comic aspect of fabula is unique to specific circumstances and serves more than as a diversion. As a practice in extemporaneous speech, it allows orators to deviate momentarily from their main arguments and involve the audience to a greater extent, relying heavily on the listener's imagination.[36] Similar to contemporary public speeches, whether encouraging fantasy and metaphors through a fabula, bringing the audience to laughter, or using direct address and diverging from the script, forges a connection with the audience, which means that the event is more likely to have an afterlife in the private spheres of its members. In the theater of narration, while narrators maintain the classical formula of historia, argumentum, and fabula, the generally comic fabula sequences comprise anecdotal moments sometimes laced with impersonations. These instances play an important role not only in how they give pause to dramatic tension but also in how they break the terse physicality of the narrators. In their comedic moments they use their bodies much more than during serious sequences, momentarily drawing attention away from the words, and focusing on the physical communication of details.

One purpose of comedy in the retelling of a drama parallels its role in classical oration to offset the seriousness. The benefits of this change-up are numerous. It affords the audience a pause to digest the material, enhances the rapport between narrator and spectator, and enlists another language, a universal physical language, in which to convey events. Paolini's *Il racconto del Vajont* (coauthored and directed by Gabriele Vacis; fig. 10) is a solemn piece based on the infamous 1963 disaster in the province of Belluno, between Veneto and Friuli, when a landslide provoked by the construction of Europe's (then) largest dam caused a megatsunami that swept away five small towns, killing more than two thousand people in less than five minutes. In 1993 when he first presented his piece, much of the inquiry regarding the circumstances of the tragedy had been swept away from public consciousness. Paolini has told of receiving copious amounts of correspondence from fans asking him to incorporate their experiences into his work, which he

Fig. 10. Marco Paolini with Gabriele Vacis in rehearsal for *Amleto a Gerusalemme, Palestinian Kids Want to See the Sea* (Limone Fonderie Teatrali di Moncalieri, Turin, 2016). Photograph by Michele Fornasero, Indyca. Courtesy of Teatro Stabile Torino—Teatro Nazionale. Though they had worked together since the 1980s on many Teatro Settimo productions, it was their partnership on *Vajont* that made them famous collaborators.

interprets as a sign that modern society has little faith in institutions amid a dwindling historic memory if they see his work as a resource for themselves.[37] It is also a sign that Paolini's publics recognize both the intrinsic value in their own stories and that they believe their stories have value for others too.

In his performance (fig. 11), Paolini points out that even in 1963 the press had so sensationalized the events into lugubrious hysteria that they circumvented a responsible journalist-driven investigation into the contributing factors. In his three-hour story he compensates these lapses by questioning what led to the tragedy and by conveying the history from heretofore silent perspectives that include the people from the region as well as the engineers and government officials who contributed toward the construction of the dam.[38] Comic anecdotal moments somewhere between the truth and hyperbole offset the ominous tragic ending to which the audience continually moves closer and closer as the play progresses.

Among the many different styles of comedy, from ironic to romantic to satirical, the one that most resonates here is from Pirandello's famous essay "L'umorismo," which revolves around the assertion that humor must exist to say something.[39] Comedy containing a message is the type with which Paolini

Fig. 11. Marco Paolini in *Il racconto del Vajont* (in front of the actual Vajont dam, 1997). Photograph by and courtesy of Marco Caselli Nirmal. This image was shot during a special televised performance (discussed in chapters 4 and 5). On a chalkboard behind him, Paolini traces important dates and events that contributed to the tragedy of the tsunami caused by the dam's construction.

works. In addition, he plays with some of the vulgarity for which Aristotle disdained comedy as a lesser form than tragedy, while he is also attracted to aspects of the stand-up comedian that lie in the figure and practices of the court jester who holds an inherent wisdom, which he reveals humbly and unspectacularly. Since the sovereign did not want someone who would challenge his authority, this stock character dressed his sagacity and criticism in humor.[40] Even if its humor is occasionally vulgar in the Aristotelian sense, it also deepens the tragic aspect of the events portrayed. The frequent presence of comedy throughout much of this tragic tale demonstrates how the tropes of classic oratory produce a dialectical tendency in the theater of narration that intersects rhetorical skill with actor-centered improvisation-oriented performance styles.

Throughout *Vajont*, Paolini carefully places comedy in the traditions of the stand-up comedian, slapstick and Aristotelian base humor that contrast with the noble heights of the tragedy more than cerebral witticisms would. Paolini embraces this aspect particularly when he impersonates the locals of Belluno. As a native son, he has additional license to do so because his humor will be seen as self-deprecating. Celestini, a Roman, mimicking the people of

Belluno, would strike a very different tone unless he first established himself from an equivalent sociocultural background. Here Paolini depicts grandmothers with guns threatening to shoot if people try to take away their land. When the water in the valley rises over what used to be their homes, Paolini depicts the citizens of Belluno running to save what they can—furniture, mattresses, and eventually door frames and roof tiles. When their old town was finally submerged, he describes how they canoed back to the site to catch any glimpses they could of the former town. He asks the audience to imagine "some guy with a hat singing *la biondina in gondoletta*." He conveys their desperation in the face of adversity with great delicacy, balancing the tragedy and absurdity of the situation. They are victims in Paolini's story, but this slightly facetious suggestion of a lone ranger singing to himself is playful and affectionate. Part of Paolini's success is in combining a mournful tribute to those who perished with a celebration of them, their routines and way of life, the local culture, and the local dialect.

In contrast to the staid poise of the orator and the limited movements normally exercised in the theater of narration, Paolini embraces a more rigorous physical routine during the comic interludes. He signals these shifts partly by altering his physicality from laconic gestures to flamboyant ones. When he recounts the first geological research on the mountain, he moves around the entire stage, hunched over to imitate scientists who are out of place in the mountains. He flails his hands when referring to the instruments the scientists are carrying:

> Maybe there were two passengers, with baggage strapped on behind, in front, all over the thing. . . . This overloaded [car] is pumping up the military road, barely making it. . . . They have valises, leather packs, picks, surveyors' gear, specimen cases, topographical recording tools . . . long red and white measure sticks fanning out on the back of the sidecar like tail feathers on a turkey's ass.[41]

Paolini's physical flamboyance enhances the farcical—fabula—qualities of his material. In the televised version, the camera switches to the laughing and applauding audience members offering proof that these interludes are successful. Akin to the formula in classical oratory, with an eloquent delivery of speech the juxtaposition of humor and foreboding tragedy resonates between the narrator and the audience, forming a relationship that will enhance the overall emotional impact.

Paolini is cautious, moreover, not to divide his depictions into political binaries. He does not utilize comedic elements to mock the officials that he holds responsible for the disaster. Yet he still privileges the local everyperson over the modernist government planner even while he is wary of positing simple oppositions. In one early scene he impersonates both a local and a managerial type who has come from Venice to observe the progress of the geological research. The joke is a play on words, involving the actual name of the town, Casso, and the vulgar name for male genitalia, *cazzo*, which also functions in Italian as a multipurpose swear word. Paolini starts his impersonation with the cantankerous Venetian, tired from his windy trip up the mountainside, rudely asking the local, "What's the name of this town, *cazzo*?"

> LOCAL: Casso.
> VENETIAN: What are you, a parrot? I asked you what the *cazzo*'s the name of this town, *cazzo*?
> LOCAL: Casso.
> VENETIAN: *Cazzo*? You calling me a *cazzo*? No, you hick, I'm calling you a *cazzo* . . .
> LOCAL: No, *cazzo*, that's the name of the town, Casso. Calm down, *cazzo*![42]

During this sequence Paolini engages in a very physical performance largely through facial gestures, shrinking his height to depict the local as meek, and turning from side to side to play the Venetian as though the two were facing each other. This is much in the vein of stand-up comedy, where the actor also solicits reactions from the spectators by occasionally looking out toward them, before returning to impersonate a character through exaggerated facial and bodily expressions.

In this scene, it would appear that the local is the subordinate character because the Venetian—already with more political and cultural authority, since he is from a large cosmopolitan city—is there to destroy the town and take the land. Paolini has the Venetian crudely put the local in an inferior status by treating him disrespectfully from the beginning, leaning forward in his stance, whereas in his portrayal of the local he leans back and throws his arms up defensively. By the end, though, the tables have turned and Paolini physically endows the local from Casso, who gradually straightens up for more height and balance, with a stronger stance than the Venetian, who does not even know the name of the town that he will obliterate. Along with his contrasting physical embodiments of the two, Paolini presents a dramatization of the larger historical point about the unfair ways that rural localities and their peoples have been sacrificed throughout history. Indeed, it is a familiar story for many cultures. Here is an instance of how Paolini rewrites history from the perspective of the masses, not the city dwellers or engineers who have no personal connection to these towns that perished in the Vajont tragedy. Paolini might be making a joke out of the town's name, but he also enunciates it. He creates a brief routine around it, with a seemingly juvenile play on words that functions mnemonically to restore Casso's place on the Italian map and within the minds of his spectators.

Historical Connections: Language of the 1970s

The ideological struggles of the 1970s in Italy based on principles and demands of feminist, labor, youth, and other movements devised their own linguistic patterns and diction that echoed through print media in magazines and journals. Rhyming sound-bite slogans abounded, from "L'utero è mio e lo gestisco io" (It's my uterus and I'm in charge of it) to "Fascisti, borghesi, ancora pochi mesi!" (Fascists, bourgeois, only a few more months!). Many political and social-political groups had their own journals from the "Trotzkjisti" ("Trotskyists" in journals such as *Quarta Internazionale*; *Bandiera Rossa*; *Falcemartello*) and workers (*Quaderni Rossi*; *Potere Operaio*; *Classe Operaia*) to the many cultural-political journals, from *Aut aut*, which focused on class history and awareness; to *Fuori!*, which addressed issues of the gay liberation movement; to *DWF* (*Donna Woman Femme*), advancing women's rights; the Marxist *Contropiano*; and *Ideologie*, which emphasized recent history and current events. Though some were ephemeral, many survived to contribute to the political and cultural climate throughout much of the 1970s. The very existence of such varied sources speaks to the complexity and heterogeneity of the many different voices that distinguish the political debates of the time.

While the political and cultural tenor of the period was immortalized in journals, other forms of literature were also evolving, including in performance-oriented ways. The youth movement's rebellion against tradition manifested itself in the rejection of the novel, though even in the early to mid-1960s with literary circles like the Gruppo '63 experimental prose was more and more frequent. By the 1970s, political protest occupied the space of the novel through linguistic choices in works by marginal writers.[43] Some texts reproduce language used by militants, as when writer-painter–factory worker Vincenzo Guerrazzi focuses on graffiti sprayed by workers in his novel *Nord e sud uniti nella lotta* (1974; *North and South United in Struggle*), or Nanni Balestrini's novel about industrial protest, *Vogliamo tutto!* (1971; *We Want It All!*), the title itself a popular slogan from the era. Many of these texts share with the theater of narration the discovery and experimentation of the relationship between the written word and oral expression.

If print media invokes content as much as it invokes method, Jennifer Burns signals the importance of testimony as a conceptual framework for many writers of the time, particularly citing *autocoscienza*, literally "self-consciousness" but meant to describe the sort of "consciousness-raising" in which feminists sought to publicly share their personal experiences. This practice with storytelling at its root ultimately led to explorations of different narrative modes, including confessional, autobiographical, diaristic, and epistolary.[44] Consciousness-raising encourages the passage from silence to spoken word, and to written word through the publishing of texts. The popularity of autocoscienza groups throughout Italy during the 1970s mirrors the historical reclamation present in the theater of narration in terms of both content (a people's history) and method (sharing personal narrative orally). With respect to writers working in the 1970s, such as Balestrini and Guerrazzi, the desire to challenge and transform conventional forms of society and politics led many to claim to be the spokesperson of certain movements, thus arrogating to themselves the plural, heterodiegetic voice of the protestors.[45] By contrast, most narrators do not attempt an overt challenge against convention or behave as spokespeople even if they regularly embody a "heterodiegetic voice," presenting different viewpoints. Rather, instead of centering themselves they blend into the other ordinary lives in the stories.

Keeping in mind the link between the experimental prose of the 1970s and the theater of narration, and Nencioni's distinctions between various spoken communications and their different relationships with texts as a framework, Celestini offers a rich example of these two dynamics in a series of works I call the "Temps Project." In this vast and versatile oeuvre that ranges across various media, Celestini explores the stories of temporary employees at the Atesia call center near the periphery of Rome. He ultimately published several different texts based on this research, staged a performance, and mounted a documentary film interspersed with short clips of himself sharing anecdotes where employees explain their situation in monologues or respond to interview questions.

One of the texts includes a novel called *La lotta di classe* (2009; *Class Struggle*) that consists of four chapters, some fantastic and some realistic, told by different characters who live in an apartment building on the outskirts of Rome, one of whom is a temp at a call center. Another text, *I precari non esistono* (2008; *Temporary Employees Do Not Exist*), which accompanies the DVD of his documentary *Parole sante* (2008; *Holy Words*), is a collage of sorts that explains the film's creation with excerpts from interviews, several newspaper and magazine articles, recent laws regarding temporary work standards, photocopies of documents from the government inspection of the Atesia call center, and even the transcript of introductory comments from the public debate when Celestini previewed the film in January 2008. Finally, Celestini created a performance from his research, which he calls *Appunti per un film sulla lotta di classe* (2007; *Notes for a Film on Class Struggle*). In this piece Celestini, often dressed casually in a pair of jeans and a button-down shirt, sits in a chair or stands at a raised microphone and tells several stories about Atesia's temporary workers interspersed with autobiographical accounts. He also reads and sometimes sings parts of his narration, accompanied by a live onstage band (fig. 12). The simple set and his delivery of the text in a rapid, nearly monotonous voice show the connection to the inner emotional state, which flickers with both the urgency of someone who is ready to fight and the weariness of someone who is tired.

The Temps Projects expand beyond performance in that—unlike Celestini's other works, almost all of which begin on the stage—the research and writing

Fig. 12. Ascanio Celestini with musician Gianluca Casadei, seated, in *Barzellette* (Teatro Vittoria, Rome, 2019). Photograph by and courtesy of Musacchio, Ianniello & Pasqualini. As he did in *Appunti per un film*, Celestini still frequently has musicians onstage with him.

first developed into a filmed documentary, then to a written assembly of promotional materials, many of which became the performance piece, and finally the crafting of a novel. Celestini does not forget the potential of new media either, since many excerpts from the project are or were once available online. The expansive methods of expression across text, film, and performance are impressive as they demonstrate the consistency of Celestini's investigative focus. His mission is to share the unjust experiences of workers in what he refers to as a modern factory, and he tackles an array of media to do so. While the film and novel are obviously not theater, they do perform gradations of the orality that narrators have developed. They represent what could be another dimension within Nencioni's framework, which concerns filmed or digital media. His audience hangs on to the ideas inherent in his story of isolation produced by contemporary capitalist society, with its borders and gated communities. More than just marketing and sales, although also those, these many different types of texts reveal a process. They demonstrate and instruct various methods for people to research and synthesize a situation.

Paolini's work has also developed into a similar multimedia enterprise. He airs almost every new production on television and sells many of the scripts with a DVD of the performance. For the most part, unlike *Parole sante*, Paolini's films and television stints are live tapings of his shows. Baliani, Curino, and Musso have also aired plays on national television channels. In much the same way that Celestini packaged miscellaneous production and promotion pieces into the book that comes with the film, Baliani and Paolini have released texts that are a mix of journals, rehearsal and performance notes, and research from when they devised the piece.[46] All of the supplementary materials that surround the productions have become a part of the extratextual layers of the theater of narration. They also present highly original gradations, from pre-text to written text to spoken text.

Along with material flexibility, the Temps Projects represents the activist potential of the theater of narration. This is especially noticeable when Celestini ends the theatrical production reciting the same story that concludes the book. He describes a temporary worker named Miss Patricia who closes down her workstation at the office and walks away from, essentially, all that is unjust. Celestini dramatizes this in an emotional and fantastical rendering of the work environment spilling into urban space. In the voice of the employee he describes leaving the bureau:

> I cross through the walls of anti-missile glass. . . . Now on the street, I cross through the anti-theft gated communities with their anti-Gypsy alarms, protected by the anti-Black iron bars with their anti-rust varnish where anti-Semitic owners who wear anti-wrinkle cream make their anti-allergy antipasti in their atomic bomb shelters. I cross through the banks under video-surveillance. I walk through the government mints where the machines print money. Every tick registers a new bill. And it's right to measure the bills with ticks because like the insects these ticks also suck the blood of the people. I cross through the walls of the military barracks, the insane asylums, the prisons. . . . Meanwhile a guard tries to stop me because I cross through her and her uniform too. She will then turn towards her superiors and say, "Captains, what should we do? This is witchcraft!" And I will respond, "No, this is class struggle."[47]

Celestini's quick and emotionless delivery connotes a two-dimensional text even as it is meant for performance. It does not exactly have the feeling of spontaneity, but it builds and crescendos into a powerful moment that preceded Zuccotti Park 2011 and any echo of the Occupy chants or Black Lives Matter, while also harking back to Clifford Odets. Celestini does not attempt to hide the literary weight of his words. He does not perform the lines as though he were inventing them then and there. Rather, he speaks rapidly in a flat monotone, contrasting the grandiosity of the magical realism with a direct and matter-of-fact delivery. By the time he hits the last few words, "this is class struggle," they resound with an unexpected precision. Preserving the pristine appearance of what Nencioni called "clean language" lends a formality to Celestini's work that the rest of the presentation (casual clothing, no noticeable set piece or props) contradicts.

The theater's ability to offer constant renewal with each performance can also work to the narrator's benefit. While Celestini's play uses anecdotes from the book and film as a base, he sometimes changes the protagonist depending on the location of the performance. As he explains, he adapts each show according to the public decrees, government inspections, and legal disputes surrounding temporary work in a given area so that they are current and relevant on a local level.[48] In Rome he might reference the Atesia employees, whereas in Bari he might invoke workers in the Barilla factories or in Faenza the conditions in the garment industries. In doing so, he takes advantage of the author-actor dimension of the theater of narration, which allows him to change the script at will. Such decisions underscore the flexibility of the genre as much as they speak to the range of political commitments. Celestini takes a local issue in the community in which he is performing and highlights its national relevance, constantly balancing the two while focusing ultimately on the experiences of individuals.

The verbal choices during the final sequence also evoke the contentious political environment of the 1970s through the clashes with state police and the fight for legal and cultural representation for marginal groups. As the employee walks through "the walls of anti-missile glass" and then through the gated communities with their many antieverything gadgets, Celestini depicts an intensely controlled military environment full of phobias and aggression. The world through which the audience or reader accompanies him is home to people who are so paranoid that they are resolutely antieverything, from other types of people (Gypsy, Black, Jewish) to aging, allergies, and even, amusingly, food, in a pun on the Italian word for the first course, "antipasto." The temporary worker in this final sequence renounces not only her job, but all of these conditions of contemporary life, including, importantly, the authority of the police, whom she walks right through as well. Such totality is particularly reminiscent of the 1970s in that people pursued many different angles of addressing the establishment in an effort to confront a multitude of unacceptable issues.

Celestini continues to evoke institutional exploitation by suggesting that financial establishments both materially and morally enervate ordinary people. As the employee walks through the state mints, Celestini broadens his original starting point from the corporate factory environment of the work space to state organizations, from asylums to prisons that exist to control people, in his Foucauldian rendering. Miss Patricia passes through them, allowing her to both acknowledge and renounce them. If she were to pass above them, it would be a denial of them, but walking right through them suggests more of a dismissal. In the book, he incorporates the other main characters from previous chapters, when Miss Patricia runs into them as they too are escaping the dystopia by walking through walls, marble columns, and fire doors in a revolt en masse. Despite the fanciful sorcery of people unaffected by the physical borders that divide a city or the social borders that divide a population, Celestini is clear about the main feature of their lives: class. This leaves the audience with the memory of what they have heard about Miss Patricia earlier in the piece. In her job, where she earns five hundred euro a month, she has three-month contracts with zero benefits. The piece becomes a tale of fairness. What is the baseline for workers' rights? What is the relationship between one's dignity and economic necessity? Why are they benefits, and not just what society accepts as normal?

This energetic, performance-oriented language has made an appearance before in Italy, and not just on Italian stages but within more structural configurations of theater artists. Once the postwar period had given way to a stable, even prospering economy by the late 1950s, many leading theater artists found themselves frustrated by their profession and what they perceived as its confounding inertia. An effort to define and reinvent the state of postwar Italian theater reached a climax with the November 1966 publication of a manifesto called "Per un nuovo teatro" ("For a New Theater") in the journal *Sipario*, still among the most important theater journals in Italy today: its contributors include many leading actors, directors, and critics. It is particularly noteworthy that this piece emerged before 1968, as it underlines the extent to which culture, and theater in particular, was in dialogue with the radicalizing political climate as it was unfolding, not just reacting to it.

The language in the manifesto reveals a combative climate, perhaps even more than the concepts the authors convey. They open by stating, "The battle for theater is something much more important than a question of ethics." They denounce the "timidity of theater," which is "subordinately" hidden under an "apparent state of flourishing" when it is, in fact, the exact opposite: moribund. They continue to lament the

> aging of and lack of adequate structure; the growing interference of political and administrative bureaucracy within the public theaters; the monopoly by powerful groups; the deafness regarding the most significant international repertoire; the total inattention for the experimental initiatives that have tried to breathe life [into the theater] over the course of these years.[49]

The accusatory rhetoric highlights the argument that quality state-run theater is suppressed under government bureaucracy and that an aggressive denial of this state of affairs blocks the creation of new work.

This type of antiestablishment tone that prevails throughout much of the struggles of '68, sometimes referred to collectively in Italian as *contestazione*, stretched into the long 1970s. Since the theater of narration came on the heels of these debates with first-generation narrators, it reproduces the discursive environment of the period. The oral dexterity and inventiveness of narrators runs across media, as Celestini's Temps Projects displays, echoing the call for ingenuity in the November 1966 *Sipario* manifesto, which itself resounds with the demands that many groups voiced in 1968. In terms of the evolution of twentieth-century theater in Italy, the theater of narration is not a part of that experimental avant-garde movement to which the authors of the manifesto allude; rather, it evolved slowly over the next forty years. Still, a similar tenacity lies even in Celestini's much later text. This time it rallies not against the state-run theatrical establishment but against an increasingly oppressive surveillance state.

The linguistic rapport between the theater of narration and the political movements of the late 1960s and early 1970s has broad implications considering that "the Left," or many left-leaning organizations, slowly lost their facility with language as the decade wore on. To say that the theater of narration recuperates that language would be to overstate the case, particularly since most narrators do not align themselves with a specific political party, but one aspect of the success of narrative theater is its ability to restore the oppositional voices reminiscent of the 1970s that the neoliberal corporate tide of the 1980s into the Berlusconi era eventually drowned out. The Left was extremely loquacious during the 1970s. One need only recall the many journals (dailies, weeklies, monthlies, quarterlies) that sprang up during the decade. Yet it ultimately failed to provide a new and sustainable political vocabulary.[50] A large part of the problem was the descent into terrorism characterized by the Red Brigades, as Baliani demonstrates in *Body of State*. In Baliani's piece, the idealism is palpable as he faithfully attends meetings, watches his infant while his partner goes to pro-choice rallies, and refers to his old friends as "comrades." He also demonstrates how, even before the kidnapping of Moro, his enthusiasm waned as the violence increased. Although Baliani does not overtly emphasize the issue of language, when he peppers his text with words that sound anachronistic, such as "comrade," he points to the fact that this type of revolutionary language did not survive.

At the heart of this idea of "the failure of the word" is the failure of language in a broader sense that connotes political and cultural communication through words as much as through ideas and actions. Enrico Fenzi, who was formally involved with the Red Brigades, also concedes this when he explains,

> Certainly, there was also this enormous and, in my opinion, decisive failure of the word, of communication on the cultural level. . . . Like all great revolutions do, [the revolutionary movements in 1970s Italy] needed to invent a new language, new dress codes, new expressions, new ideas, new images. This did not come to pass with the volume that it should have and that was the most atrocious failure.[51]

New ideas and modes of expression *did* increase and permeate during moments of that decade, including those that considered terrorism. Extremism sacrificed the very domain in which leftist contestation was at first quite effective: shaping and providing a creative vocabulary that was widely available via print media. As the presence of radicals increased, the increasing isolation and self-referentiality of leftist terrorism grew apace, along with the separation of its jargon from everyday language.[52] Where the theater of narration confronts this dynamic is through its embrace of verbal language associated with the Left, from "comrade" to "class struggle," in a number of productions. It stops short of making any requests, of calling its audience to action, yet it performs that desire by giving voice to the underrepresented.

Oral History and Journalism

Along with microhistory's ability to highlight ideological systems from new perspectives, the presence of testimony with its emphasis on language and interpersonal relationships influences the dramaturgical methodology of the theater of narration. Parallel to the discovery of microhistory, Italian historians in the 1970s reconsidered the value of oral history, both the inherent problems of ascertaining its accuracy and its unique benefits. Among the most dedicated to reclaiming the benefits of oral historiography is Luisa Passerini. She notes that this method privileges what is closer, ordinary, and normal, also underlining the significance of language in her analysis of marginalized groups. The very language of oral history, she stresses, is of ordinary people (*gente commune*), thus historians play witness to more than an educated turn of phrase and calculated diction. Rather, they hear dialects with codes from people with no official voice.[53] This cultural consciousness demands a kind of detective work both for the historian and for the narrator, who must decide on the key words or phrases they find most accurately representative. Enia clearly dramatizes this by assigning *s'asciucò* the role of emphasizing associations with the ordinary and everyday life. It is not only regional but also common vernacular.

Considering Paolini's *Vajont* in conversation with Passerini's studies points to how narrators have uniquely positioned themselves to articulate tragedy multidimensionally. Some of Passerini's early research uncovered the tension between written and spoken texts, which narrative theater exploits through its implementation of fabula and satire. In her book about working-class Turin during fascism, *Torino operaia e fascismo* (1984), Passerini explores the experiences of living under the Mussolini regime by comparing oral and written accounts. While in the process of interviewing a particular individual, she began to notice the person's storytelling rhythms. She observed the particular moments when the interviewee sped up, the repetition of particular words, and the elements of comedy that she alternated with dramatic and painful memories.[54] She realized that this comic tendency was the main difference between the person's oral account and the one written in the person's diary. The facts were the same, but the way the person told the story differed based on the medium. This finding, which corroborated with similar patterns in others' accounts, led Passerini to conclude that orally expressing one's memories veiled the most tragic elements, such as deaths and injuries, pain and fear. The interviewee revealed to her the defenses that people put in place in order to avoid the most difficult moments when they orally shared a story.[55] Much like the fabula in classical oratory, comedic interstices dramatize the tragedy by temporarily distancing it, and narrators make use of this distancing function. Passerini's observation also highlights the inherent vulnerability in performing live and sharing private histories with others. As performers, the narrators confront this exposure in every performance, but they also conjure it as they share the experiences of others and mimic their own dramatic rhythms, shifting between relief and tragedy.

As Nencioni stressed the challenge of ridding a stage performance of linguistic artificiality from its written corpus, Passerini's findings show that the "everyday" rhetorical strategy of humor can serve as a method to reach the more desirous authentic portrayal. Paolini's use of comedy clearly demonstrates these more instinctual elements of self-defense so that the structure and delivery of his performance might mirror that of actual people who experienced the 1963 Vajont tragedy. Were they to recount their stories orally, they might interrupt the heavy moments with mockery, irony, or other distancing tactics. Paolini himself, a native of the region in Italy where the Vajont dam tragedy occurred, assumes an even more intimate stance of identity with his audiences as one who shares this difficult story using similar linguistic strategies to those a local from one of the traumatized villages would.

Notably, members of the Laboratorio Teatro Settimo describe part of their early method as collecting as many testimonies (oral, newspaper, charts, and photographs) as they could in order to make a theater text. They defined the outcome not as a record of any particular event but as an exploration of how testimony reconstructs that event. They believed that collecting these varied sources and analyzing them as a whole would permit a universal truth to emerge on which they could base a new show. In creating a piece that was "near" a topic or that "surrounded" it through research and analysis of clues and seemingly insignificant details, they could demonstrate its depth from new perspectives.[56] Here their practice overlaps with microhistory and what Ginzburg described as its autoreflexive dialogic practice that emerges through investigatory methods.[57]

In addition to maintaining self-awareness during the research process, narrators also maintain a metadialogue that reflects in specific performative elements. Celestini's linguistic poetics are particularly unique as he accelerates his speech, creating tension in his casual delivery. Because of this fast pace, the audience is always aware to some extent that Celestini relays the story by varying degrees of separation. He does not strive for realism. The automated tone of his speech highlights the fact that the audience is not hearing the story from the primary source. This type of meta-awareness comments on the story's own pretenses to authenticity. Borrowing these elements from oral history and microhistory practices indicates a level of intellectual rigor and poetical direction unique to the theater of narration. Much of the dialogue in these pieces is accessible to mass audiences, since the narrators base a significant amount of their texts on actual testimony and dialect, yet the practice as a whole employs a precise historiographical methodology.

Particularly in the more activist plays, such as *Appunti per un film* or *Vajont*, narrators encroach on investigative journalism territory. The subversion of traditional presentations of drama through the counterinformation journalist style is a common feature in Celestini's, Paolini's, and Musso's more civic theater pieces. The attempt to confront issues from different angles recalls the counterinformation tendency of the 1970s, where the notion of "making information" changed so that the strategies of sharing news destabilized the traditional presentations of journalism.[58] The goal of journalism then was not only to inform the public but also to offer the reader a more multidimensional perception of the present and to reach more diverse audiences.

Dario Fo explores the notion of "Living Newspapers" in the Author's Note of the 1977 edition of his *Mistero buffo* when he refers to theater, particularly comic theater, as a primary vehicle for people to express ideas, communicate, and even provoke one another. He claims, "For the people, grotesque theater in particular has always been the first method of expression, communication and the commotion of ideas. The theater was the newspaper, spoken and dramatized by the people."[59] The classical dimensions of the historia, argumentum, and fabula triangle loom here as Fo, the jester, enacts this logic, though he does so in different ways than the narrators do, exaggerating the *fabula* and satire in his many plays in order to underline the absurdist elements of true—often tragic—situations. Although the poetics are quite distinct from Fo's, the attempt to provide information and provoke discussion is intrinsic to the theater of narration.

Both Fo's Living Newspapers and the narrators' practice of historical documentation are in some ways a response to Walter Benjamin's observations on modern storytelling. In early Teatro Settimo documents, Benjamin's name surfaces, indicating that those first-generation narrators directly engaged with his work. A key element in how narrators theatricalize history is in their ability to transform "information" beyond facts and nearer to the Benjaminian vision of storytelling. In his famed essay "The Storyteller: Reflections on the Works of Nikolai Leskov," Benjamin laments people's diminishing ability to tell stories "properly" and states that the reason for the lack in skill relates to expressions of experience. He exhibits a sense of unexpectedness and surprise along with his dismay that people are simply unable to convey experiences with each other, unable to share. For him, part of the problem lies in the role that modern technologies had in fostering a thirst for information at the expense of more timeless modes of social interaction, whose content and scope surpassed immediate concerns. His examination also turns to the listener. Technology may have corrupted the ability to tell a story, but, perhaps more importantly, does anyone care to hear one?[60]

Related, a defining element in the communicative structure of the theater of narration is the adrenalin-energized quality of an informant who conveys new information. In the 1970s, the "making" of information changed, and news-sharing strategies subverted traditional journalistic methods.[61] One of the positive outcomes of this time was the phenomenon of counterinformation that offered a different perspective from that of the mainstream newspapers, in which journalists reenvisioned what constituted relevant data. The goal of journalism became not just to inform the public but also to train the reader better to decode the underlying reality of the times. This more analytical approach also correlates with other influences from the 1970s, such as the success of semiotics, the recasting of sociology and social research, and the intense politicization of media studies and culture. Narrators subvert both historical and dramatic tradition in similar ways. Between the newfound seriousness in oral histories and Fo's Living Newspapers, echoes of a Benjaminian desire for storytelling, and both investigative and counterinformation journalism, the theater of narration pulls some strategies, rejects others, contributes to the conversations, and takes them in different directions. What emerges from these many interrelated techniques and considerations is a clear desire for human connection and dynamic perspectives. The theater of narration with its soloist intimacy and research of the underrepresented offers just this.

In a final reflection on linguistic and oral strategies, one of the most relevant patterns regarding the dialogic mechanism in the theater of narration is the tendency toward a conversational mode of engagement among certain intellectuals during the 1970s. Both Italo Calvino and Pier Paolo Pasolini had embraced political commitment early in their careers. As Jennifer Burns explores, they began publishing more front-page editorials in mainstream newspapers such as the Milan-based *Il Corriere della Sera* during the 1970s; in fact, they actually replaced the usual political commentators. This offered them a direct engagement with a large readership. As Burns points out, they also began to respond to each other in editorials in a structure of requoting and questioning, in a "You say this; why?" pattern. Burns argues that for Pasolini, this type of exchange had greater value than mere "journalism" in its capacity to provide deeper explanations to the public.[62] In addition to these explanations, these texts perform the act of questioning as Pasolini and Calvino favored dialogic prose with direct inquiry over narrative prose. Narrators mimic and adapt this practice for the stage as they perform a dialogic exchange on many levels between themselves and their research, the characters they discuss or portray, and the members of the audience. They are performing the *intellettuale impegnato*, or the politically engaged intellectual. Burns writes that "individual authors were claiming not just to be the spokesperson of the movements but to embody the plural, heterodiegetic voice of the protestors."[63] Indeed, as La Ruina shows in *La borto* when he shares the plight of southern women, or as Baliani shows when he wonders about the personal choices of his friends in *Corpo di stato*, narrators embody these variegated voices in order to demonstrate how to arrive at the critical payoffs that wrestling with different perspectives brings.

As Benjamin laments the moribund state of storytelling, he places some of the blame on print media. Journalism, he suggests, contributed to the replacement of knowledge with information. As an example, he quotes Hippolyte de Villemesant (1810–79), the founder of *Le Figaro*, who characterized the nature of information in the famous formulation "To my readers . . . an attic fire in the Latin Quarter is more important than a revolution in Madrid." Benjamin suggests the misinterpreted centrality of distance: that which is closer has more importance because it lays claim to verifiability. All that is necessary is that the information appears "understandable in itself."[64] But information does not live on, while stories that contain truth or wisdom do. Geography should not be a factor. The distance one has traveled, or the extravagance of the tale, matters no more than "listening to the [person] who has stayed at home, making an honest living," and in fact "an orientation toward practical interests" is a worthy trait of many successful storytellers.[65] The narrators, as storytellers "from home," always close to their regional origins, find ways for a method that partially invokes journalism and therefore risks spouting information, even while they include a dimension that spurs a more deep-seated and lasting knowledge.

This dynamic is especially clear in Baliani's *Corpo di stato*. As the 1998 program for the show notes, the play is closely linked to his first major theater of narration success, *Kohlhaas* (1990), because although the two are vastly different stories, they share "the conflicted relationship between the need for revolt against injustice and the acceptance of the role of the avengers."[66] Throughout the piece he quotes newspapers from the kidnapping, and he opens the show with what becomes a foreboding memory of when students occupied the school of architecture in Rome. He begins with information. But as the piece moves quickly to the end of the decade, he explores the violence of those years increasingly from personal memory.

What draws out the greater, more timeless themes is the combination of impartial journalism with his memories and commentary. Here the universal truths that Benjamin sees in the talented storyteller emerge through a combination of concrete inquiry and reflection. Themes of violence beget violence. Against headlines of skirmishes between students and police, Baliani explores his own rage while watching riot police beat his friend, followed by the seething desire to better prepare himself for future encounters. With the reflexivity characteristic of the theater of narration, he soon asks himself what that means. Should he be better armed next time?

> I'd seen a lot of pictures of murdered bodies in those years. Lots. But this time was different, I don't know why. It was as if all the others that I had tried to cancel from my memory had now come back all together, all of them, all those murdered in cold blood as they left

> their homes or walked down the steps at the university, all the victims with no way out, without a chance for a fair fight, all those killings I could never find a good reason for. How had we come to this? How'd it happen that friends, comrades from my political group, from the marches, had suddenly started talking about weapons? From one day to the next they started using technical terms from specialized magazines, as though they were infatuated with weapons. But wasn't it always the fascists who loved guns?[67]

In dramatizing the hysteria, youthful passions, and fears, from scenes of brawls with police to reading about the murder of his friend in the paper, Baliani laments the confusion of those years. He asks the timeless question about that threshold of violence and clarity. "Arms" and the very notion of engagement with weapons symbolizes the turn from the rational to chaos. The Benjaminian ability to convey a larger question is here aided by journalistic accounts that ground Baliani's story in a tangible reality, helping to explain the popularity of the theater of narration: as Villemesant acknowledged, his readers gravitated toward what they knew. The political import to which these factors accrue is that the oral dimension both gives voice to many underrepresented people and perspectives, and develops a process in which people can continue to add new layers.

While performers generally add depth to written text, especially works intended for oral practices, multiple layers of performative strategies in the theater of narration illuminate new dimensions of the logocentric. Dialect becomes an especially rich device. Its musicality and poetic figures of speech have spellbinding qualities, to the point that the language itself becomes one of the major actors onstage. Separately, accounting for the history of oratory through a classical tripartite method provides a means of unpacking the different rhetorical strategies in the theater of narration, while strengthening its links to classical traditions of the spoken word. Historia, argumentum, and fabula shift the focus from persuasion to narration; from civic to personal contexts; and from discourse to literature. Finally, if the word ultimately failed for leftist struggles of the 1970s, it was slowly revived and rehabilitated in the theater of narration. Many plays revisit central arguments of that time, but they also examine contemporary crises with linguistic approaches similar to the ones activists used in the 1970s. Their strategies unite to create stories through the specificity of lived experiences with which their audiences can identify. While most narrators continue with the staged minimalism characteristic of the practice, their use of language is complex, at times experimental, and as diversely skilled as the many itinerant troupes and commedia dell'arte performers so important to the history of Italian theater.

Chapter 4

Locating Community

In loopy cursive strokes from an inky-blue pen, a pressing question emerged: "What will the new show be?" It was June 1, 1976. In Laura Curino's personal journal, she summarizes a meeting by the members of the Laboratorio Teatro Settimo, briefly expressing her frustrations about the "lack of focus" and "emptiness" at the gathering. The encounter "limped" along, she confides, and she pinpoints the problem by posing another question. In her orderly swirls she wonders, "How to reconcile the new theater discourse with the discourse on territory?"[1] This question represents the impulse that spurred numerous endeavors for the company. As Teatro Settimo continued to search for ways to explore discourses on and relationships with territory, the possibilities assumed many different forms. Location continues to be of paramount importance in the theater of narration. Specific towns, performance sites, and public institutions are central spheres across different narrative theater productions, as the genre contemplates the ways in which public and private domains overlap, resulting in communities that are strengthened by such attention.

A variety of physical spaces—from rural territories and postindustrial urban centers to intimate interiors such as private homes—and the creation of emotional and intellectual spaces all inflect the way the theater of narration fosters community, often centered around a particular civic issue. Many of the plays themselves also concern either directly or indirectly specific lands, or human-made constructions, so that a sense of the local is present, even if the production is in a traditional theater. A number of Teatro Settimo's productions, for example, directly contemplate Settimo Torinese, while Marco Paolini's *Vajont* is specific to several small towns in Friuli Venezia Giulia, and many of his other pieces reference that region's culture and language more generally. Then there are the plays about locations such as factories (Curino's *Camillo Olivetti*), insane asylums (Celestini's *Pecora nera*), or even the disembodied world of the internet (Paolini's *#Antropocene*). Territories and locations are more than just themes. Like dialect, they are the other characters with whom narrators interact, representing the communities of individuals that most frequently inhabit them.

Two key theoretical concepts guide the arguments in this chapter. The first emerged organically from reflections by Curino and Vacis when they themselves began to conceive of their early work in Teatro Settimo as connected to the notion of a heterotopia. This framework, which reaches toward a utopia but is process-based and interrogates the journey instead of the arrival, turns out to be a particularly insightful way to appreciate the objectives of the company. It also elucidates their connection to the urban center that most of them called home, Settimo Torinese. Even more surprising, as the idea of heterotopias frames their early work, it counterpoises the utopian ideals that Curino embraces for her study of the Olivetti family. Particularly in *Camillo Olivetti*, Ivrea stands in stark contrast to Settimo Torinese, while it also demonstrates how Curino slowly processed and developed an idea over time and through different projects.

Another central aspect to much theater during the 1970s that continues in the theater of narration is what anthropologist Victor Turner defined as *communitas*. Narrators play with the ways that performance spaces can also directly enhance the potential for community growth. The custom of group work in influential practices from animazione teatrale or the companies of Dario Fo and Franca Rame as well as Jerzy Grotowski demonstrated that by uniting among themselves and then with local people, they could turn their city into their stage and thus highlight the potential of public spaces that were too often underpopulated or, in their eyes, misused. Whether they performed in the basement of a shop, or in a friend of a friend's living room, they sought to inhabit and transform both private and public spaces. With several narrators having achieved national recognition by the end of the millennium, they could have performed exclusively on proscenium stages in midsized or mainstage theaters of the largest Italian cities, charging high prices for tickets and reaping larger profits; and they do perform on those stages, but many also still opt for nontraditional theater spaces, suggesting that performance sites continue to be important to those leading the genre. Narrators are dedicated to making their theater available to people in small towns, to people with little financial resources, and especially to local populations that have direct connections to the themes of a production.

Part of Teatro Settimo's community efforts included the organization of informal encounters to discuss the state of theater in Italy, particularly the *terzo teatro* (third theater) or *teatro di gruppo* (group theater), where the terms referred to a new wave of theater. Inserting themselves into a specific largely experimental theater lineage speaks to the same international awareness that drew them to the Polish theater. In addition to Grotowski, the Living Theater (particularly Judith Malina), Tadeusz Kantor, and Robert Wilson all have important histories in Italy that were meaningful to national artists during the dawn of the terzo teatro (1968–78) and the following decade of postmodern theater. Teatro Settimo's engagement with urban space also shared some commonalities with other environmental theaters, including Kantor's theater, Allan Kaprow's happenings, and Richard Schechner's experiments. In general, the terzo teatro was preoccupied with the relationship between a performance and the space in which it takes place and aimed to stretch beyond a widely perceived cultural stagnancy.[2] These informal gatherings also have a longer history related to festivalgoing, as the famous 1967 Ivrea festival demonstrates.

Beginning with the urban productions in nontraditional spaces with their "occupy and reclaim" air, the theater of narration explores both smaller and larger sites of performance, ranging from the intimacy of a stranger's home to the building of a stage in an alpine refuge. Various factors make these site-specific productions possible from the support of national public television to festival initiatives backed by EU funds, in addition to local partners. The festival circuit creates a space where performers present new and old works, see other contemporary productions, and of course meet with other theater artists, where metaconversations about the state of theater unfurl, either organically or through predesignated meetings. While notions of territory, performance spaces, and the creation of communities were paramount first in the development of Teatro Settimo, they find continued relevance in the works of individual narrators. The genre's relationship to space reflects its subtle yet empowering politics, which advocates for grassroots human-focused experiences in contemporary society and in the creation of historical narratives.

Heterotopias: Teatro Settimo (1978–82)

In their first years as a company in the late 1970s, the Laboratorio Teatro Settimo met with other local collectives and community groups and incorporated the city into many of their early projects. They experimented with various ways to engage their territory. Almost a decade later, in 1987, Curino and Vacis provocatively referred to their attraction and revulsion to the town of Settimo, which manifested itself in a variety of public performances, as a type of "heterotopic project." This framework that they themselves identified with the distance of time offers a key window into understanding both their early efforts and their formative thinking, which influenced what would become the theater of narration. Their intention in choosing this title was to privilege the process of an unfinished project, rather than a finished work. This method is set in contrast to result-oriented expectations that would celebrate an ending, or a complete form.[3] Rather than a nonmaterial space of perfection, Foucault interprets a heterotopia as a real place, but one that maintains some aspect of the illusory.[4] Similar to how Foucault posits the notion of heterotopia against that of utopia, Curino and Vacis signal a space that fosters creation yet temporally exists before that event. In choosing this term, they imply that many of their early projects celebrated an actual place that they intended to help create but that did not yet exist. This place was the town of Settimo, though not the Settimo that they knew then. Rather, they staged the Settimo in which they wanted to live.

Teatro Settimo's theatrical practice was the inverse of a Foucauldian heterotopia. As it took shape within various organizations and public spaces, from the central public library to a parking lot that would later be a piazza, it turned real-world places created for uses other than theater into heterotopic spaces through the imaginative power of performance. Joanne Tomkins defines a stage "heterotopia" as "a location that, when apparent in a performance, reflects or comments on a site in the actual world. . . . Heterotopias are alternative spaces that are *distinguished from* that actual world, but that *resonate with* it."[5] She continues to differentiate between theater in general and heterotopic theater, arguing that theater might offer "experimental zones" that suggest different modes of living or experiencing, though without the blueprints to achieve those new practices outside of the performance. By contrast, "theater that is heterotopic depicts other possible spaces and places live in front of an audience and it offers spectators specific examples of how space and place might be structured otherwise. It points to the potential for cultural impact to be reframed."[6] Through a number of projects, including Arcircolo PEPE and the City Lab Project, both discussed in this chapter, Teatro Settimo worked in and with locations that were already a part of the actual world, not sets that reflected or commented on it. Using these preexisting places was a key part in demonstrating concrete ways in which to reenvision different uses of them. Their work is heterotopic because their theater encouraged, indeed performed, the evolution of these locations into ones geared toward the well-being of the town's citizens.

That Curino and Vacis labeled their work heterotopic also suggests that they had a predilection toward postmodern thought early on and incorporated it into their understanding of history as incomplete. This framing corresponds to the emphasis on method in the theater of narration. As the practice offers historical accounts from different perspectives, the importance is on the idea of opening new possibilities, readings, and understandings as much as it is on recuperating the specific voices often left out of official historical records. Notions of agency and power surface as Teatro Settimo and later narrators sought to understand alternative histories while gesturing toward something that could come into being, such as a city designed more for its inhabitants than for its industries. In considering the mechanics and processes of power, Curino and Vacis fashioned what Foucault would call "a new mode of exercise of power" in reference to the relationships between the real and unreal that heterotopias create.[7] The early work of Teatro Settimo on the streets of their town and in its public venues, with the retrospective framing of these endeavors as their heterotopic project, is also a manifestation of finding the value and power in gestures of potential. By working within these liminal postmodern spaces, narrators represent a nonfixedness and an openness to change.

Arcircolo PEPE and Olivetti's Ivrea

One of Teatro Settimo's most fruitful collaborative efforts during their formative years was their participation in the Arcircolo PEPE, a collective created at the end of 1978 by an eclectic group of people with a variety of entrepreneurial plans, including a graphic design company, a craft and print shop, and a pub-restaurant. They joined forces to apply for money from the region of Piedmont, the city of Turin, and other governmental sources; that is, they came together under PEPE as a starting point to obtain basic funding but also had the intention to eventually disband and function on their own.[8] Under PEPE, Teatro Settimo was able to create a legal foundation for their company with low costs and shared administrative responsibilities. There are countless letters in Laura Curino's Private Collection from Teatro Settimo addressed to various local government offices, such as the Cultural Ministry (Assessorato alla Cultura) of Settimo, Turin, and Piedmont, asking for support. While the company also earned money working with schools, and eventually through their performances, these local state funds were integral to their initial development.

The very creation of groups such as PEPE signal a reaction to the postwar climate, when the corporation first overshadowed the individual. The spirit of the day echoed in buzzwords like "creation, expansion, growth," yet these ideals did not always resonate on the ground in people's daily lives.[9] Teatro Settimo artists were among those who interpreted the so-called economic boom as a myth of the state. In an undated PEPE pamphlet amid materials from 1978 to 1981 in Curino's Private Collection, the artists voice some of these concerns. Their writing resembles a manifesto in their denunciations of greed and exploitation that belied the deceptive rhetoric of the 1960s "economic miracle." They illustrate the grotesque image of their city, which they liken to other peripheral towns of industrial metropolises which were, in their opinion, also constructed for the sole purpose of corporate profit rather than with the needs of its citizens in mind. Settimo, they insist,

> is not a city fit for humankind. It is actually the opposite; an emblematic form of the denial of human needs. Its streets, its houses, its factories and the availability of all these entities, with the relationships that result from them, are the achievements of capital. This city, like many others near Turin, Milan, or Genoa, was built and transformed to make the most money it could. In doing so (which translates to exploitation, immigration, alienation, displacement, and many other things that all of us who live in Settimo live with daily), we were saying, a person is just an object, a tool.[10]

Teatro Settimo relied on a stark juxtaposition between capitalist greed over the needs of people. Here they offer their interpretation of what led to the tense political environment of the 1970s. To them, their urban factory-scape symbolized not progress, development, and well-being but exploitation, marginalization, and alienation. Coping with these realities is a major theme in many narrative theater plays from both generations of narrators, but rarely does any artist articulate the stakes as clearly as the Teatro Settimo authors do here, with such blunt and pointed language. The group focuses acutely on their surroundings, while acknowledging their universality near other industrial metropolises, identifying precisely the pertinent issues that upset them. The next step was how to enact change.

In this same PEPE pamphlet, Teatro Settimo states its aims to restructure the cultural life of the town by arguing for a link between social climate and territory. Written along the margins in Curino's handwriting are several leading questions that the document confronts. "So is Settimo a city fit for humankind?" What, after all, might such a place look like? Industrial giants such as Fiat largely created Settimo as a residence for its employees who worked at their nearby factories, and Teatro Settimo artists asked whether it was a town on par with what modern towns should be. They also asked themselves how they could help people turn their industrial town into a more human-centered livable cultural space. They question the merits of an environment with no public parks, no creative exhibits, and no community programs for children or the elderly. Throughout the document, the authors identify the dynamics of this urban space, and they conclude that like other industrial metropolises—for example, Milan and Genoa, which were reconceived during the capitalist era for the sole purpose of economic earnings—Settimo was not constructed with its residents' quality of life in mind.

These questions continue to haunt the works of more recent narrative theater pieces, and they also frame humanistic queries concerning the environment. The very act of questioning sets up the possibility for heterotopic theater by gesturing toward a confrontation and even reconciliation with environmental awareness. It suggests the possibility of a world that does not yet exist, but could exist if only people asked these questions with more frequency and on other platforms. The questions also reflect the dystopic alternatives of their absence. What happens when no one asks, or no one pays attention to their answers? The echoes of these inquiries explain some of the success of Curino's Olivetti plays, Celestini's Temps Projects, and especially Paolini's *Vajont*, all of which chart narratives where greed and prestige threatened human well-being. Parallels in Italian society continue decades after the debuts of these shows, as Curino still travels nationally with *Camillo Olivetti* and as other narrators create new projects. As recently as August 2018, the highly trafficked Morandi bridge connecting eastern and western Genoa suffered a massive collapse, killing forty-three people, injuring many others, and terrifying a countless number. Similar to how Paolini reveals in *Vajont* that those in charge of the dam's construction ignored the warnings of geologists and other experts that it was making the area unstable, engineers, academics, and even politicians lobbied for years for the Morandi bridge's maintenance and repair, explaining in clear and urgent terms that the structure was an engineering failure and was dangerous. The bridge ultimately met a similarly ignominious fate as the Vajont dam, symbols of the ways in which environment is ignored and industry fails, sacrificing humans, and humanity.

Given her leadership role within Teatro Settimo as one of its founders and her dedication to their pursuits, mixed with her family fate of moving from the sophisticated cultural capital Turin to its outskirts when she was a young girl but old enough to take memories with her, these issues haunted Curino for much of her early career, even as she began practicing the solo theater that would come to be the theater of narration. When she wrote *Passione* in 1987, the same year that she and Vacis reflected on their projects as heterotopic, she was still processing, albeit humorously, the challenges of her childhood in the soulless city of Settimo. Just under a decade later, in the midst of writing and producing her *Olivetti* plays, she uses Ivrea, the nearby town where Camillo Olivetti set up his typewriter factories and which Adriano Olivetti helped turn into a chic, wealthy, and dynamic city, as the utopia she and her company imagined all those years prior when they wrote the PEPE pamphlet.

Examining *Olivetti* against those first descriptions of Settimo through the lens of heterotopic theater demonstrates the depth of these plays, among the most celebrated in the theater of narration. As they depict Olivetti's Ivrea, they also represent a climactic moment in the oeuvre of Curino and Vacis. The environmental and community issues with which they had grappled for nearly two decades in their art, and even longer in their lives, find solace in these two plays, along with a final resting place that demonstrates what their hopes and efforts for Settimo could look like.

They perform this ideal by way of an entirely different strategy than when they sought to bluntly expose the inhumanity of industrialization in the 1978 PEPE pamphlet, or affectionately mock it in order to highlight its absurdism, as Curino does in 1987 with *Passione*. Here Curino strives to suggest the possibility of industrial development that could be *both* technologically progressive and conscientious of human labor. Remarkably, in 1994, nearly two decades after the PEPE pamphlet, the notion of a space "fit for humankind" reappears verbatim in *Camillo Olivetti*. Early in the play, Curino marvels at the possibility of a place with acceptable living and working conditions, in the Olivetti workshops and Ivrea itself. She asks,

> How was it possible that a factory amid trees and nature existed? No walls, but glass panels, so that the workers, while they worked, could see the trees. How was it possible that a factory *fit for humankind* existed, and also a *city fit for humankind* . . . and not at the price of pollution, alienation, sickness, but simply a place of well-being with dignity in one's work, respect for people, for their bodies, their environment, their education?[11]

For Curino, Olivetti's Ivrea is what Fiat's Settimo Torinese could have been. She explicitly praises Olivetti for having achieved the coexistence of capitalist productivity with workers' well-being. Olivettian integrity was also reflected broadly in the surroundings, and indeed, when she reminisces about the Olivetti workshops, she extends her memories to encompass Ivrea. This emphasis on harmony in environment is one of the key concepts worth pondering with respect to current working cultures. Even though Curino's play is named for the single individual who built the factory, it is told by other people in his life—his mother and wife—and in their versions, the real protagonists are the factory workers, with due credit to the humble ways in which they too, as women restricted by society, nonetheless contributed to the success of the company, particularly its humanitarian and humanistic ethos. Thus, Curino performs a vision of livable spaces in which factory workers—their well-being and quality of life, but also their labor, their time and energy—had more value, as did women's labor and work.

Curino furthers this theme of well-being in the second Olivetti play. She explains that Adriano Olivetti's vision of an existence "fit for humankind" encompassed an entire culture where art, science, and capitalism endured in synchronicity. By the time she wrote *Adriano Olivetti* in 1996, she had become more accepting of the inevitable modern presence of mass industrial labor than she was in her early twenties, and rather than a full erasure of it, she highlights the possibility of a peaceful coexistence. While Camillo Olivetti was clearly interested in social reformism, it was his son's initiatives that linked industrial wealth with the creation of community service.[12] Curino explains this idea: "It was thinking that publishing and industry, society and economics, culture and social sciences could understand each other, and that this mutual tolerance could be given the name factory. Factories in this century are useful, indispensable, necessary. But maybe it is not necessary that they are also places of torture."[13] Indeed, Adriano Olivetti attempted to create such a community in his political Movimento Comunità (Community Movement), under which the people elected him mayor of Ivrea in 1956. He also created an editorial imprint under this banner, which explains Curino's reference to publishing. These political efforts reflected his core philosophy of democratic industrialism inspired by a wide range of economists and philosophers, from Joseph Schumpeter's work on enterprise to Jacques Maritain's integral humanism.[14] Curino frames Adriano Olivetti's vision around the inevitability of industry in the modern capitalist world and uses Olivetti's "humanitarian capitalism" as an ideal for which contemporary companies ought to strive. She not only values the various worker benefits, including summer camps for employees' children and public libraries for the entire city, but also the breadth of experience and practice of leisure outside the factory and the notion of community that Adriano Olivetti embraced.

Whether or not Olivetti actually achieved this lofty ideal depends on one's perspective. In the town of Ivrea there is great loyalty to the Olivetti family, and nationally they are still considered the apex of business, community, leadership, and vision, hailed as beneficent capitalists who shared their wealth with factory workers and aimed to create a work environment that promoted cultural, intellectual, and recreational habits. As they sought to improve employee benefits and to invest in the community of Ivrea, they were also attractive figures of the Italian intelligentsia and antifascist efforts. Adriano married Paola Levi, the sister of the celebrated novelist Natalia Ginzburg (mother of the microhistorian Carlo Ginzburg), and, as she famously wrote in *Lessico famigliare* (1963), Adriano himself helped important leftists such as the socialist Filippo Turati escape the fascists, an especially serious risk given Adriano's Jewish heritage.

Olivetti's critics, however, suspected that the employee benefits were meant to defuse the workers' potential dissatisfaction. Autonomists and workerists in particular, who believed in self-organization and the ability of the working class to force change in capitalist systems, recognized that by promoting an industrial culture that fostered harmonious social relations, management could deter employees from radicalizing through outside unions and political organizations.[15] Rather than hinting at any critique of the family, or performing one herself, Curino is complicit in the hagiography of Camillo and Adriano Olivetti, though her ultimate goals have little to do with them. In addition to the inclusion, finally, of the family matriarchs in their public history, she works through the environmental and community repercussions of factories, issues related to modern capitalization that have frustrated her for decades. Her glance toward the past loses sight of the fact that by the time she wrote the plays, the busy Olivetti factories that had energized Ivrea were mostly silent. The company itself did not survive the death of Adriano Olivetti in 1960, which signals the beginning of the end of its period of high productivity and creativity.[16] Curino wrote her scripts, then, in a state of nostalgia: the Ivrea she depicts had already ceased to exist by the time of her writing. It is its own heterotopia of a place that reflects the realities for which she and her Teatro Settimo members yearned, though it was already lost by the time they were fighting for change in Settimo.

City Laboratory Project, Vivapiazza, and Community Initiatives

Over the next several years, as Teatro Settimo worked through the possibilities of transforming their city into a space for the people and not machines, they devised a set of performances, workshops, and urban research projects that they called the Progetto Città Laboratorio (City Lab Project) and, in a separate initiative that followed, Vivapiazza (Long Live the Piazza). A humanistic approach to these initiatives grounded them on the streets of their city as they amassed information about the relationships that their fellow citizens created with public spaces. For the City Lab, the company created a booklet with photographs of cafés and community centers where elderly

Fig. 13. Archival photograph of Settimo Torinese from Progetto Città Laboratorio booklet (1980–81). Courtesy of Laura Curino and Federico Negro. The image depicts a central area in the city, Piazza Vittoria Veneto, with the note below that it is used exclusively for parking on Wednesdays and Saturdays, when the outdoor market takes place. It is otherwise "deserted."

and young people met. They also photographed piazzas, or town squares, and described their primary uses—mainly as parking spots and as sites for religious or political protests (fig. 13). The booklet details their findings and their plans to revitalize the city. The artists placed these descriptions around the photographs of specific locations and added notes about how the spaces might be more richly imagined.

Exercising an important element of their humanist methodology, the Teatro Settimo authors of the City Lab booklet personify spaces by treating them like characters in a story. They follow the piazzas on different days and describe the frequency with which people traffic the locations. They are curious about what happens to the spaces and how they transform when vendors set up carts to sell various goods, or during protests. One central question guides their study: "What is the life of a piazza, or this café, or that community center?"[17] Taking a macro view in their analysis, the authors do not simply portray physical spaces as central to the livelihood of the community; harking back to the concept of heterotopia, they also show how public spaces are vulnerable and can suffer. For them, the stakes could not be higher, and personifying the spaces, treating them as though they were characters in a play or literary work, helps them better understand the relationship between people and the public spaces they walk through. They discovered for themselves that space was a lens into the social life of urban and industrial towns and could reveal much about the emotional and physical well-being of their inhabitants. The underused central piazza mirrored the quality of life in its neighborhood, which was the heart of the town. Staying in that space, tracking it, photographing it, documenting its daily life, and finally thinking and writing about it and its state of abandon revealed in a particularly profound way the lonely state of the human beings who inhabited the industrial landscape. While devastating, the realization also revealed the possibility to experiment with a cure. The primary patient was the town, not the population. If the artists could minister to the city, then perhaps they could also help its inhabitants.

So began a variety of initiatives after several years of research and efforts to understand the relationship between territory and people, which had emerged as a clear priority in the earliest days of Teatro Settimo with the PEPE group, developed through the City Lab projects, and hovering years later, fully in the theater of narration form, in works such as *Passione* and the *Olivetti* plays. In the early years, Teatro Settimo's goal was nothing short of an urban transformation, and their Vivapiazza initiative during the summers from 1979 to at least 1982, memorialized in various flyers, event programs, and newspaper reviews in the Laura Curino Private Collections, accomplished just that. Over the last two weeks in July, various artist and community groups occupied the entire city center to create a wide range of events supported and organized by Teatro Settimo and their partners: the city of Settimo Torinese, the regional Ministry for Culture (Assessorato alla Cultura), and PEPE. These creative groups offered a variety of cultural workshops for all ages, from magic shows to street theater and more formally staged theater productions. An informational packet from the 1981 Vivapiazza displays a variety of mostly theater troupes and the various programs, a few paragraphs on the history of the endeavor, a map delineating the areas where events will take place (fig. 14), and the important note that all participation is welcome and free.

Teatro Settimo and their partners were able to create a striking sense of community with Vivapiazza by working through a complex web where cultural wealth meets the ordinary, all in the sphere of shared local spaces. According to *La Stampa*, the Turin-based newspaper and a leading national voice, the project fascinated the public and succeeded in creating a physical meeting ground where people could exchange ideas.[18] *La Gazzetta del Popolo* announced that Teatro Settimo had "rediscovered the piazzas."[19] The Rome-based *Il Manifesto* also claimed that through their initiatives they allowed the city, a belt of factories and dormitory houses, to breathe oxygen during those two summer weeks when it could enjoy Vivapiazza.[20] Echoing the very description that Teatro Settimo had used in their research, a staff writer for *La Stampa* noted that "the look of this piazza which is often desolate in

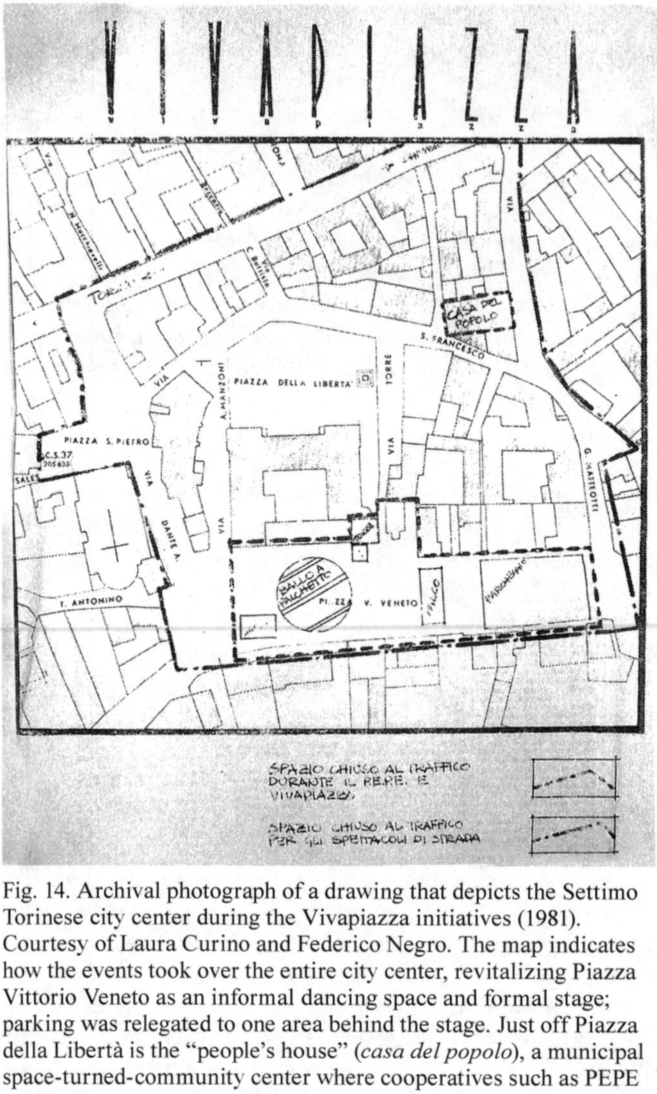

Fig. 14. Archival photograph of a drawing that depicts the Settimo Torinese city center during the Vivapiazza initiatives (1981). Courtesy of Laura Curino and Federico Negro. The map indicates how the events took over the entire city center, revitalizing Piazza Vittorio Veneto as an informal dancing space and formal stage; parking was relegated to one area behind the stage. Just off Piazza della Libertà is the "people's house" (*casa del popolo*), a municipal space-turned-community center where cooperatives such as PEPE could meet.

its vastness, normally used for parking, has been completely altered . . . in this form, the piazza recuperates its natural function as a place for meeting, enjoyment, discussion."[21] By these accounts, Teatro Settimo succeeded in its early effort to build a *storia* for Settimo by creating community around its existing urban structures. The designer Lucio Diana, one of Teatro Settimo's founders, told *La Stampa* that their idea was to recuperate sophisticated artistic traditions in the sphere of everyday life.[22] As they worked within the quotidian rhythms of their town, embracing and altering its daily pace, they began to articulate their goals in different ways.

Finally, this effort also speaks to the company's extensive dedication to study and learning from other theatrical endeavors. The press coverage and praise continued in the following year, 1982, which marked the fourth season for Vivapiazza, in a *La Stampa* article titled "When Theater Descends on the Piazza and Transforms It." That year, Teatro Settimo decided to pay homage to the rich urban theater practices developing in Poland at the time, thanks not only to Grotowski but also to group theaters such as Osmego Dnia from Poznan and Gardzienice from Lublin that also occupied public city space and worked with local "people's houses" (*case del popolo*). When the journalist asked the company why that year they were also using the Polish name "Zyvyplac" for Vivapiazza, which means the piazza that lives (or lives again), Curino responded, "Because it was from Poland where the notion that theater cannot exist without its territory emerged . . . and because in this moment, it is more important than ever, speaking of transformation, to open our eyes and turn our heart toward a country and its people, and that engagement that leads to change is certainly not made only with words!"[23] Though subtle, her personification of a single body with "our eyes" and "our heart" reveals the mentality of the collective, which had been so productive for Teatro Settimo and the other groups with whom they worked, and a signature of the Polish groups with whom they were dialoguing as they invoked Zyvyplac.

During the same interview with *La Stampa*, the artists turn the conversation into an opportunity to clarify their investment in Settimo. Curino laments that they did not receive all the funding with which they had hoped to run Vivapiazza, and Vacis explains that with just a little bit more financial support, they could have programmed productions in "spaces that remain absurdly closed."[24] It might seem brazen or youthful, but it also reveals the energy and dedication of these members as they seize opportunities to hold their city administrators accountable and challenge their values. Vacis takes a diplomatic tone when he adds that they are fortunate and grateful to have received some support from both public and private sources that agreed with their ethos, though he cautions that the relationships are fragile and have been built over years.

As the members of Teatro Settimo created more opportunities and invested in their community, their relationships with local government officials also grew. Largely thanks to their work, the publicity it brought to the area, and the enthusiasm with which it was received, the local government supported other endeavors that complemented the humanist philosophy of the theater group as they attempted to invigorate Settimo. In 1982, the region of Piedmont launched several research centers that focused on local cultures and theater arts. In addition to the Istituto Teatro e Metropoli and the Piano d'Ambiente Culturale, they also began the Atélier di Cultura Teatrale (ACT), which was designed specifically as a collaboration between the city of Settimo, the regional Ministry for Culture (Assessorato alla Cultura), and Teatro Settimo. There were practical implications in the success of launching these initiatives beyond the creative. As much as these initiatives produced opportunities for other artists, students, and community members, they were an important source of stability too, especially for Teatro Settimo, allowing the artists the time and space to focus on creating new works, and setting the stage for the 1980s as the most important decade for the company. This marks the beginning of the period when they created some of their greatest successes as a company and when individual members began to branch out with the first iterations of the theater of narration. In particular, Curino and Paolini wrote and performed *Passione* and *Gli album*, respectively, and both artists continued to collaborate with Vacis as director and writing consultant.

For their work on ACT, Teatro Settimo continued to develop their community-oriented approach as they outlined three overarching goals: community service, events planning, and research. First, they aimed to nurture a sense of civic responsibility by working with cultural organizations, gatherings, and activities for specific groups such as children. Second, they focused their goals on the formation of events such as conferences and meetings to discuss the theory and practice of theater arts in the community. Their third task, research, was directed toward gathering information on the territory, then defining that territory using coordinates of time and space. They explained that their interest in space was its "connection between cultural potential and urban structure," which complemented "the coordinate of time investigated through historical research, the possibility to characterize a cultural identity, [and] memories for a city that does not have any."[25] As these endeavors became realities, they continued to posit a connection between the urban landscape and culture, proving their dedication to Settimo as they collectively constructed a *storia* it could call its own. The proximity and appeal of engaging and even transforming public spaces as a way to rethink their utility, potential, and significance for the community continued as the theater of narration blossomed throughout the 1990s and into the current millennium.

Creating Community

As cultural laborers who both are part of an experience and view it from the outside, narrators pursue a basic practice of ethnography in the creation and execution of their productions. Their exploration of community enacts the definition of ethnography as a way of "getting to know other human beings intimately and well especially through their everyday experiences."[26] Teatro Settimo artists practiced performance as a generative act, one that brought something into being, not only a representational form. One of the most important generative acts that emerged through their investigations on territory and passed into the theater of narration is the creation and shoring up of communities, in the Turnerian sense of communitas and other ways as well.

Turner differentiates between the actual social groups of a community by using the Latin communitas to emphasize the social relationships that bind members of a community. For him, communitas represented the synchronicity (and maybe sanctity) between community and communion. He also believed that grounding communitas in experience was an essential dimension. Similarly, narrators create opportunities for their audiences with the explicit potential to develop into cohesive groups. Even if they consist of disparate individuals, that they share similar ideas with the strong sense of belonging that Turner also emphasized would lead them to identify as a homogenous collective.[27] Narrators further develop Turner's communitas into a processual action of shared agency in which people come together to experience, reflect, and generate both new histories and new futures. In the theater that Teatro Settimo created, and in the theater of narration that followed, the agency of ordinary people was an important result of their work within local landscapes and urban structures and, through those spaces, the experiences that they shared, signaling one of the principal qualifiers in the Turnerian definition of communitas.

Looking beyond established institutions, since many protesting groups deemed them ineffective, a number of communities and initiatives from this period formed not because societal programs were working, but because they came together to advocate for these structures. Teatro Settimo, for example, worked to fill a void, to create something from the absence of anything. Beyond this, their idea was purposefully nonspecific.[28] The way everyday people created communities during this period also invokes Turner's concept of liminality, the agitator of communitas. With liminality, he describes a chaotic state that exists "betwixt and between" and is a cultural manifestation of the communitas, where those transitional qualities inherent in the liminal become "definitive states of culture," which are then institutionalized, with transition as a permanent condition.[29] These tactics also manifest themselves symbolically in the theater of narration. With productions such as *Vajont*, the physical place of the dam, like the physical place of Settimo, represents not just the community of Longarone and other towns but also more generally a lost community, a vacant space, a lacuna. The genre inherited these priorities and practices that embraced the intersections of community building and communitas through urban structures from Teatro Settimo, animazione, and the work of Dario Fo and Franca Rame.

Group Work

The basic idea of Turnerian communitas, cut with a sense of that sociopolitical impulse impegno, is apparent in the formation of the many groups that came together in the cultural logic following 1968 that sought to recenter the human. It might seem ironic that the theater of narration developed into a solo theater practice, given that all of its founders from the first generation were once a part of theater groups. From Marco Baliani's activist past when he was a university student in Rome and created several theater companies, to the Teatro Settimo members, to Marco Paolini, who later joined Settimo but had previously worked with a different theater collective in the Northeast, the early efforts of first-generation narrators demonstrate the aim to combat the isolation of the individual that resulted from the alienation of industrially driven postwar Italian society. Nonetheless, during the late 1980s, as Paolini and Curino began their first solo shows and Baliani soon followed, it became clear that what was born from that group work was the relevance of the human, particularly the ordinary human. The visual synergy of the solo actor distills that realization.

The early group work was a vital component of the humanist philosophy at the center of the theater of narration and underscores the influence of 1970s culture. The practice of collectives and collaboration during that time period was itself a result of the unstable postwar society that never found any sustained momentum. While there was state-sponsored money available for small business owners and cultural initiatives, the primary funds for those enterprises were in swaths of unregulated, but not easily obtainable, public money. With World War II lingering in the recent past, the 1950s were home to major public undertakings to rebuild the country, initially with good results. There was successful growth in the iron and steel industries, the buildings of highways, and the expansion of telephone lines, all of which created the illusion of an economic boom. Granted, there was no illusion in terms of the overall economy. The period between 1953 and 1962 was a prosperous time economically, but the rub was in the expense. The programs in place that led to temporary fortune were not sustainable. By the following decade, from roughly 1963 to 1972, the government was unable to produce any profit from state-sponsored companies, and the deficits and steep losses that followed soon resulted in overstaffed bureaucracies and frequent political intraparty fighting.[30] The narrators came of age during this time, when factories were rising around them in the swelling towns of the Italian North, with their poor infrastructure, economic instability, and socioeconomic value at the expense of those who worked in them.

The very fact that PEPE was an organization that welcomed membership to almost anyone with a project made it attractive to Teatro Settimo, because it redirected their gaze away from the politicized theater world of the 1970s, where many groups associated themselves with specific political parties. As Curino once quipped, "Our only rule was, 'No weapons!' " (i.e., violent political revolutionaries were not welcome). This distance allowed them the space to develop their methods without the pressure to respond to every social issue or narrow themselves to take a political stance. Subsequent generations followed suit. Most narrative theater suggests a left-leaning ideology, but, unlike

Fo and Rame, none of the narrators associate themselves publicly with any political party or proselytize an agenda. This characteristic is a key distinction between narrators and other types of performance artists and political satirists. Rather than fomenting specific political critiques, Teatro Settimo instead committed itself to such broader goals as an inclusive environment and focused on community work. If they wanted to create a public sphere where marginalized voices could speak, they did not want it to be at the expense of groups whom they might alienate if they aligned themselves with a particular party. The core of their politics was inclusion. In the early years, during PEPE, their communities consisted of other local people, and their central commonality was their shared territory.

The PEPE environment placed the young Teatro Settimo on the same economic level as other beginning entrepreneurs. Their goal to create "a more just society that shares the aim for everyone to truly be the protagonists" emphasizes the potential of each human being, an ideal that became central to their ethos.[31] Through PEPE, they explained how they wanted to make a serious and worthy contribution to their city, one they felt was indispensable and urgent. In addition to a community where artists and entrepreneurs could strategize and help each other, PEPE offered all its members the same political autonomy that Teatro Settimo sought, and with that came both ideological and financial benefits. They conceived of creativity as "the capacity to mobilize rational, critical, and intuitive forces" for the purpose of finding new solutions.[32] This attitude helped make their work attractive to city and state councils who had discretionary funds for cultural activities. Having a civic-minded rather than policy-pushing agenda made it easier to find state support. Minimizing an overt political critique, then, was also a strategy for appealing to municipalities. Even when their shows were critical of Italian society, the creators were simply private citizens stating their views, not representatives of particular parties. PEPE was linked to a moment of prevailing demand for "agitation" when it was necessary to rethink the place of the human. Teatro Settimo wrote that it was time to understand why they lived in "these suburban ghettos" and to ask whose hands the peoples' lives were in.[33] They used PEPE specifically to create a new instrument (their theater practice) to help marginalized groups question why they were on the fringes of Italian life.

PEPE was also vital in Teatro Settimo's, and later the theater of narration's, understanding of community as having the ability to incite change through collective action. The PEPE pamphlet begins by explaining that the organization's two main principles are teamwork and volunteerism. Via collaboration and communication, the overarching goal of ameliorating Settimo offers a way to measure one's own set of priorities in the company of others. As the members of PEPE rethink public spaces, the group-oriented emphasis allows participants to rethink their own social roles and relationships to one another. The authors articulate a delicate translation of group ethics onto the individual, emphasizing that together they will learn how to cultivate and express their own cultural heritage. Setting the groundwork for an active approach, this idea of linking group work to individual cultivation recalls Teatro Settimo's view of the artist as cultural laborer. By expressing their intention to rethink the ways in which everyone can empower themselves and contribute to the building of their society, the PEPE leaders adhere to the belief that an artist is not the only member of society who can produce culture. Everyone can. The ideas expressed in the pamphlet thus complement Teatro Settimo's notion that theater can be a form of community service insofar as its message invites action.

While Teatro Settimo was able to cultivate their critical goal to build vital and creative art in the environment of PEPE, another community- and group-oriented source of inspiration came from *animatori*, who also influenced how they understood space, place, and location. Rather than performing onstage, animators opted to perform in places that were more ordinary, more central to daily life, as a sort of "social theatricalization" (*teatralizzazione sociale*).[34] While the themes of Teatro Settimo's projects were not overtly political, their early performances in piazzas were political acts in that they were attempting to "socialize" the inhabitants of Settimo toward various topical issues. This social awareness that they practiced, including their own participation in animazione projects and in group settings such as PEPE, develops some of the philosophical principles of Turner's communitas. He describes how it "breaks in through the interstices of structure, in liminality; at the edges of structure, in marginality; and from beneath structure, in inferiority" where historically those three conditions of liminality, marginality, and structural inferiority "frequently generated myths, symbols, rituals, philosophical systems, and works of art."[35] By aiming to work with groups that are on the fringes, marginalized, and treated as inferior, as factory workers, elders, and children were, both animators and Teatro Settimo artists recognized not only their need for a social theatricalization but also that their very status on the outside was the access point from which they could creatively reimagine their existence.

These efforts aiming both to strengthen existing communities and uplift excluded populations meet the twenty-first century in Marco Baliani and Lella Costa's show *~~Human~~* (2016–18) and in Gabriele Vacis's *Cuore/Tenebra* (2018; *Heart/Darkness*), both of which confront some of the current issues regarding the massive migrations into Europe through Italy. Notably, both productions return to group projects with a number of actors, even while making ample use of the monologue. Vacis joins another original Teatro Settimo member, the stage designer Roberto Tarasco, to create arresting poetic friezes on the stage, with a large cast that also pulled from local Turin high schools on alternating nights, and unusual stage properties such as a huge forty-foot balloon of the human heart that the actors gently keep afloat to a semiopaque plastic sheet hung downstage: behind this dropcloth, actors

Fig. 15. Gabriele Vacis surrounded by cast members during rehearsal for *Cuore/Tenebra: Migrazioni tra De Amicis e Conrad* (Teatro Carignano, Turin, 2018). Photograph by Andrea Macchia. Courtesy of Teatro Stabile Torino—Teatro Nazionale.

turned into ghostlike shadows or threw books at the audience (though of course the sheet would arrest their flight). Adapting Edmondo De Amicis's 1886 classic novel *Cuore* (*Heart*) and Joseph Conrad's 1899 *Heart of Darkness*, Vacis and Angelo De Matteis (who coadapted the script) meditate about love for one's country, the horrors of colonialism, and how to reconcile those concepts with the present immigration (fig. 15).

Especially important in *Cuore/Tenebra*, and rare, is the diverse cast, including Gerald Mballe, a migrant from Cameroon who is among the lucky few actually granted political asylum in Italy. Although he lacks the time and space to offer his story with real depth, he smiles to the audience while giving a monologue that explains how he got from there to here and shares his aspirations for his future. He then blends back into the group of Italians, which, in its symbolism, is perhaps more powerful than his monologue. While there is no such representation in *Human*, this play is more dedicated to demonstrating the banal racism that currently permeates much of Italy in the wake of migration, largely through Costa's monologues (which are humorous, sometimes troublingly so) as she portrays a stereotypical older woman from the Northeast who is notoriously conservative and anti-immigrant. Given the clout of Vacis, Baliani, and Costa, these group productions could signal the beginning of more migrant stories, and experiments in how best to tell them, whether in the form of narrative theater or through a larger cast.

Animazione teatrale

Reading Turner's communitas as an idea meant to reflect the binding element of groups explains some of the importance of the collaborative work of animazione teatrale that was influential for the theater of narration. As much as it was an artistic practice, animazione was also a theoretical platform that emphasized group work, involvement in the community at large, and the significance of physical space. These notions also applied to the rehearsal process, encouraging young companies to unpack and explore the practice. With respect to Teatro Settimo, one need only recall the importance of the library in 1970s Settimo Torinese, where several of the group's core members met. This specific location not only speaks to the research habit that is one of the cornerstones of the theater of narration, but also demonstrates the relevance of the library as a meeting space. By 1980, in preparation for some of their city-centered initiatives, Teatro Settimo had a rigorous work ethic that involved readings, discussions, rehearsals, and drafting letters to the Settimo city council for various permissions, and they needed a space to come together and work. The local library, which was also the site for other groups to come together and discuss social, cultural, and political issues, offered just such a setting. That other groups also took advantage of the library as a meeting place speaks to the tone and environment in which one can imagine Teatro Settimo partaking: youthful yet serious; creative and determined.

More specific to performance, the inventors of animazione also grappled with staging. Society separates artistic roles into the person who paints and the person who looks at the painting, or the person who plays an instrument and the person who listens to the music.[36] The spectators give their attention to the speaker, placing that person in a leadership position, but ritual traditions of performance recall a thick texture of social relations. Curino underlined a section of Morteo's book where he cites the work of early performance theorist Oskar Eberle, who examined life, religion, dance, and theater in primitive populations. In these cultures, it was uncommon for people to follow the events of a scene passively during a performance.[37] Rather, people participated. This remains a fundamental question in the theater of narration: How does one reimagine an active audience (not necessarily one that participates in the conventional sense—rather, one that is engaged in something more Brechtian), and what role does the performance space play in creating such an ambience? There are some simple solutions: for example, leaving the house lights on or performing outdoors, which allows narrators to emphasize collectivity by promoting the awareness among audience members that they can see (or be seen by) the person next to them as much as the performer. These choices also allow the narrator to make eye contact with audience members and address them directly.

Related to the automobile industry protests of 1969–70, factory spaces were particularly popular in animazione productions. The protests also indelibly connected animazione to Turin, home to Fiat and Alfa Romeo, where many practitioners honed the craft. During those times, the Teatro Stabile of Turin operated more independently and on a small budget. In the 1969–70 season, it hosted the Progetto di Decentramento Teatrale (Theatrical Decentralization Project) in working-class or southern migrant quarters of the city in an attempt to directly address the city's changing urban space, which was swelling with southern migrants seeking work in the auto factories. In 1970, one of the most celebrated animators, Giuliano Scabia, premiered his show

Azioni decentrate (*Decentralized Actions*) in response to the Fiat strikes of 1969, which he based on interviews. Loredana Perissinotto, a founder of the movement, described this type of work as a way to engage with the social and political realities within working-class communities. "And where are we?" she asks, "We are in school, we're around the neighborhood, we're in meetings, we're in front of the TV, we are where we are . . ."[38] So instead of disturbing those daily rhythms and asking people to interrupt their routines in order to engage in political and cultural explorations, the idea was to bring theater to them. Doing so did not mean renting local theaters or trying to create a traditional stage in the school gym. It meant inhabiting their spaces—the Fiat factory itself—and putting the factory in dialogue with the show. They did not pretend they were anywhere but in the very spaces "where they were."

As animazione used public spaces, it generated a momentum that encouraged sensitization and awareness of the spectators' social identity. By defining their working spaces as decentralized, the founding animators highlighted the choice to perform outside of theaters and in neighborhood piazzas, community centers, factories, or in schools with the aim of reaching the spectators in their environments. There are also dramaturgical reverberations, since the narrative action changes according to the needs of those who inhabit that particular space, with different spectators requiring different points of emphasis.[39] For example, in 1969 Scabia and Perissinotto produced a show called *Il teatrino di corso Taranto* (*The Little Theater on Taranto Street*) in a working-class district of Turin for children of migrants from southern Italy. Playing with puppetry and improvisation, the animators invited the kids to tell stories about their average day and their relationships with their parents. The children recalled fantastic images from their dreams and nightmares, and the performers, including Scabia and Perissinotto along with the children, transformed these stories into fables, and eventually into a show.[40] (Vacis's *Cuore/Tenebra* echoes some of this methodology in his embrace of local children from different schools for different nights of performance; it also includes video of their hopes and dreams.) In terms of dramaturgical practices, the decision to hold performances in public places required a level of fluidity and extemporaneity uncommon in traditional theater.

Morteo's dramaturgical philosophy centers around the social reverberations of theatrical practice, emphasizing the importance for animators to present a way for people to live cultural experiences and identify their own connections to culture.[41] Morteo characterizes animazione's pedagogical aims as a pass-the-baton exercise, urging animators to teach people how to be animators themselves. Narrators, however, regard their didactic interests and obligations differently, and their philosophies have evolved over time. Initially Teatro Settimo worked much more closely with the community, blurring the boundaries between making and teaching art, but now those delineations are much clearer. With the exception of formal workshops or laboratories where narrators teach their process, they have fewer distinctly pedagogical objectives and aim instead to connect their audiences to specific sociopolitical situations. Back when some of those artists were in the early days of Teatro Settimo, they saw their theater work as overlapping with forms of practicing community and building community: in addition to writing and performing plays, they would hold workshops at local schools, offer summer camps for children, and conduct storytelling practices with the elderly.

As for the animators, this act of community formation through theater of marginalized individuals is exemplified in a variety of efforts. In addition to performing in factories, on one occasion they ran a workshop with children in San Salvario, a working-class neighborhood in Turin, to create a play that recounted their lives as children of parents who worked in factories. Beyond the oral histories that the children offered, the project itself revealed that children could also create culture worthy of discussion and examination. Perhaps most famously, in 1976 as the state-run psychiatric hospitals were pried open for examination—two years *before* Franco Basaglia, the doctor leading the investigation for more than fifteen years, was able to see a law passed (honored as the Basaglia Law) declaring their end due to cruel and unusual treatment—Giuliano Scabia launched his project *Marco Cavallo: Un'esperienza di animazione in un ospedale psichiatrico* (an animazione experience in a psychiatric hospital).[42] This complex collective project, which took place in an asylum among its residents, had many aims and collaborators with different professional backgrounds and served several purposes. Using a larger-than-life papier-mâché horse that the patients built and then paraded around their facility grounds and up to their enclosed gates, their work together symbolized most stridently their desire for freedom and liberation, but also the idea that even unconfined people are in close proximity to the state of those committed. Again, deeply rooted in a humanist exploration of a social-medical system, Scabia and others helped to redefine the space of the asylum into a meditative active field of creativity and possibility.

Similarly, the authors of the PEPE pamphlet state that the opportunities they aimed to create were ones that would spur individuals' creative growth, provoke rigorous inquiry, and encourage the use of one's free time for knowledge.[43] These three goals could also describe the abstract efforts of the Marco Cavallo project. In the same vein, Teatro Settimo artists claimed that their projects were intended to incite both urban renewal and communication. All of their work, they attested, was "based on the idea of putting people in contact with each other."[44] They understood public space as an integral dimension of this idea, creating the possibility for the community to create experiences where their private lives would intertwine with one another, and how those minor encounters might unleash ideas with great creative and socially responsible potential.

As animators and, later, narrators collected histories, they also dramatized the relationship between the performance narrative and performance venue. Official theaters are for official stories. They are for popular actors who will draw big crowds, or large theater companies that can afford the overhead. While many narrators are popular and prominent, largely thanks to screen appearances, and perform in major urban venues in cities like Palermo, Rome, Milan, and Turin, they still also frequently choose spaces outside these zones and perform in smaller, lesser-known theaters. Narrators had inspirational examples regarding theaters in the work of Dario Fo and Franca Rame as well. When working in theaters on proscenium stages, narrators are keenly aware of the inherent politics in the spatial arrangement. One of Fo and Rame's companies, the Associazione Nuova Scena, wrote concisely about the drawbacks of theater layouts concerning class, equanimity, and two-way exchange. The group viewed traditional theaters as capitalist structures that reinforce economic distinctions. Regarding the actual location of theaters, they point out that in many instances the most celebrated theaters are in two or three major cities, while the remainder are in any given region's central city.

Further, major theaters often organize the seating arrangements according to class. Fo and Rame's company criticized the extravagant publicity choices that major theaters use to promote a show, believing they rendered the play a commodity rather than an experience.[45] Some aspects of these complaints are unavoidable, and some superficial. The association denounced the location of theaters because they believed that those who live outside major cities cannot access culture in the way that urban populations do. The group does not acknowledge, however, that such a setup might serve a greater, and often more diverse, population or that there might be an economic necessity for most theaters to be located in major urban areas. Their interests lie in targeting very specific populations. They are concerned not about a general populous of oppressed or underrepresented groups, but specifically about those with fewer opportunities to experience culture.

Location and arrangement of the audience area, especially when performing in more traditional theater spaces, is an important tool narrators can use to create a sense of community. Fo and Rame grappled with this and constantly worked to adjust spatial configurations to upset inherent spatial inequalities, thus indirectly offering ideas to generations of theater artists to come. At the beginning of their shows Fo often invited people with the worst seats in the back to come forward and sit on the stage. In such instances he broke the traditional space between performer and audience and conjured the carnivalesque performances in piazzas from the Middle Ages and Renaissance, where the actor performed with the public and there was less hierarchy between performer and spectator.[46] When narrators tell their stories on provisional stages, in basements of retail stores, or in factory warehouses, they too disrupt the hierarchical conventions of audience seating. Even when narrators perform in theaters, particularly smaller ones, there are open seating policies so that they can avoid arrangements that privilege those from the upper and middle classes. Creating a spatial arrangement that challenges the hierarchical setup of traditional theaters helps to equalize the narrator-audience power dynamic and enhance rapport. The spatial choices allay the inherent divisiveness involved in artistic production and illustrate how an artist can converse with a fixed space.

Sites of Performance

The intimate consideration of territory that animators and Teatro Settimo artists demonstrated continues significantly throughout the theater of narration in several specific ways: in performance spaces; thematically; and through shared events such as festivals. In these manifestations, narrators found processes that addressed themes of local/national identity by engaging with notions of the heterotopic and communitas. By performing in unconventional interiors such as private homes, and amid extraordinary exteriors directly related to the performance, narrators challenged spaces in which communitas could flourish. In the case of *Vajont* and several other productions, uninterrupted televised performances helped to memorialize the practice as it also expanded these concepts through the screen. And certainly, having the behemoth of a major state-run company like the national television organization, RAI, helped both to popularize the practice and to secure the various permissions and fees required to use some of the exterior sites and to make arrangements for substantial audiences. Among the most famous outdoor productions are Marco Paolini's *Vajont*, in front of the Vajont dam itself, dramatically lit in the night; Laura Curino's *Camillo Olivetti*, on the roof of the Olivetti cafeteria, backgrounded by one of the factories and the Olivetti home residence; and Marco Baliani's *Corpo di stato*, in the actual Roman Forum, where Caesar himself once strolled, also dramatically drowned in floodlights under a foreboding moon on the night in which it was televised.

When these performances aired nationally, with the spectacularism of their natural locations scaled down to the intimacy of private homes for millions of viewers, the territory was unmistakably a major character. Even without these extreme gestures, specific locations can still assume important roles. In *Nati in casa*, Musso immerses her midwives in the northeastern Friulian countryside, with its rugged beauty and muddy challenges as they pedal their bicycles up to the houses of birthing mothers along windy roads. Celestini celebrates and mourns the city of Rome in *Radio clandestina*, recalling its earliest days as the capital of the republic, its storied northern outskirts and the cinema there where his grandfather worked, and especially the ignoble fate of the Ardeatine caves, the final resting place for so many men. Perhaps no other play engages the author's surroundings so directly as Laura Curino's *Passione*, which satirizes, critiques, and mourns the urban landscape of Settimo Torinese, where she came of age. That play signaled the culmination of the many years she spent with Teatro Settimo, wrestling with the industrial

North's environmental and human casualties, and it marked one of the first plays that would come to define the theater of narration, as *Radio clandestina* and *Nati in casi* would in the next generation.

Finally, festivals also provide special performance opportunities for narrators, as well as a way to engage with specific territories and local lands. Whether in the mountains or by the seaside, the landscape becomes the impromptu set, contributing not just in tone and ambience but often wriggling its way into the production. Further, festivals become complex spaces of community-building for both artists and attendees in an atmosphere that extends the performance beyond itself into the time and space surrounding it. Through a variety of performance spaces, a key criterion governing venue choice is a surrounding that will aide narrators in promoting a heterogeneous public who challenges exclusionary differences. The celebration of a communal land disrupts barriers, fostering pride in one's region and creating a history for that region for people who might not be readily familiar with it. Even the more spectacular choices lend a sense of intimacy because of the deliberate connection the narrator makes with audience members.

Interiors and Exteriors: Stabat mater *and* Il racconto del Vajont

After more than ten years working together in Teatro Settimo, and with a few critically successful productions on a national scale, in addition to the many community-recognized efforts, Laura Curino, Mariella Fabbris, and Lucilla Giagnoni were the three leading sisters in the Teatro Settimo play *Stabat mater*. Directed by fellow Teatro Settimo member Roberto Tarasco, the production debuted in 1989, toured all of Italy and several other countries in Europe, and went on to win such international awards as the Edinburgh Festival Fringe First in 1991. (The same three actors would reprise their exclusive collaboration in 1996 with *Adriano Olivetti: Il sogno possibile.*) The terms of the performance dictated that they perform at a private residence in exchange for shelter for one night and food during their visit. The narrators asked the audience to make contributions toward their journey home, and the piece concerns the theme of returning to one's past. Although they never repeated this type of production, it informed their conceptions of space and community, and it remains a unique project in the history of the company at large, beyond just these three actor-authors.

The play emerged from one of Teatro Settimo's first major successes, *Nel tempo tra le guerre* (1988, *During the Time between Wars*), as a study in character based on readings of South American magical realism, particularly from stories by Isabel Allende and Gabriel García Márquez. Curino, Fabbris, and Giagnoni portrayed three sisters, each of whom has a mythical quality or power, in search of their many siblings, as many as letters of the alphabet. Gaia (Giagnoni) has been pregnant since her birth. Her mother, they say, was pregnant with a pregnant child. Demetra (Curino) has never slept and will never sleep and is always preparing for some undefined event. Meanwhile, Fosca (Fabbris) controls the family funds (and is the one who asks the audience for donations) and communicates with spirits, including that of their deceased brother. As they traveled with the show, they stayed in character throughout their entire stay at someone's home, not just during their scheduled performances of the narrative. They even incorporated the stranger's house as a stop on their journey to find their lost siblings and would also invite audience members to share a story at the end.

Their close consideration of the performance space and how to expand it was always an important aspect to Teatro Settimo from their first years together, as it continued to be in *Nel tempo tra le guerre*, the play that also birthed the central characters in *Stabat mater*. In a 2004 interview with Guccini, Fabbris reminisces on the beautiful courtyards where they erected *Nel tempo*, noting that they always performed that show in outdoor arrangements in which the architecture was specifically unique and special. Curino adds that such spaces had surprising effects on some of their objectives for the production. She describes the creation of a state of being during their performances in which the ambience was more important than the texts. The artists desired that the audience experience the act of telling a story, the behaviors and attitude of that act, the energy in the performance space, and the relationship between all of these elements, even over the actual story. Guccini responds that this objective anticipates the message in *Stabat mater*: that in taking their production into the private realm, they are emphasizing the need for and indeed the place for stories outside the formal structures of the theater, where people expect and are expected to passively listen.[47] Especially considering that they also asked audience members to share stories, the setting of the private space, the occupying of that space, also anticipates major themes in the theater of narration, which emphasizes the importance of histories from the perspective of ordinary people, as though they were sitting in their living rooms. These stories—mythic stories, national histories—have a place in the private sphere.

The conversion of a private home into a public arena as Curino, Fabbris, and Giagnoni ventured with *Stabat mater* also embraced an autonomist, even anarchist, attitude that speaks to the continued frustrations of finding support for the arts. As Curino said in a much earlier interview during the period in which they were still performing the show, "In *Stabat mater*, we have overruled the administrative bureaucracy. . . . We are doing this show without documents, without legality, without any tickets, without taxes, and even without theatres."[48] The lack of a traditional performance space was a key element of this stance, which they celebrated not only in the more technical terms that Curino mentions but also allegorically. This character-focused experiment offered an independence and freedom by turning its back, as much as possible, on the typical expenditures of theatrical productions, and in doing so it opened the artists' minds to different experiences and learning opportunities.

It was during this period, approximately six months after *Stabat Mater* began touring, when Grotowski held a ten-day workshop with Teatro Settimo in Turin. As Vacis recalls, Grotowski focused largely on the actor-spectator relationship, iterating core aspects of his celebrated Poor Theater, particularly the belief that technology need not and should not mediate this sacred relationship. His memory adds a positive spin to Grotowski's original emphasis as he conceived of the Poor Theater, which was a solution to the simple fact that theater could not compete with the technology of film and television. By the time Vacis directly encountered the Polish director, this core tenet of the Poor Theater was much more than an alternative to a fundamental problem; it was, rather, a unique and profound function of live performance. As Vacis recalls, Grotowski's main point was that all one needs to make theater is the actor and the spectator because the space between them *is* theater.[49] In the case of *Stabat mater*, that space between performers and audience was created in a location that was unconventional for both the theater and its public, further complicating the experience those parties shared.

Perhaps for the first time with *Stabat mater*, the artists involved began to articulate more intentional connections fostered in the exchanges between performer and audience in relation to the space where the action takes place. During the 2004 interview with Guccini, Curino mentions that in the intimacy of stripping away the theater, and especially the "fourth wall" distancing the actors from their publics, they found a connection in looking at their audience members face-to-face. Curino states that it affected the way they do theater as much as the way they simply exist in the world with other people. Prompted by Guccini, she also adds that shows of narration (*spettacoli di narrazione*) "come from this decisive discovery of communion."[50] Her choice of the word "communion" (*comunione*) recalls Turner's definition of communitas and conjures the sacredness of ritual. With this show in particular, and largely because of the spatial choices of performing in private residencies, Curino and her colleagues created and discovered a communion of the ordinary. Though they might recount extraordinary and magically real events, more than the stories themselves they perform the community that an intimate ambience can create, a form that offers those that inhabit the space a shared experience, as Turner suggested, of communion.

Contrasting the intimate spaces of *Stabat mater* are some of the grandiose natural settings that narrators occasionally embrace for their productions, especially televised. Curino herself did so in her production of *Camillo Olivetti* on the roof of the former company cafeteria, with the factory and the distant Alps glistening in the sunset behind her. Baliani staged *Corpo di stato* at night in the Roman Forum, dramatically awash in floodlights casting long shadows of the ancient regime as he meditated on the assassination of former prime minister Aldo Moro. Perhaps most famously, Paolini eventually set his monumental production of *Vajont* on a stage built directly in front

Fig. 16. Video still of Marco Paolini in *Il racconto del Vajont* as he points to the dam behind him. Performance televised live nationally on RAI2, October 9, 1997.

of the looming dam itself, above the towns that were washed away due to the dam's rushed construction (fig. 16). These narrators had previously performed all of these productions in a variety of locations and spaces prior to the spectacular sites, and in all three instances they were televised live, with audiences watching the productions on location as well as in their own homes, suggesting both the need for financial support from the television companies (all public and national) and the necessity Grotowski alluded to: the need for screened events to demonstrate spectacularism.

The site-specificity of the theater of narration when it chooses elaborate locations directly confronts the poetics of the postindustrial. The emphasis is less on its shocking hollowness, and more on the choice to embrace symbolic landscapes as a means of fashioning an alternative narrative or as entryways into the important work of remembering culturally important histories. This strategy contrasts the many depictions in other arts, especially cinema, of an alienated industrial society in the postwar decades, perhaps most evocatively captured by Michaelangelo Antonioni in films like *Il deserto rosso* (1964), or his meditative trilogy (*L'avventura*, 1960; *La notte*, 1961; *L'eclisse*, 1962). These artistic depictions amplify the soulless landscapes and lost souls as qualitative indicators of one dominant consequence of modernity: alienation.[51] While those cinematic works testify to the fears of a dystopia where both nature and humanity had atrophied nearly beyond recognition, the looming presence of the dam in Vajont, while menacing, is also a reckoning. Paolini confronts it, its symbolism, its own *storia* as an object and metaphor, and uses its connotations of hubris and death to find a path of reconciliation.

With its history-focused approach, the theater of narration has some provocative nuances to contribute to practices of site-specific theater, even if that term has become overused or controversial.[52] The theater and performance scholar Bertie Ferdman, for example, is highly critical of the term "site specific," believing that it has become meaningless both because it is too general and because of its neoliberal appropriation as a trendy catchphrase reborn with the sole purpose to "jolt audiences" or at least increase them.[53] Certainly, there has been a push both to move away from this term and to make it more precise, as many companies and practitioners have done (e.g., immersive theater, ambulatory performance, itinerant performance, and live installation, which moves particularly close to performance art), but it is still useful as a way to signal a theatrical practice that both occurs outside traditional theater spaces and is directly concerned with specific spaces.

As the scholars Amy Cordileone and Rachel Tuggle Whorton offer their interpretation of site-specific theater, they come close to a definition that illuminates how the theater of narration contributes to the idea. Simply but crucially, they emphasize the stories that specific landscapes hold. While they acknowledge the fundamental notions that a chosen location has the potential to shape the structure and content of a given production, and that some performances were created directly for a specific location, they stress the importance of the stories that the space is already telling. They ask, "What messages are unavoidable and what can be successfully added or removed without compromising the integrity of the space itself?"[54] Also helpful in shedding light on the theater of narration's contributions, though taking a different approach, scholar Sidney Homan has provocatively asserted that "the theater is always playing offstage" because audience members can never just be observers; rather, they imprint on a given production the different spaces that they inhabit in their lives.[55]

These ideas together—of privileging the stories that spaces are already telling, and that they are always with us offstage—point to the dialectical relationship between the theater of narration and site-specificity. As Paolini demonstrates in *Vajont*, the dam, the Friulian landscape, the rocks that fell into the pool of water behind the dam that caused the tsunami, the mountain farmers of the region, and the engineers who brought an air of big-city Venice with them when they began to tear into the local land are all and were always a part of the production. The landscape was always the central character in Paolini's story whether he narrated it from an intimate private space or a national theater or, as he did eventually, in front of the dam itself.

Experiencing the show with the dam and mountainous landscape directly behind him, however, shifts the ethereal and imaginative into the real and tangible. The audience sits in a scaffolding seating area under the stars, and Paolini, though on a platform with a few props (importantly, a blackboard on which he draws various calculations), is immersed in the enormity of the mountain on which the stage was created. Here—as with the *Olivetti* production at the factory grounds and *Corpo di stato* amid the ancient ruins of Rome—the landscape is all encompassing, ever present, the stage itself. It stretches the production far beyond the confines of a proscenium stage, as far as the eye can see, and locates itself directly on the stage *as* the stage. It is not common for productions to take place amid such grandiose surroundings. When they do, the specificity of the sites offers a rich central character, making it more apparent that the stories are about them. But even when they cannot be there in person, they are always a part of the productions.

The Festival Circuit

Another way narrators engage directly with territory is by taking part in the many festival possibilities, particularly during the summer. Theater festivals are phenomena on their own as places for the exchange of ideas among artists and venues for community building. They embrace surrounding lands and emphasize or showcase connection to territory, and they might also constitute events with commercial attraction and efforts to revitalize local economies. Historically, festivals marked a special time to rejoice and feast in the memory of an event worth celebrating, but they were also frequently associated with moments of subversion that demonstrated the fraught relationship between the state and art, where art is explored through a liberation process within a subversive celebration, or, conversely, in which spectacle is promoted with its frequent propogandist impulses.[56] In the utopic moments of creating and programming, festivals might hold "a special promise of abundance, pluralism, internationalism, and democracy," but in practice, with the interests of funders they risk folding under the pressures of a "cultivated consumerism" that looms over some festivals more acutely than others.[57] If the purest vision of a festival is an event that inspires a "collective feeling of flow and communitas" as people enjoy local life, then it may be that for most visitors the highlight of the festival is simply being a part of a communal event that concerns the experience of a collective moment and is greater than any individual experience.[58] Indeed, this experience of community is one from which both artists and audience might benefit.

Several theater festivals in particular, but also the routine practice of festivalgoing, has been important both to the development of the theater of narration and in its negotiations of cultural labor. In addition to offering performances and workshops, theater festivals in Italy—especially those organized by city councils, private theater companies, and other cultural sector sponsors—generally serve as important cultural sites. These events not only offer a series of shows but also subsidize lectures, workshops, interviews, and encourage the exchange of ideas between artists, scholars, and general members of the public. The many festival circuits in the 1970s, 1980s, and well into the twenty-first century provide an arena to assess the state of theater in Italy. They offer new companies the opportunity to display their works and give local audiences the chance to see established theater artists who might normally perform in larger urban venues. In many ways the festivals also transgress class. Thanks to the various sponsorships, many of the events are located in rural/industrial regions and are free, thus bringing a small boom to local economies.

Il Convegno sul Nuovo Teatro (1967)

One of the most important festivals in Italy in the latter half of the twentieth century took place in the summer of 1967 in the Piedmont town of Ivrea, which happened to be home to the Olivetti factories. In fact, the Olivetti Group contributed to the Convegno sul Nuovo Teatro festival, a gesture that Curino invokes during her plays when she notes the company's support for local activities. The reason the 1967 festival was particularly special was that a group of leading theater artists decided to meet there to discuss a fiery manifesto that decried the state of Italian theater. That the artists met here demonstrates the importance of the festival as a meeting space for creative thought, not only for previewing their work or testing new ideas in front of more forgiving audiences, who often attend for free because local government and organizations foot the bill.[59]

When several of these artists looked back on the conference twenty years later, most noted its importance in creating a space for people to congregate. Eugenio Barba shared that Ivrea 1967 was where he first met Dario Fo, who would then become a lifelong friend and interlocutor and would travel to Denmark for workshops at Barba's school. Leo de Berardinis, also among the most accomplished of twentieth-century Italian theater artists, states that in addition to providing a venue for one of his experimental productions involving film and television, it was at this conference that he finally met Carmelo Bene, a fortuitous pairing for the Italian avant-garde. In 1968, he and Bene went on to create a widely recognized and celebrated production of *Don Chisciotte* along with other renowned collaborators, such as the actors Eduardo De Filippo and Perla Peragallo; the set for this production was designed by Salvador Dali. Perhaps Fo himself best sums up the conference when he says that it was the "point of departure [because] at Ivrea we all met each other for the first time and we talked together."[60] The encounters in Ivrea paved the way for open dialogue that fostered collaboration between many leading artists of the postwar period. It served as a model of possibilities for artists to come and demonstrates potential outcomes that future narrators would experience themselves.

Laboratorio Teatro Settimo's Festivals

As with Ivrea 1967, a number of important festivals fostered encounters between Teatro Settimo and new artists who would come to found the theater of narration. It was at the 1982 Santarcangelo di Romagna festival, held in the small town of Santarcangelo southeast of Bologna and in six other nearby smaller towns, that Curino and Vacis discussed working with Paolini. He and Vacis had met the year before at a workshop—another important space for encounters—that Barba held at his International School of Theatre Anthropology in Volterra. Paolini invited Teatro Settimo to perform in Treviso, north of Venice, where he was based, and in turn they invited him and his company, Studio 900 di Treviso, to Settimo. He then began working with Teatro Settimo on a number of shows, including their version of *Romeo and Juliet* (1991; see p. 43, fig. 1), in which the nurse (Curino) and friar (Paolini) are the two central characters. With them and other Teatro Settimo members he also wrote one of his first monologues, *Adriatico* (1987), about the adventures of a boy at summer camp in the Northeast. That piece later became part of a larger series of monologues called *Gli album* (1992), an album of childhood memories in the Northeast, which he produced independently of Teatro Settimo, though on some of the monologues—such as *Liberi tutti*, inspired by Luigi Meneghello's important book *Libera nos a malo*—he still collaborated with Vacis (directing) and Tarasco (music design).

In addition to *La storia di Romeo e Giulietta*, Teatro Settimo also invited Paolini to act in *Riso amaro* (1988), *Libera nos* (1989), and *La trilogia della villeggiatura* (1993). By that point he and Vacis had formed a close professional relationship and had already begun work on *Vajont*, which Vacis directed. Although Paolini had worked with several other theater companies, such as Teatro degli Stracci, Studio 900, and Tag Teatro di Mestre, before collaborating with Teatro Settimo, his work with them is clearly crucial for the development of his own style and broadly for the theater of narration, which launched his own career as much as he helped found the form. The encounter at the 1982 Santarcangelo festival was what brought them all together. These networks of cultural endeavors are organized by state and city councils, along with some private sponsorship, and operate outside the more lucrative and top-down tightly controlled theater houses that hire productions for a season. Hence, they offer a new space—not so unlike the library that first brought Teatro Settimo together in 1974—for actors, writers, directors, producers, critics, and publics to meet each other and discuss ideas ranging from the possibility of collaboration to the state of contemporary theater.

The festivals in Ivrea and Santarcangelo were centered around theater, but there are two other types of festivals in which leading narrators have been and continue to be active. The first, a festival that showcases theater's civic utility, is reminiscent of the idea of the cultural laborer and some of the early initiatives of Teatro Settimo, such as the City Lab projects. The second is a type of festival that is created around a specific social issue but has chosen to include theatrical performances as a major feature, perhaps as much to draw crowds as a means of communication, in addition to other creative and intellectual initiatives that offer different angles and perspectives with which to consider specific social issues. The history of these festival styles is consistent and robust.

In a more focused endeavor, over a span of several days in 1991, in the northeastern town of Pordenone at the Scuola Sperimentale dell'Attore, Teatro Settimo performed five of their shows (*Villeggiatura*, *Novecento*, *Affinità*, *Passione*, and *Tartufo*) and participated in several critical gatherings, including a meeting titled "Towards the Heart of the Matter" ("Verso il cuore delle cose"), which involved artists and scholars such as Maurizio Buscarino, Gerardo Guccini, and the organizer, Roberto Canziani. Over the next few days Canziani and Settimo organized three other meetings specifically for high school students, called "Leaving the Twentieth Century" ("Per uscire dal ventesimo secolo"); finally, Curino held a workshop for actors, animators, and educators called "The Scene as Collective Breath" ("La scena come respiro collettivo").[61]

Still in this vein, even well after some of the first big successes in the theater of narration, several noteworthy Teatro Settimo collaborations continued to revisit animazione during the 1998 and 2000 festivals in Turin called Il Gioco del Teatro, sponsored by such private theaters as the Teatro dell'angolo and Compagnia Stilema as well as public organizations like the Regione Piemonte Assessorato alla Cultura. Similar to Ivrea and Pordenone, these festivals were also full of talks, presentations, performances, interviews, and debates about theater and its utility as a tool of social agitation.[62] And here too the attendees represented a wide assortment of individuals, including students, scholars, theater companies, and representatives from municipalities. The 2000 festival opened with *racconti danzati* (danced stories) called *Attraverso il bosco* (*Across the Woods*) by Claudio Montagna, which was billed as a production by a theater group known as CAST but was presented by Teatro Settimo as "an example of theater as a place to reflect, to confront oneself and to understand adolescents."[63] The publicity materials also included an endorsement from the cultural administrator of Piedmont (*l'assessore alla Cultura della Regione Piemonte*), Giampiero Leo, who declared that the festival "will be once again an occasion that gives space to the most interesting and established productions through diverse techniques" and that one of the festival's more beneficial aspects was its sponsorship by public organizations, cultural institutions, and artistic companies who had come together to create relationships between regional community programs and activities important to the EU.[64] Considering the leadership in events such as the Gioco del Teatro conference series, and thinking back to their early initiatives such as City Lab, Teatro Settimo demonstrates success in transforming cityscapes into places that provided opportunities for cultural dialogue. This atmosphere echoes in the theater of narration even if it is not an intentional goal of each individual narrator.

Il Festival Frontière (2018)

In addition to the festivals that discuss the state of theater, there are also festivals that focus on sociopolitical issues. The Festival Frontière, which took place over four days during the summer of 2018 in the Alps of Cuneo, a rugged region of Piedmont not many miles from the French border, placed migration center stage and invited a number of leading narrators to enrich the discussion in different ways with a variety of productions. Above all, it was an attempt to bring community together to think about migration, and the narrators played a vital role in that conversation. Performance scholar Erika Fischer-Lichte explains that "a festival aims at either affirming, and thus renewing, an existing community or at bringing about a new one. . . . Whatever the aim might be, performances always bring about a particular future."[65] This festival exemplifies the impact of the sustained work of artists who emphasized the importance of theater in community discussions, showing how theater is a vital aspect to renewing a community and creating space for a future. While its scope was sociopolitical, it demonstrates the agency of theater—how it can offer enlightened perspectives on social issues—and symbolizes the broad acceptance of this notion by the very fact that the organizers invited leading narrators to perform.

Festival Frontière was an EU collaboration between France and Italy, rendering it eligible to EU funding, which in turn served as an impetus for other regional, mostly Italian, organizations to contribute funding as well. The focus of this festival is a primary concern not only in Italy but also throughout the EU, and in many other countries around the world. Specific to the location, it sought to illuminate its attendees on the border crossings from Italy to France along those weathered and storied Alpine mountain ranges and to think broadly about how local Italian and French societies could create sustainable and stable situations for the influx of migrants pouring into Italy in increasing numbers from the early 2010s. The sheer volume of migrants and the rate at which they have entered the EU is a primary reason for the populist shift to the right, and indeed is one of the platform centerpieces of both the powerful right-wing party, la Lega, and the libertarian populist MoVimento 5 Stelle; these two forces, both virulently nationalist in their anti-immigration and anti-EU stances, formed an alliance and won control of the national government in the spring of 2018.

Frontière dramatically set its location in a remote mountain refuge called the Borgata Paraloup that was once a safe zone for partisans during the war. Nearly unreachable due to its altitude in the winter, it becomes a refreshing and peaceful oasis in the middle of the hot Italian summer. Cars had to park on lower ground, and the festival arranged for a limited van service that brought people to/from the refuge if they did not want to complete the one-hour hike by foot. The location, symbolic of borders as it is no more than thirty kilometers to France, also hides old fortresses and lookouts that speak to an era of war struggles, and the conference celebrated these forgotten secrets and their ties to the present border crisis in a number of ways. Normally the space is a stop on a trail for hikers where they can set up camp, or where people come for a weekend getaway in the mountains. There is a fully functioning kitchen and dining area and a large room with bunk beds. There are also some smaller cabins made out of stone and wood, and for these the festival programmed a variety of events, including photography exhibitions, academic panels featuring scholars who work with local immigrants, and a documentary screening.

With generous financing and collaboration, the festival organizers actually built the stage at the Paraloup refuge overlooking Cuneo specifically for this event.[66] It was here that most of the narrators performed in one-night-only shows. Laura Curino, Saverio La Ruina, Mariella Fabbris, and Beppe Rosso (a former Teatro Settimo member) were the headliners, while other performance projects included the well-known performance artist and independent journalist Carlo Infante, and even a youth troupe that had created a show about the resistance.

In a typical format for the theater of narration, Curino stood at a lectern and read excerpts from Nuto Revelli's famous book *L'anello forte* (*The Strong Ring*), an oral history of local, often poor women during the postwar period in that same mountainous region outside Cuneo. Deviating only subtly from the formal appearance of a reading, she occasionally stepped away to walk around the stage and turn her back to the audience to face the rugged landscape, as if to instruct the audience to breathe in the mountains where these women had lived their lives and left their stories for Revelli to transcribe. She also wore five different scarves throughout the show to signal the five different women whose stories she read, offering slight character variations for each. Over the next two years she would work with the director Anna Di Francisca to create a fuller performance out of the stories, which debuted only in previews at the Teatro Giacosa in Ivrea in early March of 2020, days before the country locked down due to the novel coronavirus pandemic. For this version, produced by Teatro Stabile of Turin and the Contato del Canavese, she also worked with the actress Lucia Vasini onstage in both shared and independent scenes.

Figure 17, taken during previews for the premiere in Ivrea, features an archival photograph of Paola Martinengo (1916–78), whose story, which Revelli titled "La mia sfida" ("My Challenge"), is memorialized in his book.[67] In her portrayal, in which Martinengo's photograph is projected behind her, Curino honors this touching account of a brave and independent young woman who followed her heart into a circus career that left her mostly impoverished but rich with inspiration and freedom and love. She recounts some of her struggles with poverty, particularly famine, during her early years in the circus, and the early death of her trapeze artist husband, which left her alone to raise their young children. Eventually she earned a living selling knickknacks and had enough to buy a house. When she retired, she bought herself a caravan like the one she and her husband used to live in during their traveling circus days and parked it in her courtyard. She/Curino recalls that every now and then she would walk inside the caravan and have a coffee and

Fig. 17. Laura Curino in *L'anello forte* with an archival image of Paola Martinengo provided by the Fondazione Nuto Revelli projected behind her (Ivrea, 2020). Photograph by Giorgio Sottile. Courtesy of Laura Curino and Federico Negro.

remember the days of her struggles and joys. Triumphantly, she declares that if she were to see a caravan on the road she would run after it and live her life all over again in the exact same way. In the archival image, she shows a framed photograph of the caravan. This one snapshot of the play with Curino downstage reveals not only the story of Martinengo with her prized possession, but also the story of the theater of narration, with its emphasis on ordinary people and their life experiences. Martinengo's personal narrative is moving, but through Curino it becomes a story of liberation for rural women in midcentury Italy. The newer version of the production projects several archival images, but in the early stages of the show, in the mountains of Paraloup outside Cuneo during the festival, the imagery was the land itself behind the outdoor stage.

In his festival performance, La Ruina most directly addressed the crisis of migration, particularly the psychological trauma, with *Italianesi*, a show about children of Italian military personnel born during the war in Albania, after Mussolini invaded and claimed Albania as part of the Italian Empire in 1939. Many of them and their mothers were abandoned there when their fathers returned to Italy after the war and grew up imprisoned in camps from 1945 to 1955. By their paternal association, Albania considered them "enemies of the state," though they were not welcome in Italy either. La Ruina describes them as *italianesi*: neither Italian (*italiani*) nor Albanian (*albanesi*), though also both. Like so many migrants, they are caught between cultures, nationalities, and territories. In his production, he uses the theme of imprisonment to serve together as testimony to an actual situation, and as a metaphor of the psychological imprisonment that accompanies the status of not belonging. This piece was especially pertinent to the festival given its focus on migration, but it is also a vital contribution to the oeuvre of narrative theater and Italian theater more broadly as an attempt to confront this complex and timeless issue.

Fabbris, the only headliner to perform in the dining area above the stage, presented what she billed as her tasting-play (*degustazione-spettacolo*), *L'albero delle acciughe* (*The Family Tree of Anchovies*, a show Fabbris continues to perform in her repertory; fig. 18). The set was a banquet of various anchovy dishes to which the public was invited after her monologue. Some she invented herself based on the flavors of Sicily, such as orange marmalade on toast with an anchovy (the sweet citrus complements the salty fish surprisingly well), while others were classics such as Piedmont *salsa verde*, a herbaceous mix of parsley and basil, alliums, and the anchovies used as a spread on bread. As she prepared the banquet, she recounted her loosely adapted version of Torinese writer Nico Orengo's short story "Il salto dell'acciuga" ("The Journey of the Anchovy"), which mixes popular legend and oral accounts to muse on the *via del sale*, an ancient path between Liguria and Piedmont (and parts of France) traveled by salt merchants. Fabbris works to connect North and South through her stories and flavors, celebrating the land and fruits of the sea with humorous and poignant vignettes of local people who were either a part of the anchovy trade industry or simply enjoyed eating anchovies, and with an anchovy as protagonist. Engaging with the migrations theme of the festival most uniquely through gustatory experiences as well as the oral traditions in her stories, she centered the farming culture that synergizes the tastes and colors of earth and sea in the very mountains of Paraloup.

Beppe Rosso, who played a large part in organizing the festival, performed one of his early big successes, which he developed with other Teatro Settimo members, including Gabriele Vacis, and which he has performed over five hundred times: *Dei liquori fatti in casa* (*Homemade Liqueurs*). In this narration, in which Remo Rostagno, the director and performer who has also worked closely with Marco Baliani, contributed to the writing, Rosso first conjures the literati of Piedmont, such as Cesare Pavese, Beppe Fenoglio, and Gina Lagorio, through the perfumes of the region's celebrated liquors and

Fig. 18. Mariella Fabbris in *L'albero delle acciughe* during a performance in the home of the photographer (Pozzolengo, 2017). Photograph by and courtesy of Mario Piavoli. Fabbris has collaborated on films directed by the photographer's father, Franco Piavoli.

wines, and he uses these olfactory senses to reflect and envision the hopes and dreams of the postwar generation who grew up amid these flavors. His play embraces both regional and formal Italian, exploring the borders within the country itself.

Finally, perhaps the most experimental performer at the festival, Carlo Infante (who once worked with Marco Baliani), guided tours of Paraloup and several surrounding hikes over the course of the multiday festival. His aim was to test ways that technology could enrich one's experience of this remote mountain refuge and serve as a means of connection across borders and topographies. Infante outfitted each participant with a headset, as though they were on a museum tour, though one that was more participatory. He had a microphone and used it to interview participants about what they were experiencing in real time on the hike, as well as to play famous resistance songs and to listen to readings of Nuto Revelli, the author who had documented so much of the region's life and whose words Curino turned into a play.

Festival Frontière demonstrates the utilitarian approach to theater that was always a part of Teatro Settimo's work and that clearly still marks the theater of narration. Given the substantial funding, it also speaks to a European appreciation for theater and its power to connect people and unpack an issue. As Fischer-Lichte wrote, these initiatives gesture toward a future, and this particular festival gestured toward future communities that are evolving with the influx of immigrants. Considered together, each narrator speaks to a different constituency of that community. Curino reflects on the life of women in the region and how the labors of the land influenced their lives and well-being, while Rosso cultivates the flavors of the territory and its intoxicating echoes on one's hope and ambitions. Fabbris actually offers a tasting of some of those flavors, an immersive experience that asks the audience to connect her stories with the physical world, while Infante guides his audience through the physical spaces and surrounding lands of the festival, exposing them to its history and grounding them distinctly in the present. La Ruina's production most literally addresses the theme of migration. This festival in particular demonstrates the relevance of territory for the theater of narration, and the dexterity with which the practice makes connections across local communities, their linguistic traditions, and their environs.

Narrators embrace a variety of territories and spaces that enhance the dynamics of their productions as they foster a counterpublic sphere for subaltern groups. Some of the 1970s-era ideological struggles were a result of economic slowdown and capitalist restructuring. Evinced in the public theater projects of Teatro Settimo, for whom community involvement was a constant and crucial component to their work, later generations also cultivated communities and encouraged the exchange of experiences. The heterotopias with which Teatro Settimo played point to the theories of liminality that Turner developed, emphasizing the notion of being *in progress*, with a clear goal ahead. They and later narrators wanted their communities to be partners in re-creating the city for themselves, or in rewriting histories that included them and their perspectives. For narrators, honoring the impact of ordinary people also means honoring the environments they inhabit. In this sense, narrators practice an invitation. When they are able to perform on site, the character-like presence of the location plays an especially vivid role, but even on proscenium stages, the notion of occupying and reclaiming a specific space—as a group effort, a community—is a vital aspect of the performance.

Chapter 5

Experiments with Media

With advancements in technology that occurred in the last decades of the twentieth century onward, the theater of narration joined the many other art forms and industries that explored ways media practices might enhance their work. In several instances the genre has transformed itself for established technologies: for example, airing productions in the format of uninterrupted televised specials on national networks. Narrators have also experimented with audiovideo enhancements more directly in actual productions to complement specific moments in their otherwise minimalist stage shows. In terms of new media, besides using it for publicity through social media sites, there has even been one production whose initial run largely took place on the internet: Daniele Timpano's *Aldomorto*, debuting in 2012. Given the genre's agility, inexpensive economics, and easy transportability, video, radio, and television have presented a wide range of possibilities to increase audience numbers.[1] More than that, it has challenged narrators to consider what, for them, is the most important aspect of any given production, in order to enhance it or at least carry it through a new medium.

Reflecting the theater of narration's genealogy via Jerzy Grotowski and even Bertolt Brecht, the genre works best with less invasive technology. One of the main arguments for a Poor Theater was in critical response to new technologies and the cinematizing of theater, while Brechtian epic traditions demand transparency in the use of apparatuses, in lieu of masking stage machinery. From Peter Brook to Eugenio Barba, subscribers to the idea that media projections do not necessarily enhance the intellectual power of visual spectacle in theater fall into two main scholarly conceptualizations of digital media and performance. One group, led by new media scholar Lev Manovich, conceives of technology as part of the artwork itself and, in many cases, its most innovative and creative aspect; the other insists that technology is but a means to express ideas.[2] Given its link to the Poor Theater and Epic Theater traditions, it might not be surprising that the theater of narration would embrace a more spartan approach to media. As evident in Marco Baliani's televised *Corpo di stato* (1998), however, it *is* surprising that when productions stray from this approach and attempt to compete with more cinematic visions of a play, they are unable to deliver many of the genre's hallmark attributes, including a sense of community and commonality. They are also strained as media products.

At the heart of this discussion is the relationship between live performance and so-called mediatized performance. No matter the involvement of technology in this practice known for its simplicity, the main lesson from the use of technology, whether it has enhanced as opposed to distracted from the raw text, is that it functions best when in the service of live performance. The most successful uses of media are when the additional instruments—a screen onstage or camera angles for television—do not take on a life of their own, but constantly support the dramaturgy of the narrator. The performance theorist Philip Auslander refuses to think of the two as competing binaries, as Grotowski did. Grotowski believed that the more live performance attempted to compete with mediatized performance, the greater it would fail; by contrast, Auslander emphasizes a historical and contingent reading of this relationship even while insisting on an unequivocal rivalry between varying media.[3] Approaching the subject from a viewpoint of "cultural economy," Auslander focuses on the competition between live performance and mediatized events, seeing the former as the perennial loser against cinema, and even more so against television and digital media. He acknowledges the defensive position taken up by theater aficionados, scholars, and critics, who insist that the intrinsic value and transcendence of a live performance experience is in its very resistance to commercialized media culture, though that is a specifically twentieth-century aspect of performance, since (mass) media culture is a more recent phenomenon. One reason Auslander sees this logic as untenable, however, is that media and performance have become blurred to the point where ontological differences between the two are less clear.[4]

This tension raises the stakes for the generally unspectacular theater of narration and its rapport with media. During a televised production, there is not necessarily a blurring between the live and mediated performance, but those that are successful as televised performances privilege and serve the live productions in a utilitarian way that downplays competition between the two forms. Auslander begins to move away from the rigid binary of theater/commercial media when he re-places performance and media in an almost dialectical rapport. Although he does not arrive at this conclusion, his theoretical arrangement reveals that one problem with binary-staked arguments surrounding performance and media is hermeneutical. An economic approach, whether cultural or financial, would not offer a particularly nuanced scale on which to weigh performance and media either. It would similarly point to the fact that they should not be weighed against each other but considered with respect to one another. Analyzing how the theater of narration works in a variety of ways with media offers a study of a minimalist theater practice that tactfully experiments with ways in which media can enhance performance without ever claiming or attempting to be dependent on that media. All of the productions around which this chapter centers demonstrate a variety of media uses in the theater of narration. Investigating how the genre incorporates media in staged productions, and how performances translate across different media, this chapter considers a measure of success that involves neither monetary nor cultural capital but, rather, concerns how explorations across new media reference and defer to the live performance.

There is a further duality with which to reckon: the opposition between orality and literacy, as discussed in chapter 3 with respect to Giovanni Nencioni's distinctions of the *parlato*. Generally, the two modes of communication compete as a binary, or even a hierarchy, with literacy widely praised as the more sophisticated form.[5] The advent of visual, technological, and digital media, from the cinema and television to the internet, presents an additional dimension in considering the journey of orality from spoken word to written text and now into new technologies. With the addition of new media in the theater of narration, orality competes not only with literacy but also with new modes of visuality, as well as more varied, hyperlinked and interactive types of prose. These primary, secondary, and tertiary oralities do not travel in one direction; they go back and forth to each other, mediated by each other, transforming the notion of a pure unmediated state of orality into an anachronistic reflection.

This chapter begins with an analysis of technological media in a live performance, which occurs in the theater of narration with occasional frequency, particularly since the new millennium, but is by no means ubiquitous in the genre. Some examples include the use of projected still images, some famous, some personal, as in Baliani's *Corpo di stato*; there is also the use of voice-over, as in Ascanio Celestini's *Pueblo* (2017), as well as the use of projected video superimposed on the actor and/or interacting with the performer, as in Laura Curino's *Il signore del cane nero: Storie su Enrico Mattei* (2010). It is noteworthy, however, that some productions that directly address states of technology refused to share their stages with it. Marco Paolini's *#Antropocene* (2017) explicitly addresses the loneliness of the internet age, yet his costars are a full orchestra onstage plus the famous Italian rapper Frankie hi-nrg mc, without any visual special effects. To explore the ways in which media enhancement can unthreateningly bolster the intimate minimalism in the theater of narration, an examination of projected still and moving images and enhanced sound in Laura Curino's *Santa Bàrbera* (2005) offers a dynamic case study. Curino was particularly successful in enlivening the play's complex feminist narrative, notably concerning concepts of the voice through media.

Following this discussion, the chapter turns to the presence of the theater of narration on Italian television through national public service broadcasting in order to examine the types of creative decisions deployed to make televisual style serve the live performance nature of the genre. A comparative investigation best demonstrates variances in this process, first in Paolini's *Vajont* and second in Baliani's *Corpo di stato*, which provide contrasting case studies that first aired in the 1990s. Whether present onstage or creating a new method for distribution, the use of technology in the theater of narration offers another dimension in which this already hybrid practice can adjust to and embrace different media potentialities. For a monologist genre, technology becomes both a way for narrators to expand their audience and another voice with which they must contend in their dialogic practice.

Multiple Media Performance in *Santa Bàrbera*

Laura Curino's *Santa Bàrbera* (which debuted in 2005 and is still performed in repertory; fig. 19), a production that makes significant use of sound and visual technologies, exemplifies how media and technology can function onstage. In the piece, Curino implements video projections of a modern city to offer a pathway between modern life and the story of the fourth-century saint. This decision is helpful, but not crucial to understanding the parallel. She also uses a microphone and manipulates her voice, demonstrating an essential technology in the production for its ability to amplify a feminist narrative that adds new dimensions to verbal language. In a further effort to connect this centuries-old story to contemporary experiences, Curino highlights the many extratextual layers present in *Santa Bàrbera*: from the medieval writings of Jacopo da Varazze, who chronicled the saint's story, to the sixteenth-century frescos of Lorenzo Lotto, which retell Bàrbera's tale on the walls of a chapel.[6] Notably, she incorporates a manifesto from the contemporary subculture world of "ravers" to pose a contrast with the antiquated language that evokes those older texts.

Throughout the production, the characteristics that define the theater of narration are still intact: the minimalist set; the unobtrusive costume; the solo performer who is also the author; the direct address; the occasional commentary or autobiographical reference. Diverging from this simplicity, Curino occasionally amplifies the volume of her voice through a microphone that reaches piercingly loud levels, in addition to projecting film, photographs, and a digital montage of morphing colors and shapes behind her (reminiscent of the old colorful geometric screen savers). These choices create an additional dimension that augments various ideas or themes. Most notably, with the microphone Curino is able to emphasize feminist leitmotifs, playing with different registers and sounds that do not always arrive at comprehensible language. Suddenly the piece about a fourth-century saint becomes an avant-garde political work, rich in its theoretical possibilities. In using technology to heighten the contemporary relevance of Bàrbera's story, Curino deploys these various media effects as instruments of subversive gestures.

Throughout the play Curino indirectly pays homage to feminist artists who, coming out of 1968, explored nonlinguistic, gestural means of communication. These actions were widely prevalent across the West, including

Fig. 19. Laura Curino in *Santa Bàrbera* (Bergamo, ca. 2005). Photograph by Gianfranco Rota. Courtesy of Laura Curino and Federico Negro.

in Italy, where grassroots feminism took place in the public sphere and was expressed in forms that were inherently theatrical, not simply discursive or linguistic.[7] Italian feminism of the era explicitly engaged the specific national situation with goals that ranged from the juridical (e.g., the legal right to divorce, or elective abortion) to the theoretical (e.g., the concept of sexual difference, or the "pay for housework" campaign), but it was also deeply in conversation with international currents, most notably American, French, and British feminist practices and thought.

These collaborations and inspirations were reciprocal, as renowned Living Theater artist Judith Malina demonstrates when she writes in her diaries about a play that she saw in Italy in which the women refused to speak, drawing attention to the extent to which masculine rhetoric dominated their language. In lieu of their live voices, they used physical language and a tape recording to tell their story.[8] For Anglo-American audiences, such an observation might seem rooted in the second-wave feminism of the 1960s through the early 1980s, but these arguments about gendered language and sexual difference are still prevalent today in Italian feminist thought. These emphases also help illuminate the feminist implications in Curino's choices by substantiating her use of technology as a tool to articulate a female voice that those in power have historically silenced.

In 2005, Teatro Donizetti in Bergamo commissioned Curino and fellow Settimo company member Roberto Tarasco to write *Santa Bàrbera* for part of a series they were revisiting called *Altri percorsi* (*Other Paths*).[9] The theater launched the series as a twenty-fifth "birthday" celebration from the day it first billed *Altri percorsi.* In 1980, as in 2005, the endeavor was as important for the Donizetti as it was for new theater practices in Italy, since it both mirrored the desire to uncover connections to local territories and, relatedly, indicated the theater's direct involvement with several local associations interested in regional promotion.[10]

Creating a cross-form palimpsest of sorts, Curino and Tarasco based the script on their studies of a sequence of sixteenth-century frescos about Saint Bàrbera painted by Lotto in Trescore Balneario, a northern Italian town approximately ten miles west of Bergamo. The frescoes, in turn, were based on a story in the thirteenth-century *La leggenda aurea* (*The Golden Legend*) by Varazze.[11] As the play explores, Bàrbera is a beautiful young woman whose ardently pagan father of considerable wealth keeps her cloistered in their home, protected, in his view, from the evils in the world, particularly her many potential suitors. He leaves on a business trip, directing workers to build a tower in which to keep her like Rapunzel. While he is gone, her sisterly best friend Giuliana introduces her to Christianity, and she soon becomes a convert. When her father returns, he is horrified and, in consultation with the town prefect, subjects her to many tortures and eventually executes her by his own hand.

One way *Santa Bàrbera* pushes against conventional boundaries is in its interweaving of multiple media, not just modern audiovisual technology but also the fourth-century hagiography through a thirteenth-century legend depicted in sixteenth-century frescos. To an extent, a parallel characteristic is common in the theater of narration, as when a story in a given text operates within its own binary: it promotes a core simplicity by reproducing various social rituals and narratives; at the same time, it embodies a postmodernist poetics through its complex self-referentiality.[12] The practice is more than mere narration because its process is dialectical, combining ancient modes of storytelling with postmodern theatrical ideas to create a new practice entirely its own. Curino's vast array of media only contributes to this. In addition to exploring Varazze's rendition and Lotto's frescos of Santa Bàrbera's life, Curino gives an entirely contemporary layer to the voice of her heroine by intertwining much of the alternative and relatively little-known Raver's Manifesto, a text attributed to Maria Pike and hailed as an authentic voice of the subculture gatherings.[13] In Curino's production, the sequence in which she recites excerpts from the manifesto is among the most technologically rigorous. The combination of audiovisual media with the contemporary slang in the Raver's Manifesto exemplify how Curino embraces technology to amplify her feminist interpretation of the story.

Echoing a specific moment grounded in the 1970s when psychoanalysis and feminist thought were a particularly fruitful pairing, Hélène Cixous's concepts of language and sound from her seminal essay, "The Laugh of the

Medusa," are still pertinent decades later and help to reveal important intricacies in Curino's production. In terms of the essay's structure, Cixous's own formal hybridity connects critical commentary with direct address and autobiography. Though Cixous's text was not intended for performance in the way that Curino's piece is, it has an innately performative quality as she asserts how writing is a means for women to claim autonomy. In the oft-cited opening line, "Woman must write her self," Cixous suggests that writing begins with the body and connects the act of writing to the psychoanalytic conception of the body as a site of early memory, ongoing experience, and biological drives and desires, all of which shape and have the potential to disrupt the formation of the female subject. In her exploration of different literary styles that might (almost literally) flesh out the writer, she dramatizes what she argues is an innate fluctuation and lack of fixedness in corporeal existence.

Just as one could claim that the performance Judith Malina witnessed, that of the women who refused to utter language, was reactionary and thus dependent, one could also argue that Cixous's essay supports the idea that phallocentric forms were what pushed women writers toward a breaking up of forms in order to develop the possibility of what might be designated as a "female" mode of practice. As feminist performance scholar Elaine Aston points out, such a suggestion problematically allows the concept of feminism to be determined by patriarchy.[14] After all, why should such binaries bound Cixous's—and Curino's—stylistic choices and experimental instincts, which might derive from a postmodern inclination or another impulse entirely? Rather, their feminism reflects not an insurgence against rigidity but an exploration that emanated from other sources that are not absolutely patriarchal or phalloreferential but instead are at least partially aesthetic. Similarly, Bàrbera's desire to pursue Christianity had little to do with her cloistered existence, a point Curino's play barely acknowledges. Early on in the play, she brags to Giuliana about her father's affection. Even while Giuliana points out his domineering behavior, Bàrbera is less rebellious or interested in a conversation that might bring about a more heightened awareness of her captivity than she is curious about religion.

Cixous's psychoanalytic framework invokes temporal landscapes that women must traverse in order to reaccess what they have lost in their journey toward adulthood, or, more specifically, womanhood. Woman has the difficult task of returning from afar, from a place she inhabited before her body was "frigidified."[15] The body is crucial in second-wave feminist theory, of course, and continues to be an important subject in Italian feminist discourse. In 1970s Italy the idea of female subjectivity as a perspective that linked women to a sphere of feelings grew more complex. It began to lose its pejorative connotations because it engaged a line of thinking that refused a comparative denigration of feminine subjectivity to masculine subjectivity: that is, female subjectivity, with its relationship to emotion, was not regarded now as inferior to male subjectivity, though it did remain in a realm of interiority, turning away from the goal of liberating women. Some circles of Italian feminists, such as the Milan Bookstore Collective, argued that there was a contradiction inherent in the idea of emancipation, because it was a juridical principle and not one that reflected a state of being, as the title of one of the most important books of the era attests, quoting Simone Weil: "Non credere di avere dei diritti" (Don't think you have any rights).[16] Freedom does not ensure equality. For the authors in Milan, the discourse on female subjectivity needed to shift to sexual difference in order for liberation to even have a chance.

That Bàrbera must withstand carnal tortures before her death questions distinctions between equality and liberation with respect to the somatic. As Curino narrates, "So then the prefect, full of fury, commanded that her flesh be cruelly tortured . . . so that her whole body bleeds."[17] While Christ aids Bàrbera physically, emotionally, and mentally, the prefect persistently attacks her body. Overnight her sores heal, so again he orders her body thrashed and torn and commands that hot iron plates be placed on her flesh.[18] When Giuliana begins to pray for her friend, the prefect then condemns her body to flames as well. When Bàrbera miraculously extinguishes them with her breath, the prefect orders that both women have their breasts cut off.[19] Certainly both male and female martyrs underwent much carnal torture, but the female body is further emphasized in this hagiography, as Diòscoro, Bàrbera's father, had originally locked her away to hide her beauty. Her body is the reason for her punishment, and because of it she approaches death.

Cixous's invocation of the "frigidified" body suggests that in childhood, girls experience a degree of liberation until society instills its repressive mores. Bàrbera's youth, however, is characterized by the tight control of her father, and she only expresses autonomy when she baptizes herself by dunking her head in the fountain of her garden. Curino punctuates this moment with laughter, loose physical movements such as raising her arms up in a *hallelujah* gesture, and the melodious and carefree folk version of "Over the Rainbow" sung by the Hawaiian musician Israel Kamakawiwo'ole (recorded in 1988; fig. 19). Curino, as Bàrbera, sways to the music and dances, performing her pleasure in one of the more physically acted moments in the entire play. Through Kamakawiwo'ole's audio recording, Curino uses a different medium to convey a newly "thawed out" body free of restraints and, in an offering to the story of the saint, sings along at points in Bàrbera's voice. On the screen in the background, colorful abstract geometrical shapes swirl and converge together, reminiscent of a hallucinogenic dream, weaving in the altered states of mind that the 1960s culture connotes. (Though this is surely unintentional, because the images also recall popular screen savers from the 1990s they highlight the link between technology and the oneiric that was perhaps there in those early days of home computers.) Through her embodiment of Bàrbera, Curino performs what approaches a state of religious ecstasy through the baptism, which Curino codes through the music as a freewheeling instance of countercultural liberation. While narrative theater productions do occasionally feature music, rarely does it have the force to speak for the narrator/character, but here, as when Malina witnessed the production with recorded voices in Faenza, Curino ushers in a new voice—also a mediated one—that conveys a state previously foreign to Bàrbera. The next time Bàrbera experiences a similarly ecstatic event, Curino supplements her voice technologically, using the microphone to recite excerpts from the Raver's Manifesto.

Cultural historians view the contemporary rave movement as an extension of the 1960s psychedelic music and drug culture updated with techno-dance music that replaces the rock and reggae of the 1960s. The raver motto, "PLUR," stands for "Peace Love Unity Respect," the nonviolent ideals ubiquitous in the 1960s, and one could argue that, like Bàrbera, rave culture is widely misunderstood and unfairly condemned. Curino capitalizes on this undercurrent to demonstrate the contemporary relevance of her story when Bàrbera begins to withstand her torture. Together, both Giuliana (voicing Jesus's teachings) and Bàrbera (in her state of saintly forgiveness) convey the PLUR ideals. Giuliana—whom Curino parallels to Jesus as an outcast, with her modern punk-raver attire replete with piercings and a dog collar—ultimately liberates Bàrbera through the ecstatic PLUR message expressed in the manifesto.

Cixous's idea that writing as woman means writing the body directly involves Curino in one of the few narrative theater performances that lacks overt autobiographical references. Cixous insists that "by writing herself, woman will return to the body which has been more than confiscated from her, which has been turned into the uncanny stranger on display—the ailing or dead figure."[20] Curino takes back this ailing figure by developing a rhythmic and mediated vocal strength that culminates with her recitation of the Raver's Manifesto, using a microphone to bellow this climactic chant throughout the performance space. When the prefect attempts to physically diminish Bàrbera, the tenor of Curino's voice builds toward an ecstatic sequence that precedes Bàrbera's death. Importantly, she first maintains the English that the manifesto was written in rather than translating it. In doing so, she works past the fact that her audiences will for the most part likely catch only some but not all of the meaning of the manifesto. Rather, she privileges the other sensory (namely auditory and visual) experiences that comprise the scene: "Our emotional state of choice is Ecstasy. / Our nourishment of choice is Love. / Our addiction of choice is technology. / Our religion of choice is music."[21] She then repeats the text in Italian, but her voice grows so loud, ramped up and distorted by the microphone, that the words become an echo of themselves. Rather, she performs the "addiction" of technology and "religion" of music by demonstrating how they are indispensable and intertwined in this ecstatic moment of freedom for Bàrbera, when she is no longer bound by corporeal restrictions.

In this instance, the use of the microphone and the psychedelic back-projection function as the preoedipal breaking up of symbolic order (language) even though language is among its conduits. Curino's vocal performance paves the path for transcendence when the words' distorted repetitions serve as instruments for sound and voice, like the female voice that soars across Cixous's essay. When woman speaks, "she doesn't 'speak,' she throws herself forward; she lets go of herself, she flies; all of her passes into her voice, and it's with her body that she vitally supports the 'logic' of her speech. Her flesh speaks true. She lays bare. In fact, she physically materializes what she's thinking; she signifies it with her body."[22] Curino's body, and the bodies of the audience members, reverberate through her voice, charged with a language that commands its own sounds, rhetoric, and codes, invoking a contemporary subcultural text written by a woman, Maria Pike, in celebration of rave's various ideals. Curino's appropriation of the text within the world of the play further demonstrates, perhaps finally and climactically, the third-wave inclusiveness of her feminism through a topic dominant in second-wave inquiry: that of the body.[23] As she announces "our" utopian principles, she nods to the intersectionality of third-wave feminism, which encompasses not only women but also other marginalized groups. The choice of the text also emphasizes that Curino is speaking about and addressing youth.[24]

As is common in the theater of narration, Curino's relationship to language is very specific. In this piece, as she unintentionally honors Cixous's invitation, she creates what feminist philosopher Adriana Cavarero suggested was a new language, or way of communicating. Cixous's exhortation that women must write faces a serious challenge in Cavarero's arguments about gendered language. Woman, Cavarero asserts, must "speak herself, think herself, and represent herself as a subject," yet "woman is not the subject of her language. Her language is not *hers*, therefore she speaks and represents herself in a language which is not hers, that is, through the categories of the language of the other."[25] Curino, however, as a writer and especially as a performer, is in command of *her* language and finds a way to "write woman" through the use of audiovisual media. While media have been used to various ends within the theater of narration, the example of Curino's *Santa Bàrbera* demonstrates a specific function in which audiovisual technology becomes a means to express long-held feminist ideas about the vexed relationship between women and language.

Translating Theater for Television

Television as a mode of exhibition is still a rarity in the theater of narration compared to the many live theatrical productions televised at any time of year around the country. Only a handful of narrative theater plays have been transmitted live (and occasionally taped), and they tend to be the larger

Fig. 20. Marco Paolini in the *Vajont* performance televised by RAI (1997). In this video still, the camera televising the image also captures a second camera in the bottom right closer to Paolini, standing, who has his back to it. Additionally, this Brechtian shot exposes the audience, seating arrangement, and lighting rigs.

successes, though the overall success of those plays is certainly buttressed by the recognition gained through broadcast. While the live broadcasts of theatrical productions in movie theaters has been popular recently, often by major companies such as the Royal Shakespeare Company or by major Broadway musicals, the intimacy of watching live theater amid the comforts and distractions of one's own home is a specific situation. In the case of the theater of narration, it amplifies the subjectivity and importance of one's own experiences as entryways into understanding events that had national consequences.

Paolini's *Vajont* (aired live on October 9, 1997, the anniversary of the 1963 tragedy, on RAI2; fig. 20) and Baliani's *Corpo di stato* (aired live on May 9, 1998, the anniversary of Moro's 1978 assassination, also on RAI2) both appeared on national television and offer very different examples of the challenges in translating the theater of narration into the medium of television. Analyzing them side by side demonstrates that the most engaging moments on television are those in which the camera functions in the service of the performance, rather than attempting to enhance it. This does not mean that the apparatus needs to remain hidden or that the home audience should ignore it altogether. There are a number of important, reflexive shots in Paolini's production (and others) in which the cameras catch each other as they pan or cut from Paolini to show reaction shots from the audience or the dam behind him as he references it. In doing so, they reveal the gaffers' scaffolding that carries the lighting rig, the raked seating, and the cameras and sound equipment. When the production team translates a theatrical piece into a televisual format without trying to make it a grand cinematic experience, they preserve the sense of community so crucial to the theater of narration.

Given that one central aspect of the theater of narration is its pedagogic ability to encourage ordinary people to reflect on and critique both major and minor events in national history from local perspectives, it has much in common with the origins of Italian television broadcasting. While the theater of narration is grounded in intellectual rigor, narrators also intend for it to be relevant and appeal to popular groups. In the early period of television in Italy, a related socially progressive vision unfolds through the ubiquity of theater, literary adaptations, and historical dramas that were frequently broadcast on national airwaves. Indeed, stretching further back, the promulgation of classical Italian texts and "great histories" is associated with the very forming of Italy as a nation as late as 1860, and its attempt to unify its regions under the umbrella of the Italian state. While the theater of narration is not a divisive practice, one way it differs from these nationally unifying endeavors is that even in plays that appear to celebrate local and national histories (Curino's Olivetti plays, for example), there is always an urge to explore the past from different, underrepresented angles in order to create a more varied holistic understanding.

One consistent trend on Italian television, which has remained despite major changes over the decades in both programming and the addition of cable and satellite networks, is its identity as a vehicle of public service, not just entertainment. In part thanks to this continued civic practice, when narrative theater productions air nationally, they are programmed to appeal to a wide-reaching public sphere. Even though various corporate and political decisions eventually extinguished many of the inclusive, civic initiatives that flourished during the early years of Italian television, the more recent, ongoing presence of the theater of narration on television since 1997 indicates a continued commitment toward public service broadcasting. For narrators, these initiatives have a concrete outcome on their plays, enabling them to reach many more people than they can while touring the country.

In addition to exploring the pedagogic angle inherent in public service, contextualizing televised narrative theater within the history of Italian television sheds light on some of the complicated politics behind the performances. Given that specific political parties were affiliated with certain stations, the fact that narrators have aired their shows on a variety of channels demonstrates the delicate shifts in critique that guide their style compared to someone with more obvious political intent, such as Dario Fo. Most experts categorize the development of Italian television in the postwar period, when it quickly became a household staple, into three phases: the state monopoly from 1954 to 1975, the rise of private broadcasting from 1975 to 1992, and the duopoly of the state and Fininvest media holding company from 1992 to 2012, when the rise of the internet and the apparent end of Silvio Berlusconi's on-again off-again stints as prime minister of Italy ushered in a final politicized phase.

As owner of Fininvest, and thus the largest shareholder of Mediaset, Italy's largest commercial broadcaster, which owns three of seven national channels (Italia 1, Rete 4, and Canale 5), Berlusconi enjoyed years of media monopoly. As prime minister, the range of his influence through televised media was disturbing (to say nothing of the various print media that his company also owned). He maintained supreme control over the airwaves through Fininvest while also, as head of state, presiding over the three state-owned channels: RAI1, RAI2, and RAI3. Only the national La7 remained independent. During this period, narrative theater productions mostly aired on La7, the one national channel not controlled by the government or by Berlusconi's private media company, suggesting an awareness among narrators for the need to separate from the domineering politics of Berlusconi's leadership. Turning back to the periodization of Italian television, it was during its first two periods that, unburdened by aggressive corporate and political tactics for power, the basic ideals of a public sphere in television flourished. This ideal is the one to which the televised narrative theater works aspire.

Phase 1: The State and TV (1954–75)

In the first phase of Italian television, which comprises the invention of the state-owned public service broadcaster Radio Audizioni Italiane, or Radiotelevisione Italiana (RAI) in 1954, political leaders explored the extent to which the new medium could affect public sentiments and educate the masses by extending their cultural horizons. Media scholar Milly Buonanno describes the composition of the RAI board in the 1950s as mainly intellectuals and managers who combined a predominant humanist-literary training with a moderate Catholic political orientation. She asserts that this first group of directors was more interested in how this new form could influence the masses than they were with its role as a public service.[26] They immediately recognized its power to affect large swaths of people. Adding to this line of thinking, film scholar Elena Dagrada argues that, because the Christian Democrats (Democrazia Cristiana, or DC) dominated politics for the entirety of this first period, the party was able to shape public broadcasting to advocate their views and policies and thereby maintain the Christian Democrats' hold on power.[27] These are alarming prospects even if the underlying paternalistic objective was still to broaden the cultural horizons of citizens in order to unify, modernize, and democratize the country.

Historians widely credit Sergio Pugliese, the first director of programming at RAI (from 1953 to 1965) and also a playwright and theater aficionado, with the strong presence of theater both taped and live on Italian TV. In weekly Friday evening broadcasts, Pugliese and his team introduced viewers to many classics, from the Greeks to the modern greats such as Pirandello, beginning with Goldoni's one-act *L'osteria della posta* on January 3, 1954, soon followed by *Romeo and Juliet*. These canonical choices have led some scholars, including Buonanno, Aldo Grasso, and Damiana Spadaro, to argue that his decisions spoke to a pedagogic inclination, to a RAI leadership that delighted in the thought of how television would help Italy become a more cultivated nation.[28] Indeed, these efforts were popular and reached a much wider audience than normally had the means or inclination to attend theatrical performances.

Televised theatrical productions were popular in both cities and rural towns with millions of spectators across Italy, in what journalist-turned-scholar Emilio Pozzi refers to as the "golden years" for theater.[29] Broadcasting theater led to the articulation of a medium-specific televisual language. An almost trial-and-error exploration of theater on cameras intended for TV helped to define the parameters of televisual communication and entertainment. RAI programming directors experimented with format and developed several different modes of representing theater on TV. These mainly included direct transmission, in which little changes from the stage version; translation, in which the text and production is designed only for television; and adaptations, in which the play is highly altered and serves as a type of metatext.[30] The theater of narration has almost always aired as direct transmission, but translation between the two media is nonetheless crucial. The success of Paolini's televised *Vajont* proved that it is possible for even a minimalist style of theater to transcend the stage and nonetheless attract millions of viewers while formally changing very little. The spectacularism of performing in front of the actual dam, however, was an important decision in the translation of the show for television.

Pozzi understands the early years of programming as less pedagogical and more experimental, arguing that Pugliese and his team searched for an authentic mode of communication that was specific to TV.[31] Pugliese and his colleague, Carlo Terron, were well aware that TV required its own language, just like cinema, and that there is a tension among the televisual technology, cinematic representation, and live performance. Over time Pugliese began to form opinions about what type of performances were more adaptable. He thought that because of framing, plays with fewer characters, such as those from the eighteenth century, were better suited for TV than the Roman or Greek classics with large choruses were.[32] Considering the physical dimensions of screens at the time, he believed the viewers at home could better accept an image that encompassed only a small number of characters.

Another attribute that developed out of attempts to translate theater for television, and one that has much in common with the mechanisms in the theater of narration, is hybridity. The history of theater on TV in Italy is also the history of hybrid forms, from the *teleromanzo* (miniseries) to the *teleinchiesta*. The program *Teatro inchiesta*, which premiered on November 10, 1966, was a theatrical reconstruction of historical or current events within a specifically televisual language in which an omniscient voice-over guides the audience through a nonlinear story replete with flashbacks.[33] Today this format's legacy in Italy is visible through the fusion of crime drama with reality TV in shows about missing persons and in some types of narrativized investigative journalism. It is hard not to see similarities with the theater of narration, especially with those productions that some call civic theater, such as *Vajont* and *Corpo di stato*. The mix of storytelling and mystery in these televised plays—not of how the story ends, but an alternative perspective from which it is told—provides a level of drama and suspense similar to mystery novels. Even though the genre clearly comes from theater, and actually in part because its origins are in stage performances, on TV the theater of narration continues a tradition of programming from RAI's earliest days.

Concerning the adaptation of drama that moves from theatrical performance to televised production, plays are irrevocably and profoundly changed to create a hybridization of the two forms. The end result is neither theater nor television but a *teledramma*.[34] These types of developments are of utmost importance because of their cohesive value. In her essay reconstructing the origins of domestic television drama, Buonanno argues that the *sceneggiato* (not just a screenplay but a "dramatized novel" or fiction specifically adapted for TV) was a crucial aspect of the "nation-building" strategy commonly associated with the beginning of Italian TV because of how it nationalized the Italian language in a country of regional dialects. The *teledrama* also deserves acknowledgment for its ability to convey key historical events and canonical literary texts.[35] To frame the idea more concisely, RAI promoted interconnection and nationality in the postwar climate through programs that discussed a wide range of issues via a universally accessible service.[36] This landscape of Italian TV was shaped by executives who developed the public broadcasting service with a catholic array of programs, from immensely popular quiz shows such as *Campanile sera* or *Lascia o raddoppia?* to news programs and drama.

This type of programming continued with the creation of more stations. In 1961, with the launch of the second national channel, RAI2, the new director, Ettore Bernabei (ex-editor of the Christian Democratic newspaper *Il Popolo*) also emphasized informational, cultural, and educational programs.[37] Pedagogical programming was thus part of television from the beginning, which makes the medium's development through this first period significant in understanding the theater of narration on TV, since the practice challenges many nationalist discourses by uprooting and reexamining histories that are widely considered accepted truths. The theater of narration, however, does not break with the tradition of promoting national unity just because it might be more dissident. Even as the practice interrogates the dynamics between region and nation and challenges dominant historical narratives by redefining them, it is still possible through the genre to promote a narrative of cultural unity and cooperation in its televised form.

Phase 2: Political Parties and TV (1975–92)

In the second era of Italian television, which was subject to a distribution of political influence known as *lottizzazione*, the emergence of other stations challenged the dominant programming schemes.[38] As a result of Reform Law 103 in 1975, which aimed to address pluralism of information, lottizzazione evolved as political parties, managers, and journalists shared positions of power in broadcasting. While the DC held on to RAI1, the Socialist Party took control of RAI2, and as late as 1987 the Communist Party ran RAI3. The three main political parties, armed with their own channels, regarded RAI's public role as one where each party could establish its own cultural and political influence, challenging the notion that public service media could enhance democratic practices.[39] By this time, those interested in the potential of television, whether political, cultural, or technological, advanced a more sophisticated concept of public service, articulating its prospects in two main ways: first in terms of access, and second in terms of content.

Despite the widespread criticism of lottizzazione, it nonetheless promoted a plurality of voices (even if they did not talk to one another), which is ultimately a positive step for democratic practices and public service.[40] Given these polarizing perspectives, the dominant view of television critics examining this period is that while lottizzazione came about precisely to instill plurality, it ultimately clashed with the ideal of public service by fragmenting the whole system among partisans who did not interact with each other, thus closing the door to productive exchanges.[41] As people began to better understand the communicative reach of television, it was clearly too risky to leave it entirely in the hands of a single political party. But as there was no discussion between the networks, and as they were so divided across party lines, the system did not really manage to *integrate* a plurality of voices. Even though more voices reached more of the public, they still spoke independently, encouraging division rather than a spirit of national unity through open dialogue.

Although the televisual landscape was significantly different by the time the theater of narration began to appear with some regularity on TV, this broad history, with questions about plurality of voices and integration of perspectives, sets up a perspective from which to view the theater of narration. Its inherent qualities, especially its desire to put different outlooks into dialogue and challenge dominant views, stand in sharp contrast with the fragmentation of Italian television networks, yet its presence on various channels over the years represents a successful attempt at both representing and integrating diverse voices, exactly what the stage practice aims to do across major and minor venues throughout Italy.

Phase 3: The Private Sector (1992–2012)

By the 1990s, an environment of duopoly in which the three RAI state-owned channels and the three Fininvest (Berlusconi's umbrella company) channels dominated the airwaves, making for a new kind of media homogeneity during the years when Berlusconi was prime minister. Unsurprisingly, in an era when high ratings generated advertising revenue and Italy was close to thirty years away from the era of long uninterrupted programs, RAI had to battle the contradiction between its public service mission and commercial imperatives. Increasingly, programming that once sought to engage audiences intellectually was quartered off into a niche market, whereas entertainment programming became mainstream. Instead of a push toward "quality" programming, executives were drawn toward the latter because of revenue.[42] As a result, RAI's high audience share was related to its diminishing distinctiveness in an increasingly standardized and advertising-driven media market. In stark contrast, when narrative theater productions began to air on television, they almost never had commercial interruptions, as was common for televised theater in the early days of RAI. Any productions that implicitly challenged the growth in commercialization and privatization of the broadcasting and telecommunications sectors, as the theater of narration did, put their revenue sources at risk. Its very presence, then, indicates a continued, if weakened, interest on behalf of RAI (or La7) to create a public sphere for serious conversation.

By this time, however, TV had almost fully lost its reputation as an instrument with educational possibilities; instead it was broadly seen as an integral part of the culture industry, which one could run as a competitive profitable business.[43] It was amid this environment that the theater of narration entered its televisual era with the broadcast of Paolini's *Vajont* on RAI2 on the thirty-fourth anniversary of the tragedy. The director of RAI2 in 1997 was Carlo Freccero, who had similar leadership qualities to Sergio Pugliese, the first director of RAI programming. After seeing *Vajont* in person, it was his idea that it could and should reach more people. Thanks to Freccero, other shows by Paolini, Laura Curino, Marco Baliani, Moni Ovadia, Giuliana Musso, Davide Enia, and Ascanio Celestini also soon appeared on that network or others. With these choices, which were only a fraction of RAI2's programming, Freccero and his team slightly disassociated themselves from the commercial and financial imperatives brought on by private competition that had largely replaced public service and community-driven discussions. In this way, the theater of narration made an important contribution: the practice's ongoing popularity demonstrates that a sizable audience is in fact interested in engaging with the nuanced and rigorous discourses the genre proposes. A close examination of two highly successful narrative theater pieces helps demonstrate how a successful translation from the stage to television preserves this quintessentially democratic goal.

The Theater of Narration, Televised

In 2001, there was a major blockbuster film laden with special effects about the Vajont disaster, starring the well-known Italian actress Laura Morante as the journalist Tina Merlin. Titled *La diga del disonore* (*The Dam of Dishonor*; it was translated for release in France as *La folie des hommes* or *The Whim of Men*, which pointedly reflects the issues of blame and responsibility that Paolini takes up much more directly than the film, or even its Italian title, does), it dramatized the political corruption behind the tragedy that Paolini examines in his play. By industry standards, despite all its technological savvy and special effects of a digitized tsunami wiping out seven villages, the film was a flop. Meanwhile, the taping of Paolini's show in 1997, with few constructed visual effects, was a great success both for him personally and for the theater of narration as a dramatic form, since it increased popular interest in the genre. In a loose parallel, Auslander notes that comedians and club owners in the 1980s were surprised to discover that viewers responded with a desire to see individuals perform live after seeing them perform on a TV show. In this instance, "mediatized performance became the referent for the live one."[44] While *La diga del disonore* was just a tedious film that did not incite discussion or palpable interest, the televising of Paolini's play actually boosted the live performances, as evidenced by his continued success with both *Vajont* and his other plays in theaters around the country and with many reappearances on TV. Several channels, including RAI2, RAI3, and La7, have shown his work to great critical acclaim, as the case of the *Il sergente* premiere in 2007 demonstrates. Over 1.2 million watched the show, or 5.5 percent of all viewers on the night it aired, which was a record for La7 and illustrates how televisual productions reached audiences far vaster than national theater tours could.[45]

In the televised *Vajont*, a decision to build a stage in front of the actual dam added a startling affective dimension. While spectacular settings are not uncommon in televised productions of the theater of narration, their very presence suggests an effort to compensate for the genre's lack of spectacle, even if its minimalist style is a characteristic that critics widely celebrate. Similarly, while Baliani has performed *Corpo di stato* in a plethora of humble locations, the televised version was set dramatically amid the ancient ruins of Rome in the heart of the city. The inherent drama in these sets adds a tactile realism to both the in-person and televised performances, but it also introduces risk. Media scholar Giorgio Simonelli notes that theater of narration plays often have moments of dramatic intrigue that include political-military dynamics fraught with cover-ups, as the genre embraces rereadings of history. Pointing out that 2 to 5 million viewers watch the theater of narration each time a production airs, he suggests that these theatrically televised events could be as frequent as once a month and even replace RAI2's *Palcoscenico*, which only offers the same bland, homogenized theater productions that fare poorly on both TV and in theaters.[46] The contrast between the average televised theater production and a televised narrative theater production suggests that the genre is effective at translating itself for the small screen, even as it maintains its minimalist aesthetic. Part of this relates to its inherent hybridity, which allows for its adaptability to different forms and media, but most of its success is due to its emphasis on empowering spectators/viewers to reevaluate historical perspectives, privileging their point of view.

The use of spectacular settings has become a common characteristic of Paolini's televised productions, but this is not necessarily true of the entire genre. For example, Giuliana Musso's *Nati in casa*, which aired on RAI3 in 2004 and again in 2018 on RAI5, was taped during an intimate indoor production on a small stage with characteristic minimalism, rather than being staged in the birthing centers, hospitals, or Friulian mountains that are so much a part of her story. One of the risks inherent in favoring grandiose surroundings for television adaptations is that they set a visual standard, which might denigrate future productions that cannot meet such an expectation. Simonelli ties all of Paolini's TV work inextricably back to the *Vajont* production. Since it aired on the anniversary of the tragedy and took place in front of the dam at the exact time of day the disaster occurred, the adaptation possessed an inherent drama that, because it was the first experience of the theater of narration on television, became part of the standard mode of presentation for the genre. For Simonelli, the emotional height of the piece has no match.[47] Yet what makes the practice so successful in both its medial form and its stark live performances is the drama in the subject itself.

The argument that *Vajont*, as the very first theater of narration production to air on TV, reached unattainable heights places Paolini himself in a particularly difficult position, as if all of his future productions must meet the expectations he set with *Vajont*. To an extent, there is proof of this battle in many of his televised shows, which continue to take advantage of surroundings that are impossible for most live performances except in special circumstances and with significant funding. In *Miserabili: Io e Margaret Thatcher* (*Miserables: Margaret Thatcher and I*, which he began performing in various forms in 2006, and in a more final version by 2009), Paolini intertwines perspectives from both macro- and microeconomics to reflect on deregulation and the growth of precarious labor during the 1980s in Italy and elsewhere. It is a very typical narrative theater piece in the sense that Paolini rigorously researched the topic; he examines not a particular event but, rather, a specific historical period marked by economic change; there are moments of autobiography, especially via a character that he brings back from the earlier highly autobiographical piece *Gli album*; with the exception of the musicians, he is the sole performer onstage who speaks directly to the audience; and at the end of the show, he actually solicits comments from audience members (which was included in the live national broadcast), starting a conversation that will ideally carry on without him.

On November 9, 2009, the performance aired live and uninterrupted on the national station La7 (the only one historically *not* tied either to the government, like the RAI channels, or to Berlusconi's private media companies) from the Taranto Container Terminal at the port of Taranto in one of the country's most historic sites of economic trade, off the southern heel of the boot in Puglia. The containers themselves are industrial objects, fixtures of mundane everyday life, though here monumentalized through their staging. They also represent global trade, with all its fraught connotations. The symbolism of this location is powerful and affective too, conjuring a long view of historical trade and war as far back as the Second Punic War in the third century BC, when the Carthaginians and Romans fought to control Tarentum, through World War II, as a site of military operations. It adds to the production's grandiosity as well as stimulating the visual sense, which normally receives much less attention in the theater of narration. Is Paolini chasing the ghost of *Vajont*? To some degree, yes. The Taranto port, despite its stature as a major source of trade, is not tantamount to the mountains of Vajont, where the actual tragedy took place though it is movingly allegorical. When *Vajont* portrayed its pathos in the spectacle of the set and surroundings, it recounted a deep and specific tragedy in Italian history with which the more ruminative thinking behind *Miserabili* cannot compete despite the thoughtful staging and location.

Vajont

Adhering to his typical working pattern, Paolini developed *Vajont* slowly, first performing it after dinner for friends in September 1993.[48] By the time the production aired on RAI2 in 1997, he had presented it over two hundred times in a plethora of venues, many of them nontraditional (i.e., not theaters). In March 1994, less than six months after his first postdinner performance, he recorded a version of the play on the Milan-based left-leaning radio station Radio Popolare following an earlier theatrical performance.[49] It was a moment that confirmed there was something special about the show. The radio program began around midnight and ended at 2:30 a.m., but to his surprise he maintained such a large audience that he accepted callers until 4 a.m.[50] In addition to the obvious exposure to an audience that was not the typical mainstream theater audience, the radio broadcast also allowed Paolini to continue the exhibition of his show on his own terms in low-pressure situations. It gave him time to let the production grow and change in small ways and to understand it both in terms of its theatrical staging and in a language suitable for radio and eventually for television.

While his live show gained momentum through word of mouth, particularly in artistic and intellectual circles—people such as Carlo Freccero, the director of RAI2, attended a performance—Paolini still chose spaces that were nontraditional, rarely entering theaters. As he explains, this was not because he was antiestablishment per se, but because he felt that the show worked better in more intimate venues. Within two weeks of accepting Freccero's proposition to air the piece on national television, new offers were pouring in for Paolini to perform *Vajont* at festivals and in theaters nationwide. As he says, "*Vajont* exploded in theaters," which he found distressing given his insistence on maintaining an intimacy in this story, an intimacy that also become a hallmark of the theater of narration. He admits that the televised performance killed something in the theatrical version, without elaborating on what precisely that was.[51] What bothered him was probably his sudden and growing fame, because with more recognition, Paolini became an auteur of sorts. Yet part of his appeal after the televised performance was that same essence of intimacy that he held so sacred in his live performances.

The October 9, 1997, televised version of *Vajont* was a live direct transmission, not a taped or adapted-for-TV version of the original theater piece. Both Gabriele Vacis and Felice Cappa adapted the production for television. Cappa, who has had a career as a journalist, director, and overall collaborator with illustrious artists, including a number of narrators along with Dario Fo and Franca Rame, would go on to become a key figure in finessing the presence of many other televised theater of narration plays, including *Olivetti* and *Corpo di stato*. For this first and thus high-stakes production, the team decided that they would use seven cameras to alternate perspectives from center, left, and right, zooming in for close-ups of both the performer and audience, and would also take extreme long shots of the audience, the stage, and the surroundings, including, of course, the star: the dam itself. Most shots are direct medium or high angles, an important distinction from the confusing low angles in Baliani's production, which took more liberty with cinematic aesthetics. One of the advantages of direct transmission is its incorporation of the physicality and sacredness of the actual stage, which the viewer sees on the screen. Everyday life, normalcy, and that conversational colloquial tone characteristic of the theater of narration are all also typical of live broadcast TV, working to the genre's advantage.

The very first shot is of a paper map that centers on Venice and the surrounding area. The camera slowly zooms out and pans northwest to Longarone and Erto, two of the nearby towns affected by the disaster. This shot then dissolves from the paper map into several establishing landscape shots of the dam itself, zooming out into an extreme long daytime shot of the mountaintop, where the dam still exists, and panning to the valleys below. That shot then dissolves into a close-up of the dam at night, awash in floodlights. At this point the feed switches to live transmission from the recorded footage, and the audio begins to pick up the low hum of chatter and coughs as the audience awaits the beginning of the performance. All the while, the opening credits run. The camera pans to Paolini, shown with audience members in front of him and the dam lit behind him; he utters his first words in the center of the frame. Until Paolini speaks, the only sounds are water trickling down rocks, and the rustles from the audience.

For the next minute, the camera follows his few movements on the stage, keeping him framed in the same way, occasionally switching to medium shots of audience members as he interacts with them by gesturing toward them and looking directly at them. A minute and a half into Paolini's opening, archival images replace him as he provides voice-over, along with a shortened running text in subtitles, stating the bare facts of what happened exactly thirty-four years before. That first sequence of extra materials lasts thirty-six seconds before shifting back to Paolini. At one point his performance is superimposed over the wreckage. For the next four minutes the image of Paolini continues to be interrupted by old footage in clips of ten to twenty-five seconds. These patterns quickly turn redundant, but in their simplicity, they demonstrate how the televisual language has preserved the minimalism of the performance genre. The images of people recall found footage or documentary, and while they honor those local families, they also signal that in the unspectacular lives of ordinary people lies the key to the *storia* of the Vajont tragedy.

Unlike the experience of sitting in the audience, multiple camera setups allow the viewer at home to see Paolini from different angles and at different distances. Since the cameras also capture reaction shots from the audience at different moments throughout the production, they also allow the viewer an element of sharing and witnessing that mimics the collective experience of the in-person theatrical performance. The cameras imitate movements of the eye, but they surpass human vision when they offer close-ups of Paolini or fly toward the dam. Although the cameras may enhance and build on the live performance, they still reaffirm the in-person experience more than they try to go beyond it. The reference is still the stage performance, even if Paolini's team must adapt and create a new televisual language.

The televised presentation does incorporate materials that are not present in the staged versions. Here, too, the decision was to streamline, offering only simple and minimal information. Early in the show, and contributing to the building momentum, there are several cuts to still images or archival newsreels: drawings of old maps, still photographs of the actual newspaper headlines that Paolini references, photographs from those newspapers, and old footage from the aftermath of the disaster. Most of these images appear in the first ten minutes, with decreasing frequency as the performance continues. Though this extra visual material is sporadic and unobtrusive, including such imagery, particularly of the flood's aftermath, offers some benefits. As Grasso points out, it contributes to Paolini's dexterity, since most contemporary audiences had either never witnessed those raw scenes, even in the newspapers, or had long since forgotten them. In the immediate aftermath of the disaster, some of the photographs or reels may have even been censored.[52]

Paolini, Vacis, Cappa, and their team thus found a way to utilize one of television's main strengths—its potential for intimacy, which also happens to be a key strength of the theater of narration. On stage such images and footage might distract, but on television, when they become the entire screen, they bring with them an immediacy and utility that works specifically for the medium without sacrificing the intimate qualities of the performance genre. The footage also establishes a scholarly tone that underlines the erudition of the genre and enhances its ties to microhistory. Showing these primary sources, the audience at home is exposed to the anthropological research that the genre both embraces and mimics. In one sequence of archival footage, people help an older woman walk over debris by holding her arms on either side. She is dressed in black, as though for mourning, and at one point she looks directly at the camera. The expressive pain that registers across her face in a shot of no more than three seconds is potent, if brief. This type of material capitalizes on the ways that TV can enhance or offer another dimension to the theater of narration without usurping what live performance can offer.

These sequences also show how real people personalize the event, a phenomenon microhistorians describe as witnessing the intimate affects of ordinary people. In the preface to his book on witchcraft, Carlo Ginzburg discusses how the "rich variety of individual attitudes and behavior" emerging from the sources so enveloped him that he risked losing sight of the larger project. He explains that "the principal characteristic of this documentation is its immediacy. . . . The voices of these peasants reach us directly, without barriers."[53] When the exhausted woman stares into the camera, filling the entire television screen at home, there is a new proximity to the Vajont disaster. Even if there were a screen onstage onto which Paolini projected the images, it would still only be a part of the audience's focus, as other details of the theatrical experience frame any screens on a stage. By creating a televisual language through the inclusion of raw footage, however, Paolini and his team maintain a direct intimacy with the at-home audience that is different from his rapport with the audience before him at the site of a stage, while still preserving many of the characteristics of that encounter. Such a gesture also harks back to the public education efforts at the roots of early Italian television. In bringing this history of Vajont into the homes of so many and telling it in a new way twice over (i.e., the story itself offers new perspectives, and the medium of television revises the theatrical production), Paolini and his team demonstrate their continued commitment to public dialogues.

Corpo di stato

Just seven months after *Vajont*'s television debut in 1997, RAI broadcast live a performance of Baliani's *Corpo di stato* on another important anniversary for Italians: May 9, 1998, marked twenty years since the Red Brigades assassinated former prime minister Aldo Moro and since the Mafia murdered anti-Mafia activist Peppino Impastato. In one of his most minimalist narrator roles, rarely adding even a single prop in his productions or donning any suggestion of a costume, Baliani completely changed tactics for television by embracing technical adjustments to remarkable effect. At first glance, it might seem as though there are few differences between the stage-to-TV transitions of *Vajont* and *Corpo di stato*, yet there are several key modifications that result in one main distinction: Baliani and his team's attempt to dramatize the production and its underlying ideas through televisual (ultimately cinematic) means, which largely detract and distract from the core of the piece. This is particularly surprising given that Paolini and Baliani shared some creative staff, most notably Cappa, who had demonstrated such deft handling of the transition from theater to television with *Vajont*. Reminiscent of Simonelli's judgment of *Vajont* as spectacularly charged by emotion and novelty, Cappa seemingly competes with himself in this second attempt at televising the theater of narration by trying to enhance the emotional resonance of the show to surpass even that of *Vajont*.

In his review of RAI's *Corpo di stato*, the critic Gualtiero Peirce at *La Repubblica* (Rome), the major national newspaper, addresses the comparison immediately. Quite simply, he states that Baliani's piece did not create the same "magic" as Paolini's. It did not create the same "televisual fusion." He also notes that it had about half the viewership as *Vajont*, which reached over a million sets (at an almost 7 percent market share).[54] In his view, this discrepancy is partially due to the fact that *Vajont*'s tragic power stems from a natural disaster—the landslides that triggered the tsunami—while the tragedy in *Corpo di stato* is caused by humans and told in a very personal autobiographical manner. In Peirce's reading, Paolini largely aims to correct that prevailing view of nature's whimsy by providing evidence of human error. Meanwhile, the violence of the 1970s and particularly the dramatic kidnapping and eventual assassination of Moro are innately more dramatic, full of much more scheming and politics than is apparent in *Vajont* (though Paolini attempts to reveal much scheming and politics surrounding the building of the dam); and the charged killings are much more nationally resonant than the *Vajont* story, which took place in the distant Friulian Mountains of northeastern Italy.

Rather, the two main missteps with Baliani's televised production revolve around its location and the camerawork. Instead of enhancing the theatrical experience or simply providing ways to let it seep through the images, the televised production competes with the performance through the hyperbolic background in the ancient government buildings of Augustus's Forum. Worsening the situation, erratic and low-angle camera movements are all too frequently employed, in addition to the creation of long creeping shadows that are more typical of film noir and horror films, thanks to excessive floodlighting against the depths of night. A third potential issue is the extent to which the performance styles between Paolini and Baliani differ. Although both pieces address tragedies, Paolini has a more jovial accessible air, at least in the beginning of his story and later with comedic renditions of various personas, so that by the time he narrates the tragedy, the audience has an affection for him. Baliani, on the other hand, is severe from beginning to end. That *Corpo di stato* has enjoyed much success on the stage for decades refutes such an assertion, so it appears that he was directed for the televised performance to embody a more stately, distant, and harsher presence. That persona is precisely the opposite of the demeanor typical of narrators, who are eager to communicate and work with their audiences, and specifically of Baliani, who in *Corpo di stato* typically presents an intimate and sympathetic side of a compassionate young man, achingly eager to do the right thing.

As the quintessential symbol of Rome and the political heart of the nation, there is a compelling rationale in the choice of the ruins, specifically the Forum of Augustus, just north of the Roman Forum, for Baliani's live broadcast. It evokes the depths of the past as well as dramatic leitmotifs from his text, such as justice, betrayal, and human frailty. It also serves as a material contrast to the use of contemporary media, such as the soundtrack and photographic stills from the 1970s that appear in a brief interlude during Baliani's stage performance on a screen upstage.[55] The production opens in a beautifully lit panning shot of the ruins, with the Temple of Jupiter twinkling in the background. A textual overlay announces the live transmission from Augustus's Forum. As a recording of the musician and political activist Joan Baez singing the old folk song "Fare Thee Well" begins, cameras switch to different shots—some offer close-ups, others provide panoramas—of the crumbling ancient structures.

The black sky hangs like a curtain in the background, playing a particularly important and surprising part in evoking the sense of a theater. As though it were the wings of a stage set, it both frames and cuts off the world in which the action takes place. As the camera pans to a luminous full moon overhead, it too evokes a single bright spotlight, and although floodlights and human-made equipment cast long shadows, the camera suggests that it is, rather, the work of the foreboding light that emanates from the sky. The opening is nothing short of spectacular, like the image of the dam in *Vajont* or the factories of Ivrea for RAI's *Camillo Olivetti*, but unlike in those productions, here it is too poetic and abstract, clashing with and even upstaging the play. Baliani's tale confronts a specific moment in the past, using autobiography critically as a way to analyze an unambiguously violent shared history. The Forum represents power and politics, the possibility of an ideal republic: the promise of democracy, with its brilliance but also its weaknesses, corruption, and downfall. It is also layered with centuries of myths, plays, novels, revised histories, personal visits, and various tales woven into its remaining structures in ways that are impossible to comprehend or disassociate fully. Such imbrication and invisible layering betray the directness of the genre. The theater of narration is concerned with new dialogues that uncover lesser-known facts, yet this location confounds that process with both mystery and overdetermined meaning.

Further, the space was not conducive to the in-person performance, forcing Baliani away from his audience members in order to thrust him closer to the cameras, or bringing him so absurdly close that he addressed only a handful of spectators at a time. He complains in his published diaries how terrible it was at times to be unable to engage with the audience, as some of them were almost placed behind him so as to give the visual sense of community, even while he was directed to look only at the camera.[56] This *sense* of community reveals more of an attempt than a successful execution. The producers clearly understood the importance of communal engagement for the piece, but functionally they were thinking only in terms of the visual presentation for the at-home viewers, and in fact alienated the actual audience onsite, which in turn affected Baliani. By comparison, Paolini looked at both the audience and the cameras throughout his performance, and the cameras also showed numerous audience reaction shots, which created community between performer, audience, and at-home spectator. According to Baliani, Maria Maglietta—his longtime partner both professionally and personally, who directed the piece—intimated that the production team was making decisions that were not consistent with the spirit of the text. She protested the location, citing its grandiloquence and rhetorical pedantry, but Cappa insisted. She did at least convince the producers to avoid the great staircase, where they considered having Baliani stand, looking down on the audience.[57] Still, the producers found a way to incorporate the dramatic angles that a staircase would have created by placing the cameras low, so that everything seemed larger and looming, including Baliani. The end result was that an exquisite and important stage piece celebrated for its confessional intimacy was transformed into a televisual language cluttered with an ill-fitted baroque set instead of one that would have supported the mechanisms at work.

After a little over a minute into the opening sequence, the camera pans from a shot of the moon to the first image of Baliani. In a medium close-up, pillars of the ancient Forum frame him as he looks down directly at the camera with a stern expression (fig. 21). The camera here is angled low, making the ruins behind him appear even larger as he glares at the spectators watching from home. The actual audience present before him does not appear in the opening. Their experience is more akin to watching the taping of an episode with an actor who speaks to the apparatus that has drawn his attention away from them, rather than meeting at a midway point in which the narrator both acknowledges the audience and at times directly addresses the camera for the audience at home. Besides the location of the Forum, this technical aesthetic is one of the production's most miscalculated choices. Like the low-level lighting, the low-angle shots are also reminiscent of horror and noir films that dramatically overwhelm the spectator through harsh angles to create imposing figures on screen. When the cameras draw Baliani to look down on them, he morphs into an Orwellian authority rather than the sympathetic voice working through a complicated history rife with personal political conflict that is his usual stage persona.

Helpfully, throughout the performance the cameras also capture Baliani in medium long shots that are framed at eye level, but despite his own instincts

Fig. 21. Video still of Marco Baliani in *Corpo di stato* televised nationally from the Forum of Augustus, Rome, on RAI2, May 9, 1998.

and the protests of Maglietta, he was directed to speak almost exclusively to the camera, at the expense of the onsite audience. Perhaps Baliani, Cappa, and others (it appears that Maglietta, who pleaded a different argument, struggled to be heard) meant to convey the authority of the state, which is certainly a leitmotif in the play. While that logic might explain shooting the ruins and performer in such a haunting way, it is a manipulative choice. The formal differences between *Vajont* and *Corpo di stato* highlight the difficulty and risks in translating the theater of narration for television. By and large the productions are quite similar. Both embrace a spectacular space, use multiple cameras, incorporate archival footage or photographs, and maintain the primary focus on the narrator in a mode of direct address. Yet the slight differences with which Baliani's team aimed to enhance the drama of the production reveal two very different productions: the stage and screen versions of *Corpo di stato* differ from one another as much as *Vajont* and *Corpo di stato* themselves do.

Finally, there are some narrators who experiment with a variety of media in the same piece, demonstrating a continued urge to revise, reinvent, and reinvest in the practice. Celestini exhibits a curiosity regarding technology and media that is particularly explorative. Besides regular appearances on satirical programs or talk shows in which he frequently tests short excerpts of new projects, many of which then appear on his YouTube channel, as well as his range of film work (in the roles of both actor and director), on several occasions he has developed a stage production into a film that is truly independent from the live version; adding another layer, some of these works have aired on television. Celestini experiments with the developmental order of his creative projects, whether they are from theater to film (as most of his cases are), or from film to theater. His Temps Project is one of the best examples of the range of media within which he works. His choices fracture the project in many ways and offer different layers to his central idea about precarious pay and labor through documentary film, live performance, a novel, and a scrap book of sorts sold with the film that culls various research and preparation materials, including interviews and published editorials.

The performance, *Appunti per un film sulla lotta di classe*, with its string of anecdotes interspersed with live music, functions as a prequel to the film. Celestini narrates the content as much as he shares anecdotes from interviews relating to the film's development. The performance's publicity tagline casually states, "It is not a play, but is exactly what the title says it is" (i.e., "Notes for a Film on Class Struggle"). The line that follows the tag confounds this idea: "A play by and with Ascanio Celestini." This project not only highlights Celestini's journey across media but also demonstrates the evolving life of a text, exemplifying how the theater of narration can be read as a form that intrinsically questions what constitutes a play and explores how other media can contribute to this practice.

More broadly, the diverse use of media in the theater of narration reflects an inherent hybridity even within its rigid minimalist presentation. Whether present in a stage show, or used as a new way of exhibition, media interacts most effectively when it privileges the live production, unless it is completely rewritten and scripted for new media, like Celestini's works. The visual imagery and sound in *Santa Bàrbera* help to clarify Curino's complex rendering of female agency, while the cameras in *Vajont* offer an intimacy to the at-home spectator, who cannot smell the humidity in the air or choose when to shift their focus from Paolini to the mountainous region surrounding them. By contrast, Baliani's production buries its most meaningful elements of human connection under distracting pretense by emphasizing the drama inherent in this play that confronts state-level terrorism, kidnapping, and assassination. The harsh camera angles from above and below draw long shadows, extending the reach of the tragic elements, whereas the play on its own is mostly concerned with the interiority and individual experience of such large-scale assaults. Narrators still experiment with media in their famously minimalist genre, but they also demonstrate that simplicity does not have to mean pretechnology. By deferring to the original stage production, a variety of media can draw attention in meaningful ways not to their own form but to the narrative performance.

Conclusion

✦

Politicizing History

In examining the history of the theater of narration, this study has also analyzed how the artists themselves were thinking about history. Through their specific performance practice, these artists create a process of history making that illuminates the ways in which history itself is a theater of narration. By presenting interpretations of events and people, the theater of narration urges its audiences to see how the everyday stories that ordinary people tell themselves and share with others are the narratives, the very microhistories, that devise broad understandings of national events. Ordinary individuals can and should tell their stories of the disasters and well-known figures that foreground their lived experience. As they do, this process of everyday storytelling alters the public dimensions of the event. The very art form that narrators have created is inherently didactic: aspects of each performance show how individuals have the power to recount the legacies of history, the famous figures whose voices and achievements have inspired or revolted them, the private ways in which those publics reverberate in their thoughts and experiences.

This position is a radical departure from a rational, top-down epistemology of history, favoring instead a microform of history that is responsive to the involuntary memories, personal feelings, and associations that experience engenders. Identifying narration as the shared element between theater and this conception of history, narrators recognized theatrical performance as the perfect vehicle to collectively complicate a shared past. If cultivated, such an experiential approach has the potential to bolster the collective sharing of narratives. By stripping away many of the spectacular elements of theater and instead reinvigorating a classically inflected dramaturgy of the word, narrators privilege the embodied acts of listening and, from there, re-creating. As a dramatic practice, the form they have shaped is personal yet also, since it is minimalist, easily transferable and commanding. Narrators center themselves in their staging and thereby perform the idea that the human should be at the center of historical inquiry and construction.

What takes place onstage relates both to specific histories and to a method of history making. There is a dialectical practice that revises existing histories into new ones, a didactic method that teaches its audiences and viewers how to do so themselves, a framework with which to comprehend a specific event, and the historical praxis to reconstruct it. As the micro and macro perspectives begin to intertwine, a new version of both a private and a public past takes shape, and the theater, with its power to bring people in physical proximity to focus on a shared topic ushers forth new understandings of collective pasts. When narrators, as cultural laborers, devise a story and perform it for an audience, one of the main events in that specific time-space is the unfurling of both a story and a history through micro accounts, dialogue, and imaginative practice.

Building on the relationship between memory, feeling, experience, and expression made famous by anthropologists Victor Turner and Edward Bruner, D. Soyini Madison emphasizes how in performance what was once personal reality becomes shared, and with that "we have arrived at the threshold of performance evolving from experience. Experience becomes the very seed of performance."[1] For the theater of narration, personal experience—and especially the way one's subjectivity influences the interpretation of a public event—also becomes the seed of public histories constructed from a private place of feeling. From this perspective, the past is recognized as a much more open-ended space than top-down histories would suggest. There is a magnanimous gesture in such a notion, one that offers the weight of value to people who are typically insignificant, even subaltern, within major historical narratives. When they shape those very narratives, though they themselves do not feature directly in them, they have a specific claim to a public history. Given the reclaiming power of this practice, there is the need for future productions to cast their net more widely to encompass more members of their society deserving of representation—particularly migrants and racial minorities, but also people with different levels of ability, both cognitive and physical. The current leaders of the practice might endeavor not to share these stories themselves but to empower those who live these histories to share them.

The theater of narration politicizes history and historical thinking by destabilizing it. Though the context of each production surrounds actual, often controversial, historical realities, since the practice embraces a theatrical medium to recuperate history, it frequently invents minor details. This is particularly evident with the imaginative aspects that reflect the artistry of the practice, such as when Camillo Olivetti rides his bicycle to protests; when men sing folk songs in canoes at the site of the Vajont dam; when a woman in labor converses with her midwife. These moments benefit the cohesion, drama, and dynamism of the narrative, but they likely emerge from the mind of the narrator, not a historical source. Even as an art form, this aspect raises profound questions and implications in the climate following the 2016 US election. When Donald Trump took office, sending shock waves across the globe with the accompanying presence and manipulation of "fake news," the theater of narration began to bear a heightened responsibility in its ambition to shed new, revisionist light on public histories with the help of both personal and imagined details. How narrators will navigate this issue is an open-ended question, but the fact that they are not politicians and do not typically take overtly political positions keeps their work in the realm of cultural production even if it is implicitly a political act to encourage increased agency among their audiences for the formation of personal and collective national histories.

As a provocation, and as a future study, one might consider how these intersections point to the centrality of performance in politics, from reality stars such as Donald Trump to the 2019 election of the comedian Volodymyr Zelensky in the Ukraine, and to the rise of the Five Star Movement in Italy. In considering not just how performance is political but also how politics is highly performative, Italy offers a wealth of material. The year 2013 presented an especially pertinent time, with both the highly theatricalized process of electing a new pope, and national elections that voted into Parliament the insurgent party of Beppe Grillo, a performer and satirist who has become famous for criticizing national scandals involving Italy's elite. By the 2018 elections, only five years after he crossed explicitly into the realm of politics with his MoVimento 5 Stelle (Five Star Movement, or M5S), the party had enough votes to create a coalition that positioned its members at the head of the government.[2] A provocateur since the late 1970s, Grillo was barred from publicly owned television in 1986 (just as Dario Fo and Franca Rame had been in 1962) for making an infamous joke on the popular Saturday night variety show *Fantastico* suggesting that all socialists were thieves (the Italian Socialist Party was dominant at the time; its leader, Bettino Craxi, was prime minister).[3] Even as Grillo's jesting critique of the ruling socialists was met with laughter, it was utterly shocking in its bluntness, stating what was widely believed yet none dared say.

It took more than five years after that, in judicial investigations known as the *mani pulite* (clean hands), for officials to address the high-level fraud, which uncovered widespread corruption, earning the country the moniker "Tangentopoli" (Bribesville). After many months of investigations, people could no longer tolerate the corruption and took to the streets. As the investigations continued into 1993, in a particularly searing and orchestrated act of protest imbued with performance, one morning when Craxi and his entourage were leaving his residence at the Hotel Raphaël in Rome crowds threw coins at them, shouting, "Prendi anche questo!" (Take this too!).[4] More than chants to make their frustrations known, the performative gesture with the coins demonstrates the overlap between politics, performance, and action. The lasting references to that period of politics in the minds of many Italians are these cultural victories against corruption. Rather than the politicians themselves or the investigations that brought them down, the historical narratives revealed in Grillo's irreverent joke, and in passionate but calculated acts such as throwing the coins outside Hotel Raphaël, convey the emotional and lived nuances of the event.

For Grillo, that type of abrupt whistleblowing earned him trust broadly among ordinary people who saw his actions as brave and honest. Even if everyone knew about the corruption, his groundbreaking polemic against Craxi and the Socialist Party demonstrated his ability to expose a scandal publicly before journalists or actual investigators could. It appeared as though no one else was willing to face, or capable of facing, the mass corruption of career politicians, and this became a position that foregrounds the platform of his confusing populist party. To some, M5S appears to have a progressive stance, because it promotes a younger generation through its ranks and addresses issues of (at least) gender diversity, as in the 2016 mayoral successes of M5S candidates: Rome elected Virginia Raggi, and Turin elected Chiara Appendino, both women in their thirties who were also mothers of young children when they took office to lead two of the country's most culturally and economically valuable cities. The party's promotion of environmental awareness and widely accessible technology also appeals to progressively minded youth and adults. Yet the party is anything but transparent in its leadership and infamously joined the Far Right Lega Nord party to form the coalition that would hold a majority of representatives in 2018. Together these parties are virulently anti-immigrant and anti-European. Grillo, an actual performer by profession, exemplifies the ways in which highly visible acts can be appropriated for political gain. He began his career in satire by exposing corruption, but eventually he turned to dramatic performative acts—swimming across the Strait of Messina in 2012, for example—as a way to raise awareness for his political campaign above all else.

When Grillo was banned from television in 1986, he continued his national tours in performance spaces and on soapboxes in piazzas. His desire to open public spaces for his shows free of charge shares similarities to narrators' efforts to stage widely accessible productions, as in the early public work of Teatro Settimo, and narrators' continued presence at summer festivals in small towns across Italy. Grillo, however, wanted to reach more people than he could on national tours, and in an ironic twist of fate, being barred from television lead him to think creatively about a new platform. His upstart campaigns coincided with the rapid expansion of the internet and eventually social media, and Grillo was among the first public figures—well ahead of the grassroots movements in the United States that surged Barack Obama to victory in 2008—to create a presence online. The digital environment he embraced enabled him to disseminate widely his charged counternarratives. Eventually with the help of the visionary internet entrepreneur with whom he cofounded M5S, Gianroberto Casaleggio, and later his son Davide Casaleggio, who has continued in a leading role in M5S, Grillo established a web-based infrastructure that controls the party and, since 2018, the Parliament.[5] Trump, too, embraced the digital sphere as a weaponized system of communication through his ubiquitous use of Twitter, with its brief, casual, and simple format, to reach his supporters as directly and quickly as possible, bypassing long-established media structures. It is in this context, outside of established checks, that he has infamously and seemingly without consequence been able to rewrite history for his own political gain.

In the face of such populist and political uses of social media, perhaps it is no surprise that narrators remain largely dedicated to live and in person performances, even as they explore new ways to present their work and reach disparate audiences. The narrators' work does, however, share at least one aspect at the heart of Grillo's political and cultural production, and to an extent also with Trump's. Both narrators and politicians such as Grillo and Trump perform the confrontation between official and unofficial information. When Paolini performs *Vajont*, he explicitly asks why the vast majority of journalists and government officials never bothered to scrutinize what caused the landslide and who was at fault. Why did questions and investigations not follow after public mourning? Before creating a political party, Grillo asked the same questions in one of his routines that anticipated the bankruptcy scandal of Parmalat (one of Europe's largest bankruptcies). He wondered why he was the one to break the story. "The real catastrophe is information: It is serious that these things come out with us, comedians, and not with the press, who arrives afterwards."[6] The difference between the narrators and the Grillo of M5S, is that narrators synthesize how this confrontation between information and misinformation affects the ordinary individual, and they fundamentally encourage critical questioning. Politicians like Trump, by contrast, stage controversy around information in order to sow paranoia and distrust, ultimately destabilizing communal bonds in order to profit from the discord. In a marked difference, narrators aim to empower people individually and collectively, while these politicians increasingly move in authoritarian and supremacist directions. Such different paths from parallel roads ultimately point to the wide-reaching impacts, as well as ethical stakes, at the heart of the theater of narration's radical amalgam of politics, history, and performance. For narrators, part of performing new narratives of history means practicing a theatrical form that also politicizes the relative present.

Beyond Italy and outside the explicitly political sphere, there are also instances in which other theater practitioners in similar genres worth comparing have risked creative embellishments that greatly harmed their credibility for truth telling. Mike Daisey's nearly career-ending *The Agony and the Ecstasy of Steve Jobs* (2011) has very close formal resemblances to the theater of narration, but rather than inventing inconsequential details that would enrich the narrative properties of his story, Daisy invented facts, misrepresented individuals, and maligned cultures to which he had no personal connections. In the show, Daisey sits at a desk for most of the performance and juxtaposes his own affinity for Apple products with his experiences researching their production in exploitative Chinese factories, particularly

Foxconn's Shenzhen facility. Similar to Grillo, Daisey's piece anticipated a long exposé by the *New York Times* that uncovered dubious practices in the mammoth factory that produces most of the world's electronics (not just Apple's). Daisey asked vital questions about reconciling one's consumerist predilections with the knowledge that they fuel low wages, inhumane working conditions, and massive multinational corporate profits. After a popular hour-long episode of Daisey's show aired on *This American Life*, the WBEZ Chicago production team belatedly investigated their doubts regarding the veracity of some of his claims. The discovery that he had fabricated parts of his story led to an entirely new episode about the responsibilities of journalists to fact-check and the responsibilities that artists have when they claim their work is research-based truth. The narrators—as well as Grillo, Fo and Rame, and artists such as Daisey—walk a line between art and activism, where narrators linger but tend to privilege the ethical and communal bonds of their art. Their works have political consequences, and their empowering of ordinary people is a political act in and of itself, but they are not campaigning for themselves or for a party or even the service of any particular agenda. They raise awareness and pose questions, offering their work to others who can pursue policy changes if they so desire.

Considering the pieces that the narrators keep in their repertory and those that they have newly created, the main characteristics that the theater of narration developed largely from the work of Laboratorio Teatro Settimo continue to form its defining features. The formal ones—actor-author, solo performer, minimalist mise-en-scène—are easy to recognize. Those attributes that truly define the genre—autoethnography and the narrator as cultural laborer, the regional linguistics and gradations of orality, local territories and the notions of community that reflect in the performance space—are more subtly woven into the practice's fabric. These concepts and techniques shift the focus from dominant traditional narratives to the experiences of individuals and what they can reveal about society in its many layers and infinite complexities. Contextualizing the genre's origins with Teatro Settimo and the long 1970s further sheds light on the practice's proximity to microhistory and how its founders developed their own theories about who and what constitutes the making of history. At the end of an evening's performance, an audience member might reflect on what was once a familiar narrative, but slowly, perhaps in retelling it to someone else, their own memories intermingle. Now there is a new account of a familiar story, which includes the spectator's personal history layered onto that of the narrator's. The narrator has given a popular history back to the populace. The familiar past event morphs once more, forming the newest interpretation. Within this most recent version lingers the dawning awareness that no one *storia* is final.

NOTES

Introduction

1. Laura Curino and Gabriele Vacis, *Camillo Olivetti: Alle radici di un sogno* (Milan: Baldini & Castoldi, 1998), 23. All translations are my own unless otherwise noted.

2. Some of those included indoor and outdoor recreation spaces, cafeterias with notable chefs, libraries, buildings designed by award-winning architects, temporary housing with architectural advice centers for private housing, health care, child care, summer camps, and even cultural hours with some of the nation's leading artists and intellectuals, such as Vittorio Gassman and Pier Paolo Pasolini.

3. More than 3.5 million viewers tuned in to watch this live production, and soon after a transcript of the play published by Paolini and the director Gabriele Vacis by the presitigious Garzanti press topped the country's bestsellers lists for several weeks. Stefano Curti, "A 'Floating' Audience for Marco Paolini's TV Show on Venice History, Sept. 10," *Playbill*, Sept 9, 1998, https://www.playbill.com/article/a-floating-audience-for-marco-paolinis-tv-show-on-venice-history-sept-10-com-77240.

4. The two existing book-length studies on the theater of narration, both in Italian and both consisting of interviews for approximately half of the books, are Gerardo Guccini, *La bottega dei narratori: Storie, laboratori e metodi* (Rome: D. Audino, 2005); and Simone Soriani, *Sulla scena del racconto* (Arezzo: Zona, 2009). Preceding their translation of Marco Baliani's *Corpo di stato*, Nicoletta Marini-Maio and Ellen Nerenberg offer a concise introduction to the theater of narration in English in which they consider briefly history. See Nicoletta Marini-Maio and Ellen Victoria Nerenberg, "Critical Introduction. Corpses and Coups: On Body of State," in *Body of State: The Moro Affair, a Nation Divided*, by Marco Baliani, trans. Nicoletta Marini-Maio, Ellen Victoria Nerenberg, and Thomas Simpson (Madison, NJ: Fairleigh Dickinson University Press, 2012), 1–21.

5. Diana Taylor, *The Archive and the Repertoire: Performing Cultural Memory in the Americas* (Durham, NC: Duke University Press, 2003), 24.

6. Ladurie's studies, which descended from the Annales school, famous for its macro breadth of historical inquiry, is an example of the overlap in macro- and microhistory that seeps through many works of narrative theater. Ladurie rose to international attention with his first major study published in 1966, *Les paysans de Languedoc*, in which he borrows from techniques in the social sciences and psychology to analyze seemingly banal remnants such as copious tax records as a basis for sweeping theories that put agricultural problems in conversation with cultural practices to tell the story of a region over three hundred years. Yet only nine years later, in 1975, he published his best-known study, *Montaillou, village occitan de 1294 à 1324*, which is microhistorical in scope and shares many

commonalities in both technique and subject as Ginzburg's famous *Il formaggio e i vermi*, from just a year later. Emmanuel Le Roy Ladurie, *The Peasants of Languedoc,* trans. John Day (Urbana: University of Illinois Press, 1977); Emmanuel Le Roy Ladurie, *Montaillou: The Promised Land of Error*, trans. Barbara Bray (New York: George Braziller, 2008); Carlo Ginzburg, *The Cheese and the Worms: The Cosmos of a Sixteenth-Century Miller*, trans. John and Anne C. Tedeschi (Baltimore: Johns Hopkins University Press, 2013).

7. I am thinking here of major successes from film classics such as Gillo Pontecorvo's *The Battle of Algiers* (1967) to Gianfranco Rosi's lauded documentary *Fuocoammare* (*Fire at sea*) (2016) and of the many Italian writers (if problematically often referred to as "migrant writers") from Igiaba Scego (born in Rome of Somali descent) to Amara Lakhous (born in Algeria).

8. Marco Paolini, Laura Curino, Marco Baliani, Giuliana Musso, and Davide Enia have all had works nationally televised, while Ascanio Celestini has appeared regularly as a guest on various variety programs, where he often performs vignettes or excerpts from full-length pieces. Regarding weekly magazines, in February 2006 *L'Unità* released six DVDs with each issue under the series Teatro Incivile, organized by the narrator Mario Perrotta and the journal's dance and theater critic, Rossella Battista. The series included DVD versions of plays by narrators including Perrotta, Celestini, Enia, and Musso. In January 2010, *L'Espresso* (in collaboration with the Rome-based newspaper *La Repubblica* as the same company owns both media) released seven plays on DVD, all by Marco Paolini, and then in 2012 released ten issues with works by Ascanio Celestini.

9. Michel de Certeau, *The Writing of History*, trans. Tom Conley (New York: Columbia University Press, 1988), 102.

10. Richard Schechner, *Performance Studies: An Introduction* (London: Routledge, 2013), 28.

11. Schechner, *Performance Studies*, 28.

12. Gail Reekie, "Michel de Certeau and the Poststructuralist Critique of History," *Social Semiotics* 6, no. 1 (1996): 48, https://doi.org/10.1080/10350339609384463.

13. Schechner, *Performance Studies*, 28.

14. Thomas Postlewait refers to these moments as "partial truths [that] can be attained, verified, and justified" and that acknowledge the challenges of historical inquiry. Thomas Postlewait, *The Cambridge Introduction to Theatre Historiography* (Cambridge: Cambridge University Press, 2009), 23; Similarly, Freddie Rokem asserts that "performing history is obviously a hybrid notion—creating a bridge between performance and history—at times it moves closer to the fiction and even allegorical pole . . . and at others closer to the pole of historical accuracy and documentation." Freddie Rokem, *Performing History: Theatrical Representations of the Past in Contemporary Theatre* (Iowa City: University of Iowa Press, 2002), 7.

15. Giuliana Musso, "Nati in casa," in *Senza corpo: Voci dalla nuova scena italiana*, ed. Debora Pietrobono (Rome: Minimum fax, 2009), 17–52.

16. Michel-Rolph Trouillot, *Silencing the Past: Power and the Production of History* (Boston: Beacon, 1995); Marisa J. Fuentes, *Dispossessed Lives: Enslaved Women, Violence, and the Archive* (Philadelphia: University of Pennsylvania Press, 2016).

17. Hayden White, "Introduction: Historical Fiction, Fictional History, and Historical Reality," *Rethinking History* 9, nos. 2–3 (2005): 147, https://doi.org/10.1080/13642520500149061.

18. Rebecca Schneider, *Performing Remains: Art and War in Times of Theatrical Reenactment* (New York: Routledge, 2011), 100, emphasis in the original.

19. Rokem also addresses the topic by combining embodiment with the vital connection between historiography and narrative via the actor. This individual, whom he terms a "hyper-historian," has the ability to meld the imaginative that accompanies creative endeavors with a scientific level of investigation in order to embody a historical figure from the past. Rokem, *Performing History*, 12–13.

20. Saidiya V. Hartman, *Scenes of Subjection: Terror, Slavery, and Self-Making in Nineteenth-Century America* (Oxford: Oxford University Press, 1997).

21. In addition to Certeau and White, see, for example, Keith Jenkins, *Rethinking History* (New York: Routledge, 1991); Beverley C. Southgate, *History Meets Fiction* (New York: Routledge, 2014).

22. Rokem, *Performing History*, 3.

23. The ability to convey a nuanced perspective with the label "the years of lead" is challenging, even if the term was originally coined in German for the purpose of emphasizing weight in order to underline the heaviness of the decade. With the passage of time, translations into Italian and English exaggerate the play on words beyond the original intention. For a more detailed explanation of the term, see Pierpaolo Antonello and Alan O'Leary, *Imagining Terrorism: The Rhetoric and Representation of Political Violence in Italy 1969–2009* (London: Legenda, 2009), 11n1.

24. On January 24, 1966, students met in a general assembly (a fairly new tactic at the time) and decided to strike against a recent top-down decision from Rome that altered the name and length of the sociology degree. See Phil Edwards, *More Work! Less Pay! Rebellion and Repression in Italy, 1972–77* (Oxford: Oxford University Press, 2009), 6–7; M. Klimke and J. Scharloth, *1968 in Europe: A History of Protest and Activism, 1956–1977* (New York: Palgrave Macmillan, 2008), 87–89; Gerd-Rainer Horn, *The Spirit of '68: Rebellion in Western Europe and North America, 1956–1976* (Oxford: Oxford University Press, 2007), 77–81.

25. Between 1969 and 1980 there were 12,690 incidents of terrorist violence in Italy, with 597 terrorist groups engaging in radical activity. Charles Townshend, *Terrorism: A Very Short Introduction* (Oxford: Oxford University Press, 2011), 68–69.

26. Jonathan Dunnage, *Twentieth-Century Italy: A Social History* (London: Longman, 2002), 172. Rather than what students perceived as the flimsy bandages of the Gui bill, they desired a radical reorganization of the Italian university system that would address various problems: from the technical (such as overcrowding), to the pedagogical (reducing the authority and authoritarian stature of the professoriate), to inadequate funding. Gui's bill offered modest changes such as increasing faculty hiring and opportunities for working-class students, but also proposed to restrict enrollments in several disciplines in order to solve the overcrowding problem, perhaps its most controversial measure. See also Stuart J. Hilwig, *Italy and 1968: Youthful Unrest and Democratic Culture* (Basingstoke, UK: Palgrave Macmillan, 2009), 14–15; Stuart J. Hilwig, "The Revolt against the Establishment: Students versus the Press in West Germany and Italy,"

in *1968: The World Transformed*, ed. Carole Fink, Philipp Gassert, and Detlef Junker (Cambridge: Cambridge University Press, 1998), 338–40.

27. For a thorough understanding of this season, see Robert Lumley, *States of Emergency: Cultures of Revolt in Italy from 1968 to 1978* (London: Verso, 1990), 207–41.

28. For a critical investigation of the Bologna massacre and other organized acts of violence, see Anna Cento Bull, *Italian Neofascism: The Strategy of Tension and the Politics of Nonreconciliation* (New York: Berghahn Books, 2012).

29. Films such as *Buongiorno notte* (dir. Marco Bellocchio, 2003, loosely based on the 1998 memoirs of Anna Laura Braghetti, the *ex-brigatista*, or ex-member of the Red Brigades, the far left group that frequently resorted to violent actions), *La meglio gioventù* (dir. Marco Tullio Giordana, 2003), and *Romanzo criminale* (dir. Michele Placido, 2005, based on the 2002 novel by Giancarlo de Cataldo) not only deal with specific terrorist events, from kidnapping to bombings, but also contemplate their political ramifications.

30. The former refers to an attempt to control the masses through the use of fear, propaganda, and disinformation and is largely associated with right-wing institutions. The latter reflects the attempt to find common ground between the major parties of the Christian Democrats, which was the dominant party in postwar Italy until it disbanded in 1994, and the Italian Communist Party (PCI). Aldo Moro, the prime minister who was kidnapped and eventually assassinated by the Red Brigades in 1978 and who is the subject of numerous works, including Marco Baliani's *Body of State*, was heavily involved in these talks, but when he was kidnapped they eventually crumbled. Antonio Negri argues that the PCI suffered considerably due to these two situations, since party members fractured ties with social movements as they became politically marginalized. Eventually the party itself morphed into the bureaucratic power-hungry organization that it never intended to be. In retrospect, it is clear that these events contributed to the end of the radical Left more broadly: to communism both as a viable political party and a philosophy, which is particularly significant in Italy because the PCI was the strongest communist party in postwar Western Europe. See Antonio Negri, "Reviewing the Experience of Italy in the 1970s," *Le monde diplomatique*, n.d., http://mondediplo.com/1998/09/11negri.

31. Anna Cento Bull and Adalgisa Giorgio, eds., *Speaking Out and Silencing: Culture, Society and Politics in Italy in the 1970s* (London: Legenda, 2006); Ruth Glynn, "Trauma on the Line: Terrorism and Testimony in the *anni di piombo*," in *The Value of Literature in and after the Seventies: The Case of Italy and Portugal*, ed. Monica Jansen and Paula Jordão (Utrecht: University of Utrecht Igitur Publishing and Archiving, 2006), 317–35.

32. For a thorough examination on media representation of women during the Berlusconi era, see Danielle Hipkins, "'Whore-Ocracy': Show Girls, the Beauty Trade-Off, and Mainstream Oppositional Discourse in Contemporary Italy," *Italian Studies* 66, no. 3 (November 2011): 413–30. The activist and author Lorella Zanardo has been one of the most visible presences to explore media representation, particularly with the powerful documentary *Il corpo delle donne* (Women's bodies), which she offers free for download in Italian but is also available with subtitles in a number of different languages on the website http://www.ilcorpodelledonne.net/. It is an excellent teaching resource.

33. Enrico Palandri, "The Difficulty of a Historical Perspective on the 1970s," in Cento Bull and Giorgio, *Speaking Out and Silencing*, 119.

34. For a thorough history, including the myths, of this law and the infamous Italian *manicomi*, or insane asylums, see John Foot, *The Man Who Closed the Asylums: Franco Basaglia and the Revolution in Mental Health Care* (London: Verso, 2015).

35. Marco Belpoliti, *Settanta* (Turin: Einaudi, 2010), 287–88; Piero Camporesi, introduction to *La scienza in cucina e l'arte di mangiar bene*, by Pellegrino Artusi, 2nd ed. (Turin: Einaudi, 2001), xv–lxxviii; Pellegrino Artusi, *La scienza in cucina e l'arte di mangiar bene* (Turin: Einaudi, 1970); Alberto Asor Rosa, *Scrittori e popolo* (Rome: Samonà e Savelli, 1966).

36. Giovanni Levi, "On Microhistory," in *New Perspectives on Historical Writing*, ed. Peter Burke (Cambridge, UK: Polity, 1991), 93–94.

37. Lawrence Stone, "The Revival of Narrative: Reflections on a New Old History," *Past and Present*, no. 85 (1979): 3–24. Notable responses or later references to the article include Carlo Ginzburg, "[The Possibilities of the Past]: A Comment," *Journal of Interdisciplinary History* 12, no. 2 (1981): 277–78; James West Davidson, "The New Narrative History: How New? How Narrative?," *Reviews in American History* 12, no. 3 (1984): 322–34; E. J. Hobsbawm, "The Revival of Narrative: Some Comments," *Past and Present*, no. 86 (1980): 3–8; Sarah Maza, "Stories in History: Cultural Narratives in Recent Works in European History," *American Historical Review* 101, no. 5 (1996): 1493–515.

38. Belpoliti, *Settanta*, 295–96.

39. Carlo Ginzburg, "Microhistory: Two or Three Things That I Know about It," trans. John and Anne C. Tedeschi, *Critical Inquiry* 20, no. 1 (1993): 22, http://www.jstor.org/stable/1343946.

40. This particular meeting with Celestini, on April 27, 2018, occurred shortly before a performance of his *Pueblo* at the Teatro Franco Parenti in Milan. By the time we walked around the corner from the theater to a café, there was only an hour or so left before curtain, and I was concerned that we would not have much time to visit. In disbelief I kept looking at the clock on my phone that was recording the interview as the minutes brought us closer and closer to showtime. People on their way to see the performance passed us on the street, laughing, pointing, asking to shake his hand. As I continued to inquire if it was okay with him that we were cutting it so close, he assured me not to worry. At some point I understood why: he was using our conversation as the warm-up. All of the stories he told me, the way he told them hopping along the tangents, was how he practiced. He explicitly stated that his rehearsal method consisted of talking for hours just like that, sitting in a chair in a room. Now he was rehearsing in front of me, and soon he would perform for an entire audience in a very similar register, loosely following his script.

41. In addition to Taylor and Schneider, see, for example, Anthony Jackson and Jenny Kidd, *Performing Heritage: Research, Practice and Innovation in Museum Theatre and Live Interpretation* (Manchester: Manchester University Press, 2011); Mike Pearson and Michael Shanks, *Theatre/Archaeology* (London: Routledge, 2001); Deirdre Heddon, "Performing the Archive Following in the Footsteps," *Performance Research* 7, no. 4 (January 1, 2002): 64–77, https://doi.org/10.1080/13528165.2002.10871893. From historians' perspective, see Carolyn Steedman, *Dust: The Archive and Cultural History* (New Brunswick, NJ:

Rutgers University Press, 2002); Antoinette Burton, *Archive Stories: Facts, Fictions, and the Writing of History* (Durham, NC: Duke University Press, 2006).

42. Elin Diamond, "Performance in the Archives," *Theatre History Studies* 28 (2008): 22–23.

43. Juliet Guzzetta, "At Work, at Home: Women, Labor, and Laura Curino's Olivetti Plays," in "From Otium and Occupatio to Work and Labor in Italian Culture," special issue, *Annali d'Italianistica* 32 (2014): 291–306.

44. Samuel Ravengai, "Performing the Archive and Re-archiving Memory: Magnet Theatre's Museum and Reminiscence Theatre," *South African Theatre Journal* 28, no. 3 (September 2, 2015): 219, https://doi.org/10.1080/10137548.2015.1046398.

45. Pier Giorgio Nosari, "I sentieri dei raccontatori di storie: Ipotesi per una mappa del teatro di narrazione," *Prove di Drammaturgia* 1 (2004): 11–12.

Chapter 1

1. Elin Diamond, *Performance and Cultural Politics* (London: Routledge, 1996), 1.

2. Gerardo Guccini, "Teatro di narrazione," *Hystrio* 1 (January 2005): 3–4.

3. While most European theaters are historically author-centered, Italian theater is largely actor-centered with the exception of a few important playwrights such as Carlo Goldoni and Luigi Pirandello. The theater of narration extends the long-standing tradition of the actor-author in Italy, best exemplified in the commedia dell'arte, demonstrating how those populist roots assumed an especially strong political potency in loosening the grip of directors who had assumed much authority in twentieth-century Italian theater.

4. See Guccini, "Teatro di narrazione"; Simone Soriani, "Mistero buffo, dal varietà al teatro di narrazione," in *Coppia d'arte: Dario Fo e Franca Rame con dipinti, testimonianze e dichiarazioni inedite*, ed. Concetta D'Angeli and Simone Soriani (Pisa: Pisa University Press, 2006), 117–22. Along with his portrayals of the *zanni* (servant characters in the commedia dell'arte), and excerpts from Angelo Beolco (*il Ruzzante*), Fo also reinvented aspects of *giullarata* or *giullaresca* for a modern audience. Ronald Scott Jenkins, *Dario Fo and Franca Rame: Artful Laughter* (New York: Aperture, 2001), xi. *Giullarata*, a derivative of the Latin *ioculator* (joker, jester) is a popular style from the Middle Ages, where the *giullari* were itinerant players, mostly of the lower classes, who worked within oral traditions. They included a wide variety of performers, such as musicians, dancers, acrobats, jugglers, and actors. Traditions of the *giullari padani* (from the Po region) often created pieces that were meant to be told by one person. Soriani, "Mistero buffo, dal varietà al teatro di narrazione," 108.

5. Elisabetta Povoledo, "Italian Monologues with a Message," *International Herald Tribune*, March 16, 2007.

6. Oliviero Ponte di Pino, *Il nuovo teatro italiano, 1975–1988: La ricerca dei gruppi, materiali e documenti* (Florence: La Casa Usher, 1988), 7.

7. Elisabetta Povoledo, "In Italy, Memories Are Made of This," *New York Times*, September 12, 2005, sec. Arts, https://www.nytimes.com/2005/09/12/arts/in-italy-memories-are-made-of-this.html.

8. Antonio Scuderi, "Dario Fo and Oral Tradition: Creating a Thematic Context," *Oral Tradition* 15, no. 1 (March 2000): 27.

9. Fo and Rame also translated this "everydayness" in alternative performance spaces such as piazzas, in addition to theaters, nodding to forms of *teatro minore* ("minor theater" or "secondary theater" such as circuses, popular farces, and street theaters) that stress an engagement with the popular. This is another commonality with Teatro Settimo and narrators, but not necessarily attributable to Fo and Rame.

10. Mario B. Mignone, "Dario Fo, Jester of the Italian Stage," *Italian Quarterly* 85 (Summer 1981): 47.

11. Soriani, "Mistero buffo, dal varietà al teatro di narrazione," 104. See also Simone Soriani, *Dario Fo: Dalla commedia al monologo, 1959–1969* (Pisa: Titivillus, 2007).

12. It is particularly egregious that although Fo contributed to some aspects of the writing or editing of Rame's several monologue plays about women (translated in *Female Parts* and *A Woman Alone and Other Plays*), he is regularly credited as the sole author.

13. For a more detailed analysis of this moment, see Juliet Guzzetta, "The Lasting Theatre of Dario Fo and Franca Rame," *Theatre History Studies* 37, no. 1 (2018): 257–77, https://doi.org/10.1353/ths.2018.0013.

14. Franca Rame and Dario Fo, *Tutta casa, letto e chiesa* (Milan: F. R. La comune, 1981); Dario Fo and Franca Rame, *Female Parts: One Woman Plays* (London: Pluto Press, 1981); Franca Rame and Dario Fo, *A Woman Alone and Other Plays* (London: Methuen Drama, 1991).

15. Jerzy Grotowski and Eugenio Barba, *Towards a Poor Theatre* (New York: Routledge, 2002), 18–19.

16. Guccini, "Teatro di narrazione," 5.

17. Gabriele Vacis, *Awareness: Dieci giorni con Jerzy Grotowski* (Milan: BUR, 2002), 5.

18. Teatro Odin, "Transcript from Televised Interview of 'Un'ora con Jerzy Grotowski,'" January 5, 1976, box 1976, Laura Curino Private Collections (*hereafter* LCPC), Settimo Torinese, Turin.

19. Anna Stomeo, *Intrecci: Teatro-educazione–new media* (Lecce: Amaltea Edizioni, 2006), 109.

20. For information on this movement in France, see "Formations des animateurs," *Association Technique pour l'Action Culturelle (ATAC)* 74 (February 1976); Raymond Toraille, *L'animation pedagogique* (Paris: Éditions Esf, 1973); Frédérique Letourneux, *Les métiers de l'animation* (Paris: L'Étudiant, 2007).

21. Stomeo, *Intrecci*, 115.

22. Gian Renzo Morteo and Anna Sagna, *L'animazione come propedeutica al teatro* (Turin: Giappichelli, 1977), 3, 5.

23. Carol Martin, *Theatre of the Real* (London: Palgrave Macmillan, 2013).

24. Ryan Claycomb, "(Ch)Oral History, Documentary Theatre, the Communal Subject and Progressive Politics," *Journal of Dramatic Theory and Criticism* 17, no. 2 (2003): 110.

25. Rokem, *Performing History*, 3.

26. Gary Fisher Dawson, *Documentary Theatre in the United States: An Historical Survey and Analysis of Its Content, Form, and Stagecraft* (Westport, CT: Greenwood, 1999), 162.

27. Claycomb, "(Ch)Oral History," 96.

28. Gerardo Guccini and Claudio Meldolesi, "Editoriale: L'arcipelago della 'nuova performance epica,'" *Prove di Drammaturgia* 10, no. 1 (2004): 3–4.

29. Gerardo Guccini, "Recitare la nuova performance epica," *Acting Archives Review: Rivista di studi sull'attore e la recitazione* 1, no. 2 (2011): 65–67. For an in-depth study of nonprofessional actors who perform, see Ulrike Garde and Meg Mumford, *Theatre of Real People: Diverse Encounters at Berlin's Hebbel Am Ufer and Beyond* (London: Bloomsbury Methuen Drama, 2016).

30. Laboratorio Teatro Settimo, "Laboratorio Teatro Settimo" (1977), box 1977, LCPC.

31. Fabio Ugolini, "Settimo Torinese: Quarant'anni fa il Laboratorio Teatro Settimo," *12alle12*, April 9, 2014, https://12alle12.it/settimo-torinese-quarantanni-fa-il-laboratorio-teatro-settimo-56452.

32. Ugolini, "Settimo Torinese."

33. Ugolini, "Settimo Torinese."

34. Laboratorio Teatro Settimo, "Qual'é la storia del Laboratorio Teatro Settimo?" (1982), box 1982, LCPC.

35. Gabriele Vacis, "Il disegno e la casa," *Prove di Drammaturgia* 1 (March 1996), https://archivi.dar.unibo.it/files/muspe/wwcat/period/pdd/num03/num03.html. All issues of this journal from 1995–2007 are available at https://archivi.dar.unibo.it/files/muspe/wwcat/period/pdd/annate.html.

36. Vacis, "Il disegno e la casa."

37. Alessandro Portelli, *The Order Has Been Carried Out: History, Memory, and Meaning of a Nazi Massacre in Rome* (New York: Palgrave Macmillan, 2003), 15.

38. Gerardo Guccini, "Lettera a Laboratorio Teatro Settimo sull'esplorazione e le carte," *Prove di Drammaturgia* 1 (March 1996), https://archivi.dar.unibo.it/files/muspe/wwcat/period/pdd/num03/num03.html.

39. Roberto Canziani, *Dedica: Laboratorio Teatro Settimo* (Pordenone: Associazione Provinciale per la Prosa, 1995), 14.

40. Schneider, *Performing Remains*, 6, emphasis in the original.

41. Schneider, *Performing Remains*, 6–7.

42. Ginzburg, "Microhistory," 21–22.

43. Levi, "On Microhistory," 106.

44. Vacis, "Il disegno e la casa."

45. Matti Peltonen, "Clues, Margins, and Monads: The Micro-Macro Link in Historical Research," *History and Theory* 40, no. 3 (2001): 349, http://www.jstor.org/stable/2677970.

46. Carlo Ginzburg, "Clues: Morelli, Freud, and Sherlock Holmes," in *The Sign of Three: Dupin, Holmes, Pierce*, ed. Umberto Eco and Thomas Albert Sebeok (Bloomington: Indiana University Press, 1983), 109; translation modified to change "symptoms" to "signs." For the Italian, see Carlo Ginzburg, "Spie: Radici di un paradigma indiziario," in *Crisi della ragione*, ed. Aldo Giorgio Gargani (Turin: Einaudi, 1979), 28.

47. Ginzburg, "Microhistory," 28, 33.

48. Vacis, "Il disegno e la casa."

49. Laboratorio Teatro Settimo, "LTU3: Appunti per l'avvio del terzo laboratorio di trasformazione urbana. La ricerca storica" (1981), box 1981, LCPC.

50. Laboratorio Teatro Settimo, "LTU3."

51. Laura Curino, "La vicenda del testo," *Prove di Drammaturgia* 1 (March 1996), https://archivi.dar.unibo.it/files/muspe/wwcat/period/pdd/num03/03.html.
52. Hayden White, "Interpretation in History," *New Literary History* 4, no. 2 (1973): 281, http://www.jstor.org/stable/468478.
53. White, "Introduction," 149.
54. White, "Introduction," 147–48.
55. Though he rarely returns to them, those first plays include *Cicoria: In fondo al mondo, Pasolini* (1998–99), written by, directed by, and starring Celestini and Gaetano Ventriglia; and the *Milleuno* trilogy: *Baccalà, il racconto dell'acqua* (1999), *Vita morte e miracoli* (1999), and *La fine del mondo* (2000), all written by, directed by, and with Celestini.
56. Ascanio Celestini, *Radio clandestina: Memoria delle Fosse Ardeatine* (Rome: Donzelli, 2005), 24.
57. Alessandro Portelli, "Preface," in Celestini, *Radio clandestina*, 9–17.
58. Levi, "On Microhistory," 93.
59. Celestini, *Radio clandestina*, 38.
60. Celestini, *Radio clandestina*, 51.
61. For a meticulously researched account of this history, see Ian Campbell, *The Massacre of Debre Libanos: Ethiopia 1937. The Story of One of Fascism's Most Shocking Atrocities* (Addis Ababa: Addis Ababa University Press, 2014).
62. Povoledo, "Italian Monologues with a Message."
63. Celestini, *Radio clandestina*, 74.
64. Alessandro Portelli, *The Death of Luigi Trastulli and Other Stories: Form and Meaning in Oral History* (Albany: State Univesity of New York Press, 1991), 51.
65. Celestini, *Radio clandestina*, 90, 91.
66. Celestini, *Radio clandestina*, 92.

Chapter 2

1. Kevin Landis and Suzanne Macaulay, *Cultural Performance: Ethnographic Approaches to Performance Studies* (London: Palgrave Macmillan, 2017), 38.
2. Morteo and Sagna, *L'animazione come propedeutica*, 5.
3. Curino and Vacis, *Camillo Olivetti*, 23, emphasis in the original.
4. Morteo and Sagna, *L'animazione come propedeutica*, 5.
5. Morteo and Sagna, *L'animazione come propedeutica*, 6.
6. Morteo and Sagna, *L'animazione come propedeutica*, 9.
7. Ponte di Pino, *Il nuovo teatro italiano, 1975–1988*, 7.
8. Ronald Scott Jenkins, preface to *Body of State: The Moro Affair, a Nation Divided*, by Marco Baliani, trans. Nicoletta Marini-Maio, Ellen Victoria Nerenberg, and Thomas Simpson (Madison, NJ: Fairleigh Dickinson University Press, 2012), ix.
9. Rokem, *Performing History*, 13.
10. The influence of factory worker protests as one powerful engine of revolt during much of the 1960s and into the 1970s, with the "hot autumn" of 1969 perhaps the apex, cannot be overstated. Notably, it held enormous influence both on a practical scale, in terms of bodies protesting on the street, and for the philosophical advances in thought that it inspired in various leftist Marxist movements, including workerism and autonomism, that attracted philosophers such as Antonio Negri. Mario Tronti's *Operai e capitale* (Workers and Capital)

(Turin: Einaudi, 1966) was particularly influential, as was the journal that he began with Raniero Panzieri and Romano Alquati (who later wrote critiques of the Olivetti corporation), *Quaderni Rossi* (Red notebooks) and later on his own, the journal *Classe Operaia* (Working class).

11. David Forgacs, *Italian Culture in the Industrial Era, 1880–1980: Cultural Industries, Politics, and the Public* (Manchester: Manchester University Press, 1990), 130.

12. Lumley, *States of Emergency*, 112–15.

13. Jean Baudrillard, *Fatal Strategies*, trans. Philip Beitchman and W. G. J. Niesluchowski (London: Semiotexte/Pluto, 1990).

14. Jennifer Burns, "A Leaden Silence? Writers' Responses to the *anni di piombo*," in Cento Bull and Giorgio, *Speaking Out and Silencing*, 89. For further articles on interpretations of violence surrounding Moro see Antonello and O'Leary, *Imagining Terrorism*; Ruth Glynn and Giancarlo Lombardi, *Remembering Aldo Moro: The Cultural Legacy of the 1978 Kidnapping and Murder* (London: Legenda, 2012).

15. Alessandro Portelli, *The Battle of Valle Giulia: The Art of Dialogue in Oral History* (Madison: University of Wisconsin Press, 1997), 232–33.

16. Portelli, *The Battle of Valle Giulia*, 362–63.

17. Vincenzo Binetti, "Marginalità e appartenenza: La funzione dell'intellettuale tra sfera pubblica e privato nell'Italia del dopoguerra," *Italica* 74, no. 3 (1997): 360.

18. Monica Francioso, "Impegno and Ali Baba: Celati, Calvino, and the Debate on Literature in the 1970s," *Italian Studies* 64, no. 1 (2009): 109–10.

19. Lumley, *States of Emergency*, 63.

20. Ernst Bloch, *Traces*, trans. Anthony A. Nassar (Stanford, CA: Stanford University Press, 2006), 6.

21. Marco Baliani, Alessandra Ghiglione, and Fabrizio Fiaschini, *Marco Baliani: Racconti a teatro* (Florence: Loggia de' Lanzi, 1998), 37, 75.

22. Edward M. Bruner, "Experience and Expressions," in *The Anthropology of Experience*, ed. Victor Witter Turner and Edward M. Bruner (Urbana: University of Illinois Press, 1986), 3.

23. Bruner, "Experience and Expressions," 9.

24. Craig Gingrich-Philbrook, "Autoethnography's Family Values: Easy Access to Compulsory Experiences," *Text and Performance Quarterly* 25, no. 4 (October 2005): 299, https://doi.org/10.1080/10462930500362445.

25. For an initial consultation of the well-studied field of autoethnography, see Norman K. Denzin, *Interpretive Autoethnography*, 2nd ed. (London: Sage, 2014), https://doi.org/10.4135/9781506374697; Robin M. Boylorn, Mark P. Orbe, and Carolyn Ellis, *Critical Autoethnography: Intersecting Cultural Identities in Everyday Life* (Walnut Creek, CA: Left Coast Press, 2013); Tami Spry, "Performing Autoethnography: An Embodied Methodological Praxis," *Qualitative Inquiry* 7, no. 6 (2001): 706–32, https://doi.org/10.1177/107780040100700605.

26. Barbara Myerhoff, "'Life Not Death in Venice': Its Second Life," in Turner and Bruner, *The Anthropology of Experience*, 261.

27. Giuseppe "Peppino" Impastato (1948–78, Cinisi, Palermo) was a political activist who fought local Sicilian mafia crime through political and cultural

means (such as public shaming on the radio) and fought for the rights of peasants and the unemployed. He was murdered by the Mafia on the same day that Moro's body was discovered.

28. Bruner, "Experience and Expressions," 12.

29. Marco Baliani, *Body of State: The Moro Affair, a Nation Divided*, trans. Nicoletta Marini-Maio, Ellen Victoria Nerenberg, and Thomas Simpson (Madison, NJ: Fairleigh Dickinson University Press, 2012), 27.

30. Baliani, *Body of State*, 27.

31. Baliani, *Body of State*, 31–32.

32. The "strategy of tension" refers to the ways in which the Far Right, possibly including parties in both the Italian and foreign governments such as the United States who feared leftist platforms, manipulated and controlled the public through panic and terror especially during attacks such as the 1969 bombing of Piazza Fontana in Milan.

33. Bruner, "Experience and Expressions," 4.

34. Victor Turner, "Dewey, Dilthey, and Drama: An Essay in the Anthropology of Experience," in Turner and Bruner, *The Anthropology of Experience*, 36.

35. Edward M. Bruner, "Ethnography as Narrative," in Turner and Bruner, *The Anthropology of Experience*, 153.

36. D. Soyini Madison, *Critical Ethnography: Method, Ethics, and Performance* (Thousand Oaks, CA: Sage, 2011), 10, emphasis in the original.

37. Richard Schechner, "Magnitudes of Performance," in Turner and Bruner, *The Anthropology of Experience*, 363.

38. Laura Curino, Roberto Tarasco, and Gabriele Vacis, *Passione* (Novara: Interlinea, 1998), 59.

39. Elements of this analysis are revised from an earlier article. See Juliet F. Guzzetta, "A Presentation of Herself: Laura Curino's Passions in Everyday Life," *Spunti e Ricerche* 25 (2011): 116–30.

40. Erving Goffman, *The Presentation of Self in Everyday Life* (Garden City, NY: Doubleday, 1959), 238–39.

41. Lynn C. Miller, Jacqueline Taylor, and M. Heather Carver, *Voices Made Flesh: Performing Women's Autobiography* (Madison: University of Wisconsin Press, 2003), 4.

42. Ryan Claycomb, *Lives in Play: Autobiography and Biography on the Feminist Stage* (Ann Arbor: University of Michigan Press, 2012), 2.

43. Miller, Taylor, and Carver, *Voices Made Flesh*, 4.

44. Madison, *Critical Ethnography*, 5, emphasis in the original.

45. Gingrich-Philbrook, "Autoethnography's Family Values," 299.

46. Gerardo Guccini and Michela Marelli, *Stabat mater: Viaggio alle fonti del teatro di narrazione* (Bologna: Le Ariette Libri, 2004), 14.

47. Della Pollock, *Remembering: Oral History Performance* (New York: Palgrave Macmillan, 2005), 5.

48. Roberto Canziani, "Giuliana Musso, storie di provincia e vite qualunque," *Hystrio*, no. 2 (2014): 52.

49. Martha Rose Beard, "Re-Thinking Oral History—a Study of Narrative Performance," *Rethinking History* 21, no. 4 (October 2, 2017): 531, https://doi.org/10.1080/13642529.2017.1333285.

50. Joan Wallach Scott, foreword to *Autobiography of a Generation: Italy, 1968*, ed. Luisa Passerini, trans. Lisa Erdberg (Hanover, NH: University Press of New England, 1996), xii.
51. Giuliana Musso, "Nati in casa," in *Senza corpo: Voci dalla nuova scena italiana*, ed. Debora Pietrobono (Rome: Minimum fax, 2009), 26.
52. Pollock, *Remembering*, 2, emphasis in the original.
53. Pollock, *Remembering*, 3.
54. Ascanio Celestini, "Il vestito della festa: Dalla fonte orale a una possibile drammaturgia," *Prove di Drammaturgia* 2 (2003): 23.
55. Baliani, *Body of State*, 25.
56. Baliani, *Body of State*, 25.
57. Luisa Passerini, *Storia e soggettività: Le fonti orali, la memoria* (Florence: La Nuova Italia, 1988).
58. Passerini, *Storia e soggettività*, 11–12.
59. Goffman, *The Presentation of Self in Everyday Life*, 128.
60. Musso, "Nati in casa," 48.
61. Musso, "Nati in casa," 49–50.
62. Eugenio Barba, "An Amulet Made of Memory: The Significance of Exercises in the Actor's Dramaturgy," *TDR* 41, no. 4 (1997): 130, http://www.jstor.org/stable/1146664.
63. Gerardo Guccini, "Racconti della memoria: Il teatro di Ascanio Celestini," *Prove di Drammaturgia* 2 (2003): 20–21.
64. Bruner, "Experience and Expressions," 17.

Chapter 3

1. Donatella Fischer, ed., "Introduction," *The Tradition of the Actor-Author in Italian Theatre* (London: Legenda, 2013), 1–2.
2. Paolo Puppa has mentioned the "particular coincidence between the rise of fascism—with its ambition to regulate the masses—and the parallel rise of the director." He notes how directing implies the imposition of a hierarchical strategy on performances, greater prominence to the director's name over the actors, and the prioritizing of disciplined acting over individual performances and decisions. Paolo Puppa, "The Actor-Narrator," in Fischer, *The Tradition of the Actor-Author in Italian Theatre*, 158. Such a rise also coincided with the opening of many state-run theaters throughout Italy, *teatro stabili*, which was in many ways a positive and hard-fought endeavor, though one that similarly resulted in concentrations of power.
3. Hermann W. Haller, *The Other Italy: The Literary Canon in Dialect* (Toronto: University of Toronto Press, 1999), 42–43.
4. Marvin Carlson, *Speaking in Tongues: Languages at Play in the Theatre* (Ann Arbor: University of Michigan Press, 2006), 62–63.
5. Haller, *The Other Italy*, 54, 41.
6. Carlson, *Speaking in Tongues*, 102.
7. Haller, *The Other Italy*, 42.
8. Joseph Farrell and Paolo Puppa, *A History of Italian Theatre* (Cambridge: Cambridge University Press, 2006), 383.
9. Paolo Puppa, *Il teatro dei testi: La drammaturgia italiana nel Novecento* (Turin: UTET libreria, 2003), 206.

10. Eduardo De Filippo is among the most celebrated Italian playwrights (and performers), and he frequently wrote in his native Neopolitan. Nino Martoglio, the Sicilian from Catania, was also heavily influential, especially for Pirandello. See Haller, *The Other Italy*, 39–53.

11. John Haycraft, *Italian Labyrinth: Italy in the 1980s* (London: Secker & Warburg, 1985), 14.

12. Puppa, "The Actor-Narrator," 158.

13. For Emma Dante's Sud Costa Occidentale Enia wrote *Il filo di Penelope* and *Una stanza con nessuno dentro*.

14. For statistics see the Fondazione Iniziative e Studi Multietnicità, https://www.ismu.org/dati-sulle-migrazioni/.

15. In publishing this work with the small Sicilian press Due Punti in a lightweight pocket-sized edition, rather than with the Rome-based Fandango Libri, with whom he published his previous works, Enia supports local business and reaches local inhabitants more directly.

16. Davide Enia, *Mio padre non ha mai avuto un cane* (Palermo: Duepunti Edizioni, 2010), 7.

17. Enia, *Mio padre non ha mai avuto un cane*, 33.

18. Enia, *Mio padre non ha mai avuto un cane*, 33.

19. Enia, *Mio padre non ha mai avuto un cane*, 34.

20. Enia, *Mio padre non ha mai avuto un cane*, 35.

21. Carlson, *Speaking in Tongues*, 63.

22. Angela Albanese, *Identità sotto chiave: Lingua e stile nel teatro di Saverio La Ruina* (Macerata, Italy: Quodlibet, 2017), 54.

23. Saverio La Ruina, *Teatro: Dissonorata, La Borto, Italianesi* (Pisa: Titivillus, 2014), 94–95, 106–7. This publication includes side-by-side translation from the dialect into the Italian. The English translation is my own.

24. La Ruina, *Teatro*, 116–17.

25. Antonio Gramsci, "Angelo Musco," *Avanti!*, March 29, 1918, sec. Cronache teatrale, http://www.quartaparetepress.it/2012/03/30/gramsci-cronache-teatrali-dallavanti-angelo-musco/.

26. Haller, *The Other Italy*, 45–46.

27. Albanese, *Identità sotto chiave*, 65.

28. Puppa, *Il teatro dei testi*, 159.

29. Nosari, "I sentieri dei raccontatori di storie," 11.

30. When scholars credit Dario Fo as the grandfather of the theater of narration, they are often quick to point out a major exception in Fo's hyperanimated theater. Famous for his commedia dell'arte style physicality, Fo is the antithesis of narrators in this respect. Largely remembered for the elasticity of his facial expressions with which he endows his characters, and his full-body physicality of flailing arms and leaping across the stage, he maintains several somatic traditions associated with the court jester and commedia, including dimensions of pantomime and an exaggerated sometimes grotesque performance style. Verging on slapstick at times, he calls on traditions that invoke "vulgar" Roman comedies revised in the commedia dell'arte, where physical expression and spontaneity is relied on so heavily that improvisation takes the place of the script. In these practices, Fo reinstates the hegemony of the action over the word—the opposite

of what the theater of narration offers. In his "Grammelot" language skits, for example, he speaks in complete gibberish but is nonetheless able to communicate an entire story through intonation and physical expression. Words are rendered unnecessary. Fo exemplifies a "pure state" of orality, in which sounds do not accrue to words, yet meaning is still communicable. His rejection of the sacredness of the text also aligns him critically with performance theory, with its embrace of the three-dimensional stage world over a singular focus on the script. While narrators do not favor a script per se, they favor spoken language over physical communication, in some instances barely using their performance spaces. In contrast to Fo, narrators draw attention to the value of the spoken word by helping the listener concentrate their attention free of distraction on what they are saying, not what they are doing. See Simone Soriani, "In principio era Fo," *Hystrio* 1 (January 2005): 17–22; Simone Soriani, "Dario Fo, il teatro di narrazione, la nuova performance epica: Per una genealogia di un 'quasi-genere,'" *Forum Italicum* 39, no. 2 (Fall 2005): 620–48; Antonio Scuderi, "Dario Fo and Performance Theory," *Italian Culture* 12 (1994): 239–46.

31. Giovanni Nencioni, *Di scritto e di parlato: Discorsi linguistici* (Bologna: Zanichelli, 1983). See especially the chapter "Parlato-parlato, parlato-scritto, parlato-recitato," 126–79.

32. Nencioni, *Di scritto e di parlato*, 129.

33. Nencioni, *Di scritto e di parlato*, 131, 133.

34. Soriani, *Dario Fo*, 18. In a dialectical reading, Plato explains in the third book of the *Republic* that tragedy and comedy are wholly imitative types (mimetic), the dithyrambis (hymns sung to Dionysus) wholly narrative (diegetic); and their combination is found in epic poetry.

35. Païvi Mehtonen, "Poetics, Narration, and Imitation: Rhetoric as Ars Applicabilis," in *The Rhetoric of Cicero in Its Medieval and Early Renaissance Commentary Tradition*, ed. Virginia Cox and John O. Ward (Leiden: Brill, 2006), 295.

36. Mehtonen, "Poetics, Narration, and Imitation," 301.

37. Povoledo, "In Italy, Memories Are Made of This."

38. As with many of Paolini's plays such as *I-TIGI Canto per Ustica* (2000), *Gli album* (1987), and *Il sergente* (2004), *Vajont* was not only taped but was also aired uninterrupted on national television across Italy.

39. Luigi Pirandello, *L'umorismo e altri saggi* (Florence: Giunti, 1994).

40. Don L. F. Nilsen, "The Evolution of Stand-Up Comedy: From the Middle Ages to Post-modernism," *Journal of Evolutionary Psychology* 21, nos. 1–2 (2000): 35.

41. Marco Paolini and Gabriele Vacis, *The Story of Vajont*, trans. Thomas Simpson (Boca Raton, FL: Bordighera, 2000), 9.

42. Paolini and Vacis, *The Story of Vajont*, 22, emphasis in the original.

43. Jennifer Burns, "Facts, Fictions, Fakes: Italian Literature in the 1970s," *New Readings* 6 (July 2012): 4.

44. For more on autocoscienza, see Paola Bono and Sandra Kemp, *Italian Feminist Thought: A Reader* (Oxford: Blackwell, 1991), 9–11; Libreria delle donne di Milano, ed., *Non credere di avere dei diritti: La generazione della libertà femminile nell'idea e nelle vicende di un gruppo di donne* (Turin: Rosenberg & Sellier, 1987), 32–35; Nanni Balestrini and Primo Moroni, *L'orda d'oro,*

1968–1977: La grande ondata rivoluzionaria e creativa, politica ed esistenziale (Milan: Feltrinelli, 1997), 479–88.

45. Burns, "Facts, Fictions, Fake," 4–5.

46. Paolini, for example, published *I quaderni del Vajont* (The notebooks of Vajont), a thin volume of materials and progress reports during his research for the production. Baliani wrote an entire book called *Ho cavalcato in groppa ad una sedia* (I rode on the back of a chair) (2010) about his experience creating *Kohlhaas* to coincide with the release of a DVD of the production on its twentieth anniversary.

47. Ascanio Celestini, *Lotta di classe* (Turin: Einaudi, 2009), 228–29.

48. Ascanio Celestini, *I precari non esistono* (Rome: Fandango, 2008), 107.

49. Corrado Augias et al., "Per un nuovo teatro," *Sipario* 247 (November 1966), http://www.trax.it/olivieropdp/mostranew.asp?num=44&ord=4.

50. Antonello and O'Leary, *Imagining Terrorism*, 2.

51. Sergio Zavoli, *La notte della repubblica* (Milan: Mondadori, 1992), 218.

52. Antonello and O'Leary, *Imagining Terrorism*, 2.

53. Luisa Passerini, ed., *Storia orale: Vita quotidiana e cultura materiale delle classi subalterne* (Turin: Rosenberg & Sellier, 1978), vii–viii.

54. Luisa Passerini, *Torino operaia e fascismo* (Bari: Gius. Laterza & Figli SpA, 1984), 14–16.

55. Passerini, *Torino operaia e fascismo*, 16.

56. Laboratorio Teatro Settimo, "LTU3."

57. Ginzburg, "Clues," 24.

58. Massimo Veneziani, *Controinformazione: Stampa alternativa e giornalismo d'inchiesta dagli anni Sessanta a oggi* (Rome: Castelvecchi, 2006), 43.

59. Dario Fo, *Mistero buffo: Giullarata popolare* (Verona: Bertani, 1977), 5. It is noteworthy that in the 2003 edition *grottesco* was replaced with *comico* ("comic" instead of "grotesque") and *popolo* with *classi inferiori* ("lower classes" instead of "the people"). Franca Rame is also added as the editor, suggesting that these changes might have been hers, though she was likely involved with earlier editions just not as prominently recognized. Dario Fo, *Mistero buffo: Giullarata popolare*, ed. Franca Rame (Turin: Einaudi, 2003).

60. Walter Benjamin, "The Storyteller: Reflections on the Works of Nikolai Leskov," in *Illuminations: Essays and Reflections*, ed. Hannah Arendt, trans. Harry Zohn (New York: Schocken, 1969), 83–109.

61. Veneziani, *Controinformazione*, 43.

62. Burns, "Facts, Fictions, Fake," 2–3.

63. Burns, "Facts, Fictions, Fake," 5.

64. Benjamin, "The Storyteller," 84.

65. Benjamin, "The Storyteller," 86.

66. Marco Baliani, *Corpo di stato: Il delitto Moro* (Milan: Rizzoli, 2003), 64B.

67. Baliani, *Body of State*, 31.

Chapter 4

1. Laboratorio Teatro Settimo, "Cosa sarà il nuovo spettacolo?," January 6, 1976, box 1976, LCPC.

2. Valentina Valentini, *New Theatre in Italy: 1963–2013*, trans. Thomas Simpson (New York: Routledge, 2017), 123.

3. Guccini and Marelli, *Stabat mater*, 19.

4. Michel Foucault, "Of Other Spaces," trans. Jay Miskowiec, *Diacritics* 16 (Spring 1986): 24. Foucault's idea leads to an understanding of theater in general as a space that plays the unreal as though it were real, and indeed he acknowledges that a heterotopia is "capable of juxtaposing in a single real space, several sites that are in themselves incompatible," which is what theater does when it presumes space anywhere other than a theater ("Of Other Spaces," 25). For an extensive genealogy of Foucault's thinking on heterotopia and analysis of its key features, see Joanne Tompkins, *Theatre's Heterotopias: Performance and the Cultural Politics of Space* (London: Palgrave Macmillan, 2014), 20–24.

5. Tompkins, *Theatre's Heterotopias*, 1, emphasis in the original.

6. Tompkins, *Theatre's Heterotopias*, 3.

7. Michel Foucault, *Power/Knowledge: Selected Interviews and Other Writings, 1972–1977*, trans. Colin Gordon (Brighton, UK: Harvester, 1980), 38.

8. Lizbeth Goodman and Gabriella Giannachi, "A Theatre for Urban Renewal," *New Theatre Quarterly* 7, no. 25 (1991): 27–28, https://doi.org/10.1017/S0266464X00005169.

9. Portions from this discussion were previously published. See Guzzetta, "At Work, at Home."

10. Laboratorio Teatro Settimo, *Theatre's Heterotopias*, box 1978 (1978), LCPC.

11. Curino and Vacis, *Camillo Olivetti*, 35–36, emphasis in the original.

12. Patrizia Bonifazio and Paolo Scrivano, *Olivetti Builds: Modern Architecture in Ivrea* (Milan: Skira, 2001), 23.

13. Laura Curino and Gabriele Vacis, *Adriano Olivetti: Il sogno possibile* (Milan: IPOC, 2010), 43.

14. Francesco Novara, Renato Rozzi, and Roberta Garruccio, *Uomini e lavoro alla Olivetti* (Milan: Mondadori, 2005), 22.

15. Elisabetta Bini, Ferdinando Fasce, and Toni Muzi Falconi, "The Origins and Early Developments of Public Relations in Post-War Italy, 1945–1960," *Journal of Communication Management* 15, no. 3 (2011): 215. The autonomist thinker Romano Alquati, who was influential in the discourses on workerism, particularly in Piedmont, embraced a "practice of inquiry" with Olivetti employees regarding their workplace experiences. The idea behind the practice is that no one would know more about capitalist exploitation than the workers themselves, so they should be the ones to articulate it. This study led Alquati to question the fundamental differences of working for this social employer (Olivetti) with respect to other companies, such as Fiat. For a helpful overview on the practice of inquiry, see Asad Haider and Salar Mohandesi, "Workers' Inquiry: A Genealogy," *Viewpoint Magazine* 3 (2013), http://viewpointmag.com/2013/09/27/workers-inquiry-a-genealogy/#fn1–2809. In a similar gesture to Alquati's practice of inquiry, three scholars interviewed former Olivetti workers at the turn of the twenty-first century about their experiences in the factories. While the former employees express gratitude and loyalty to Olivetti, they thinly mask an undercurrent that questions the potentially repressive aspects of the company's widely perceived cultural and intellectual munificence. Some of them speculate that the in-house labor union, Autonomia Aziendale, was designed to create distance from more working-class organizations that might promote class conflict just at the

moment when the work of a new generation of foundational leftist intellectuals including Alquati, Antonio Negri, Renzo Panzieri, and Mario Tronti was taking shape. For the interviews, see Novara, Rozzi, and Garruccio, *Uomini e lavoro*. Special thanks to Jim Carter for discussions regarding the Olivetti Company.

16. Only four years later in 1964, the Olivettis lost their majority share when they sold the company to a holding group of various Italian conglomerates including Fiat, Pirelli, and Mediobanca, who shared control with Adriano's eldest son, Roberto. Additionally, they sold the most promising wing altogether, the electronics division where they had begun developing mainframe computers, to General Electric.

17. Laboratorio Teatro Settimo, "Fase 0, 1, 2: Progetto Città Laboratorio" (1980–81), box 1980, LCPC.

18. "A Settimo 'Viva la piazza!,' " *La Stampa*, July 28, 1981, Sera edition, sec. Spettacoli.

19. "Settimo riscopre le piazze," *Gazzetta del Popolo*, July 15, 1981, sec. Cinema, teatro, musica, mostre.

20. R. M., "Cavalcata eroica del teatro in piazza," *Il Manifesto*, July 17, 1981, sec. Le Immagini.

21. P. G., "Che la festa cominici . . . sulla piazza settimese," *La Stampa*, July 21, 1981, Sera ed., sec. Spettacoli.

22. P. G., "Che la festa cominici . . . sulla piazza settimese."

23. "Quando il teatro scende in piazza e la trasforma," *La Stampa*, July 16, 1982, Sera ed., sec. Spettacoli.

24. "Quando il teatro scende in piazza e la trasforma."

25. Laboratorio Teatro Settimo, "Atélier di Cultura Teatrale" (1982), Correspondence, box 1982, LCPC.

26. Landis and Macaulay, *Cultural Performance*, 38.

27. For an insightful study on participatory theater that considers mimesis, methexis, and communitas, see Samy Azouz, "Amiri Baraka's Participatory and Ceremonial Theatre: From Mimesis to Methexis," *Journal of Dramatic Theory and Criticism* 29, no. 2 (2015): 25–41, https://doi.org/10.1353/dtc.2015.0002.

28. To this extent, their notions of community call to mind Giorgio Agamben's theorization of uprisings, with the absence of specific demands other than to combat authoritarianism. Though the narrators and early Settimo artists were less interested in discussions of identity than Agamben was, their postmodern inclination toward an open scheme calls to mind some of his conceptions of community. See Giorgio Agamben, *The Coming Community* trans. Michael Hardt (Minneapolis: University of Minnesota Press, 1993).

29. Victor Witter Turner, *The Ritual Process: Structure and Anti-structure* (Chicago: Aldine, 1969), 95–97.

30. Paul Ginsborg, *Storia d'Italia, 1943–1996: Famiglia, società, stato*, trans. Marcello Florese (Turin: Einaudi, 1998), 340–42.

31. Laboratorio Teatro Settimo, "L'Arcircolo PEPE Pamphlet" (1978), box 1978, LCPC.

32. Settimo, "L'Arcircolo PEPE Pamphlet."

33. Settimo, "L'Arcircolo PEPE Pamphlet."

34. Stomeo, *Intrecci*, 111–12.

35. Turner, *The Ritual Process*, 128.

36. Morteo and Sagna, *L'animazione come propedeutica*, 9.
37. Morteo and Sagna, *L'animazione come propedeutica*, 9.
38. Lodovico Mamprin, Gian Renzo Morteo, and Loredana Perissinotto, *Tre dialoghi sull'animazione* (Rome: Bulzoni, 1977), 16.
39. Stomeo, *Intrecci*, 115.
40. Stomeo, *Intrecci*, 116.
41. Morteo and Sagna, *L'animazione come propedeutica*, 5.
42. Giuliano Scabia, *Marco Cavallo: Da un ospedale psichiatrico la vera storia che ha cambiato il modo di essere del teatro e della cura* (Merano: Edizioni Alpha Beta Verlag, 2011). The title of the project honors Italo Calvino's short story collection *Marcovaldo*, or *The Seasons of the City*, which follows the humble title character as he attempts to navigate an unfamiliar and hostile society.
43. Settimo, "L'Arcircolo PEPE Pamphlet."
44. Goodman and Giannachi, "A Theatre for Urban Renewal," 28.
45. Dario Fo and Vittorio Franceschi, *Compagni senza censura* (Milan: Mazzotta, 1970), 5–6.
46. Soriani, "*Mistero buffo*, dal varietà al teatro di narrazione," 107.
47. Guccini and Marelli, *Stabat mater*, 98.
48. Goodman and Giannachi, "A Theatre for Urban Renewal," 31.
49. Vacis, *Awareness*, 5.
50. Guccini and Marelli, *Stabat mater*, 125–26.
51. Russell King, *The Industrial Geography of Italy* (London: Routledge, 2015), 234.
52. For a rich history of the term and essays seeking to push the boundaries of the definition, see Anna Birch and Joanne Tompkins, *Performing Site-Specific Theatre: Politics, Place, Practice* (London: Palgrave Macmillan, 2012).
53. Bertie Ferdman, *Off Sites: Contemporary Performance beyond Site-Specific* (Carbondale: Southern Illinois University Press, 2018), 5.
54. Amy Cordileone and Rachel Tuggle Whorton, "Site-Specific Theatre: New Perspectives on Pedagogy and Performance," *Research in Drama Education: The Journal of Applied Theatre and Performance* 20, no. 3 (2015): 298, https://doi.org/10.1080/13569783.2015.1059267.
55. Sidney Homan, "Introduction: What It Can Mean to Play Offstage—and Why," in *Playing Offstage: The Theater as a Presence or Factor in the Real World* ed. Sidney Homan (London: Lexington Books, 2017), vii.
56. Jacqueline Martin, Georgia Seffrin, and Rod Wissler, "The Festival Is a Theatrical Event," in *Theatrical Events: Borders, Dynamics, Frames*, ed. Vicki Ann Cremona et al. (Amsterdam: Rodopi, 2004), 97.
57. B. Meersman et al., "Theater Festivals and Their Audiences: A Forum," *Theater* 41, no. 1 (2011): 79, https://doi.org/10.1215/01610775-2010-024.
58. Willmar Sauter, "Introduction: Festival Culture in Global Perspective," *Theatre Research International* 30, no. 3 (October 2005): 238–39, https://doi.org/10.1017/S0307883305001495.
59. As previously discussed in the section on Celestini's "Temps Projects" (chapter 3), in the November 1966 issue of the theater journal *Sipario*, many leading artists from Carmelo Bene and Giuliano Scabia to Carlo Quartucci and even the critic Franco Quadri called for a new theater (*un nuovo teatro*), declaring the 1967 Ivrea festival the place where they would convene to devise fresh

methods and practices. Artists such as Luca Ronconi and Dario Fo did not sign the manifesto, but were present at the Ivrea gathering. The manifesto inspired a cross-disciplinary call to action with signatories from other artists including the musician Sylvano Bussotti and the film directors Marco Bellocchio and Liliana Cavani.

60. Francesco Bono, "Dossier Ivrea 1967 le opinioni di chi partecipò: I ricordi di Ambrosino, Bajini Barba, Calenda, Capriolo, De Berardinis, Fo, Mango, Moscati, Ricci, Ronconi, Scabia, Trionfo," Ateatro: Webzine di cultura teatrale, April 27, 2007, http://www.ateatro.org/mostranotizie2bis.asp?num=108&ord=11.

61. Canziani, *Dedica*, 7.

62. Some examples of these sessions include "theoretical reflections" such as "1968/69 La nascita del progetto 'Animazione' al Teatro Stabile di Torino" by Nuccio Messina (director of the magazine *Primafila*); "Dal teatro all'animazione. Dall'animazione al teatro" by Patrizia Mattioda; and "Il corpo animato" by Claudia Allasia (dance critic). "Il gioco del teatro: Convegno 'l'animazione trent'anni dopo.' Vetrina del teatro ragazzi e giovani," April 21, 1998, box 1996–99, LCPC.

63. "Il gioco del teatro: Vetrina del teatro ragazzi e giovani," April 17, 2000, box 2000, LCPC.

64. "Il gioco del teatro."

65. Erika Fischer-Lichte, "Culture as Performance," *Modern Austrian Literature* 42, no. 3 (2009): 7.

66. The organizers were the Fondazione Nuto Revelli, which preserves and celebrates the works of this local writer, once partisan leader, most famous for collecting oral histories of the people who lived in the mountains outside of Cuneo, especially women, in addition to the Turin-based ACTI Teatri Indipendenti Azione del progetto MigraACTION, and cofinanced largely by the EU's Programma di Cooperazione Territoriale Transfrontaliera Interreg V A Italia-Francia ALCOTRA 2014–2020.

67. Nuto Revelli, *L'anello forte* (Turin: Einaudi, 2018), 61–63.

Chapter 5

1. Guccini, *La bottega dei narratori*, 14.

2. For a helpful overview of these two perspectives, see Steve Dixon, *Digital Performance: A History of New Media in Theater, Dance, Performance Art, and Installation* (Cambridge, MA: MIT Press, 2007).

3. Philip Auslander, *Liveness: Performance in a Mediatized Culture*, 2nd ed. (New York: Routledge, 2008), 1.

4. Auslander, *Liveness*, 6–7.

5. For a succinct introduction to the historical rapport between orality and literacy see Marina Spunta, *Voicing the Word: Writing Orality in Contemporary Italian Fiction* (Bern: Peter Lang, 2004), 13–15.

6. Varazze (ca. 1230–98) was a member of the Dominican order who eventually became archbishop of Genoa. Around 1260 he compiled hagiographies that became very popular in the late medieval ages through the Renaissance.

7. Sharon Wood, "Women and Theater in Italy: Natalia Ginzburg, Franca Rame, and Dacia Maraini," *Romance Languages Annual* 5 (1993): 343.

8. Karen Malpede, *Women in Theatre: Compassion and Hope* (New York: Drama Book Publishers, 1983), 215–17.

9. For a detailed discussion of how *Santa Bàrbera* came to fruition, see Maria Grazia Panigada, "Introduction," in *Santa Bàrbera*, Laura Curino and Roberto Tarasco (Bergamo, Italy: Teatro Donizetti and the Assessorato alla Cultura del Comune di Bergamo, 2008), 9–13.

10. Some of the seminal theater of narration pieces, such as Marco Baliani's *Kohlhaas* (1991), made their national debuts there, and Laboratorio Teatro Settimo also staged several significant productions at the Donizetti, such as *Elementi di struttura del sentimento* (1980). In addition, Curino performed some of her most important pieces there over the years.

11. Lotto's (ca. 1480–1556) frescos depicting Saint Bàrbera's story are in the small chapel known as the Capella dell'Oratrio Suardi.

12. Guccini and Marelli, *Stabat mater*, 13.

13. As in *Santa Bàrbera*, the manifesto often appears unattributed, though based on a copyright record in England from 2001 Maria Pike claims authorship. Little is known about the author. Though some websites now attribute the Raver's Manifesto to Pike, in the past it circulated anonymously.

14. Elaine Aston and Sue-Ellen Case, *Staging International Feminisms* (Basingstoke, UK: Palgrave Macmillan, 2007), 46.

15. Hélène Cixous, "The Laugh of the Medusa," *Signs: Journal of Women in Culture and Society* 1, no. 4 (1976): 877.

16. Libreria delle donne di Milano, *Non credere di avere dei diritti*. This book was translated in English with a much less exciting title though it emphasizes its main theoretical contribution: Milan Women's Bookstore Collective, *Sexual Difference: A Theory of Social-Symbolic Practice* (Bloomington: Indiana University Press, 1990); For a related and brief summary in Italian, see also Serena Palieri, "A proposito di femminismo," *L'Unità*, April 16, 2009, http://www.unita.it/italia/a-proposito-di-femminismo-1.28317.

17. Curino and Tarasco, *Santa Bàrbera*, 35.

18. Curino and Tarasco, *Santa Bàrbera*, 37.

19. Curino and Tarasco, *Santa Bàrbera*, 37.

20. Cixous, "The Laugh of the Medusa," 880.

21. Curino and Tarasco, *Santa Bàrbera*, 42.

22. Cixous, "The Laugh of the Medusa," 881.

23. For a thorough analysis of the relationship between the second and third waves, see Catherine Harnois, "Re-presenting Feminisms: Past, Present, and Future," *NWSA Journal* 20, no. 1 (2008): 120–45.

24. For detailed analyses of feminist intersectionality, a notion that generally questions the relationship between gender and other social categories, especially race and class, see Kimberlé Crenshaw, "Mapping the Margins: Intersectionality, Identity Politics, and Violence against Women of Color," *Stanford Law Review* 43, no. 6 (July 1991): 1241–99, https://doi.org/10.2307/1229039; Devon W. Carbado et al., "Intersectionality: Mapping the Movements of a Theory," *Du Bois Review* 10, no. 2 (Fall 2013): 303–12; Leslie McCall, "The Complexity of Intersectionality," *Signs: Journal of Women in Culture and Society* 30, no. 3 (2005): 1771–1800.

25. Adriana Cavarero, "Towards a Theory of Sexual Difference," in Kemp and Bono, *The Lonely Mirror*, 194, 197.

26. Milly Buonanno, *Italian TV Drama and Beyond: Stories from the Soil, Stories from the Sea* (Chicago: Intellect, 2012), 15.

27. Elena Dagrada, "Television and Its Critics: A Parallel History," in *Italian Cultural Studies: An Introduction*, ed. David Forgacs and Robert Lumley (Oxford: Oxford University Press, 1996), 224.

28. Buonanno, *Italian TV Drama and Beyond*, 15; Aldo Grasso, *Storia della televisione italiana* (Milan: Garzanti, 2000), 862; Damiana Spadaro, *Il teatro in televisione da Eduardo De Filippo a Dario Fo. Il teleteatro: Sviluppo, tecniche e esperienze* (Florence: Firenze Atheneum, 2004), 23. Other canonical works of theater that aired on RAI included plays by Chekhov, Gogol, Ibsen, Molière, O'Neill, and Shaw.

29. Emilio Pozzi, "Prefazione," in *Il teatro in televisione: Regia e registi dalle prime trasmissioni in diretta all'alta definizione*, ed. Giorgio Tabanelli (Rome: RAI ERI, 2002), 15.

30. Grasso, *Storia della televisione italiana*, 861.

31. Pozzi, "Prefazione," 14.

32. Tabanelli, *Il teatro in televisione*, 311–12, 316–17.

33. Grasso, *Storia della televisione italiana*, 861, 865.

34. Spadaro, *Il teatro in televisione*, 9–10.

35. Buonanno, *Italian TV Drama and Beyond*, 14.

36. Matthew Hibberd, "The Reform of Public Service Broadcasting in Italy," *Media, Culture and Society* 23, no. 2 (2001): 234.

37. Dagrada, "Television and Its Critics," 236.

38. Lottizzazione describes the way in which any one entity can be split up into minor parts. This occurred with other state conglomerates in Italy around the same time, including ENI, the Italian oil and gas company; ENEL, the Italian energy provider; and the Institute for Industrial Reconstruction, which played a role in refinancing banks and private companies. Here I use the term only to refer to the state-run television networks under RAI, which first divided into two, and eventually three (RAI1, RAI2, RAI3).

39. Cinzia Padovani, *A Fatal Attraction: Public Television and Politics in Italy* (Lanham, MD: Rowman & Littlefield, 2005), 4.

40. With respect to the development of the three main state channels, since the DC had solely controlled RAI from 1953 until 1975, presenting a wide variety of political perspectives had not been possible until the parceling out of stations across the political parties themselves, but some were not convinced by this rationale. The main criticism of lottizzazione during the time was that allocating a national channel to each main political party challenged the standard view that objectivity meant an absence of political bias, since all the channels now had political parties at their helm. Paving the way for the logic of privatization, that argument insisted on a situation in which no party, rather than several major parties, would have so much control over television. Meanwhile, the counterargument sought to persuade the public that it was precisely the multiple party system that exposed audiences to multiple viewpoints. Instead of refraining from party propaganda, lottizzazione allowed the main parties a forum for their political views.

41. Grasso, *Storia della televisione italiana*, 841.

42. Cinzia Padovani and Michael Tracey, "Report on the Conditions of Public Service Broadcasting," *Television and New Media* 4, no. 2 (2003): 139–40.
43. Dagrada, "Television and Its Critics," 244.
44. Auslander, *Liveness*, 34–35.
45. Rita Celi, "La7 sorprende nella sfida degli ascolti con 'Il Sergente' di Marco Paolini," *La Repubblica*, October 31, 2007, sec. Spettacoli e cultura, http://www.repubblica.it/2007/10/sezioni/spettacoli_e_cultura/sergente-paolini/ascolti-la7/ascolti-la7.html.
46. Giorgio Simonelli, *Ci salvi chi può: Cronache della TV italiana dal 2000 a oggi* (Turin: Effatà, 2009), 195–96.
47. Giorgio Simonelli, *I peggiori anni della sua vita: La televisione italiana nel nuovo millenio* (Turin: Effatà, 2004), 37.
48. For a detailed description of that first performance, see Marco Paolini and Oliviero Ponte di Pino, *Quaderno del Vajont: Dagli album al teatro della diga* (Turin: Einaudi, 1999), 16–17.
49. Radio Popolare in Milan is part of a tradition of left-leaning stations that emerged during the 1970s and include, perhaps most famously, Radio Alice in Bologna, which later became Radio Radicale; Radio Aut in Palermo lead by Peppino Impastato, the young activist that Baliani honors in *Corpo di stato* for speaking publicly against the Mafia, who then murdered him; and more recently Radio Blackout in Turin, emerging from protests in occupied universities in the late 1980s and early 1990s known as *il movimento della pantera* (the panther movement).
50. Paolini and Ponte di Pino, *Quaderno del Vajont*, 50–51.
51. Paolini and Ponte di Pino, *Quaderno del Vajont*, 43, 71.
52. Grasso, *Storia della televisione italiana*, 863, 866, 871.
53. Carlo Ginzburg, *The Night Battles: Witchcraft and Agrarian Cults in the Sixteenth and Seventeenth Centuries*, trans. John and Anne Tedeschi (Baltimore: Johns Hopkins University Press, 1983), xvii.
54. Gualtiero Peirce, "Corpo a corpo fra video e teatro," *La Repubblica*, May 11, 1998, sec. Spettacoli.
55. R. S. Jenkins, preface to *Body of State*, ix.
56. Baliani, *Corpo di stato*, 101.
57. Baliani, *Corpo di stato*, 81–82.

Conclusion

1. Madison, *Critical Ethnography*, 168.
2. The capital "V" in "moVimento" stands for an Italian vulgarity, in this instance directed toward members of Parliament, euphemistically translatable as "take a hike."
3. For a taping of the joke, see "Beppe Grillo e i Socialisti—1986—Per questo fu cacciato," YouTube video, 0:30, posted August 20, 2007, https://www.youtube.com/watch?v=W7oKQtBfTT8.
4. For a taping of this event, see "Bettino Craxi sotto una pioggia di monetine," YouTube video, 1:44, posted August 30, 2013, https://www.youtube.com/watch?v=JCELIWzRFkg.
5. See, for example, Alessandro Dal Lago, *Clic! Grillo, Casaleggio e la demagogia elettronica* (Naples: Cronopio, 2013).

6. "Grillo sentito sul crac Parmalat 'Ho portato pure Fiat e Telecom,'" *La Repubblica*, January 16, 2004, sec. Economia, http://www.repubblica.it/2004/a/sezioni/economia/parmalat6/grillo1/grillo1.html.

BIBLIOGRAPHY

Agamben, Giorgio. *The Coming Community*. Translated by Michael Hardt. Minneapolis: University of Minnesota Press, 1993.

Albanese, Angela. *Identità sotto chiave: Lingua e stile nel teatro di Saverio La Ruina*. Macerata, Italy: Quodlibet, 2017.

Antonello, Pierpaolo, and Alan O'Leary. *Imagining Terrorism: The Rhetoric and Representation of Political Violence in Italy 1969–2009*. London: Legenda, 2009.

Artusi, Pellegrino. *La scienza in cucina e l'arte di mangiar bene*. Turin: Einaudi, 1970.

"A Settimo 'Viva la piazza!' " *La Stampa*. July 28, 1981, Sera ed., sec. Spettacoli.

Aston, Elaine, and Sue-Ellen Case. *Staging International Feminisms*. Basingstoke, UK: Palgrave Macmillan, 2007.

Augias, Corrado, Giuseppe Bartolucci, Marco Bellocchio, Carmelo Bene, Cathy Berberian, Sylvano Bussotti, Antonio Calenda, et al. "Per un nuovo teatro." *Sipario* 247 (November 1966). http://www.trax.it/olivieropdp/mostranew.asp?num=44&ord=4.

Auslander, Philip. *Liveness: Performance in a Mediatized Culture*. 2nd ed. New York: Routledge, 2008.

"Autoethnography." Special issue, *Journal of Contemporary Ethnography* 35, no. 4 (August 2006).

Azouz, Samy. "Amiri Baraka's Participatory and Ceremonial Theatre: From Mimesis to Methexis." *Journal of Dramatic Theory and Criticism* 29, no. 2 (2015): 25–41. https://doi.org/10.1353/dtc.2015.0002.

Balestrini, Nanni, and Primo Moroni. *L'orda d'oro, 1968–1977: La grande ondata rivoluzionaria e creativa, politica ed esistenziale*. Milan: Feltrinelli, 1997.

Baliani, Marco. *Body of State: The Moro Affair, a Nation Divided*. Translated by Nicoletta Marini-Maio, Ellen Victoria Nerenberg, and Thomas Simpson. Madison, NJ: Fairleigh Dickinson University Press, 2012.

———. *Corpo di stato: Il delitto Moro*. Milan: Rizzoli, 2003.

———. *Ho cavalcato in groppa ad una sedia*. Pisa: Titivillus, 2010.

Baliani, Marco, Alessandra Ghiglione, and Fabrizio Fiaschini. *Marco Baliani: Racconti a teatro*. Florence: Loggia de' Lanzi, 1998.

Baliani, Marco, and Remo Rostagno. *Kohlhaas*. Assisi: Edizioni Corsare, 2001.

Barba, Eugenio. "An Amulet Made of Memory: The Significance of Exercises in the Actor's Dramaturgy." *TDR* 41, no. 4 (1997): 127–32. http://www.jstor.org/stable/1146664.

Baudrillard, Jean. *Fatal Strategies*. Translated by Philip Beitchman and W. G. J. Niesluchowski. London: Semiotexte/Pluto, 1990.

Beard, Martha Rose. "Re-Thinking Oral History—a Study of Narrative Performance." *Rethinking History* 21, no. 4 (October 2, 2017): 529–48. https://doi.org/10.1080/13642529.2017.1333285.

Belpoliti, Marco. *Settanta*. Turin: Einaudi, 2010.

Benjamin, Walter. "The Storyteller: Reflections on the Works of Nikolai Leskov." In *Illuminations: Essays and Reflections*. Edited by Hannah Arendt, translated by Harry Zohn, 83–109. New York: Schocken, 1969.

Bini, Elisabetta, Ferdinando Fasce, and Toni Muzi Falconi. "The Origins and Early Developments of Public Relations in Post-War Italy, 1945–1960." *Journal of Communication Management* 15, no. 3 (2011): 210–22.

Binetti, Vincenzo. "Marginalità e appartenenza: La funzione dell'intellettuale tra sfera pubblica e privato nell'Italia del dopoguerra." *Italica* 74, no. 3 (1997): 360–74.

Birch, Anna, and Joanne Tompkins. *Performing Site-Specific Theatre: Politics, Place, Practice*. London: Palgrave Macmillan, 2012.

Bloch, Ernst. *Traces*. Translated by Anthony A. Nassar. Stanford, CA: Stanford University Press, 2006.

Bonifazio, Patrizia, and Paolo Scrivano. *Olivetti Builds: Modern Architecture in Ivrea*. Milan: Skira, 2001.

Bono, Francesco. "Dossier Ivrea 1967 le opinioni di chi partecipò: I ricordi di Ambrosino, Bajini Barba, Calenda, Capriolo, De Berardinis, Fo, Mango, Moscati, Ricci, Ronconi, Scabia, Trionfo." Ateatro: Webzine di cultura teatrale, April 27, 2007. http://www.ateatro.org/mostranotizie2bis.asp?num=108&ord=11.

Bono, Paola, and Sandra Kemp. *Italian Feminist Thought: A Reader*. Oxford: Blackwell, 1991.

Boylorn, Robin M., Mark P. Orbe, and Carolyn Ellis. *Critical Autoethnography: Intersecting Cultural Identities in Everyday Life*. Walnut Creek, CA: Left Coast Press, 2013.

Bruner, Edward M. "Ethnography as Narrative." In *The Anthropology of Experience*, edited by Victor Witter Turner and Edward M. Bruner, 139–55. Urbana: University of Illinois Press, 1986.

———. "Experience and Expressions." In *The Anthropology of Experience*, edited by Victor Witter Turner and Edward M. Bruner, 3–32. Urbana: University of Illinois Press, 1986.

Bull, Anna Cento. *Italian Neofascism: The Strategy of Tension and the Politics of Nonreconciliation*. New York: Berghahn Books, 2012.

Buonanno, Milly. *Italian TV Drama and Beyond: Stories from the Soil, Stories from the Sea*. Chicago: Intellect, 2012.

Burns, Jennifer. "Facts, Fictions, Fakes: Italian Literature in the 1970s." *New Readings* 6 (July 2012).

———. "A Leaden Silence? Writers' Responses to the *anni di piombo*." In *Speaking Out and Silencing: Culture, Society and Politics in Italy in the 1970s*, edited by Anna Cento Bull and Adalgisa Giorgio, 81–94. London: Legenda, 2006.

Burton, Antoinette. *Archive Stories: Facts, Fictions, and the Writing of History*. Durham, NC: Duke University Press, 2006.

Campbell, Ian. *The Massacre of Debre Libanos: Ethiopia 1937. The Story of One of Fascism's Most Shocking Atrocities*. Addis Ababa: Addis Ababa University Press, 2014.

Camporesi, Piero. Introduction to *La scienza in cucina e l'arte di mangiar bene*, by Pellegrino Artusi, 2nd ed., xv–lxxviii. Turin: Einaudi, 2001.

Canziani, Roberto. *Dedica: Laboratorio Teatro Settimo*. Pordenone: Associazione Provinciale per la Prosa, 1995.

———. "Giuliana Musso, storie di provincia e vite qualunque." *Hystrio*, no. 2 (2014): 52–53.

Carbado, Devon W., Kimberlé Williams Crenshaw, Vickie M. Mays, and Barbara Tomlinson. "Intersectionality: Mapping the Movements of a Theory." *Du Bois Review* 10, no. 2 (Fall 2013): 303–12.

Carlson, Marvin. *Speaking in Tongues: Languages at Play in the Theatre*. Ann Arbor: University of Michigan Press, 2006.

Cavarero, Adriana. "Towards a Theory of Sexual Difference." In *The Lonely Mirror: Italian Perspectives on Feminist Theory*, edited by Sandra Kemp and Paola Bono, translated by Giuliana De Novellis, 189–221. London: Routledge, 1993.

Celestini, Ascanio. "Il vestito della festa: Dalla fonte orale a una possibile drammaturgia." *Prove di Drammaturgia* 2 (2003): 21–26.

———. *I precari non esistono*. Rome: Fandango, 2008.

———. *Lotta di classe*. Turin: Einaudi, 2009.

———. *Radio clandestina: Memoria delle Fosse Ardeatine*. Rome: Donzelli, 2005.

Celi, Rita. "La7 sorprende nella sfida degli ascolti con 'Il Sergente' di Marco Paolini." *La Repubblica*, October 31, 2007, sec. Spettacoli e cultura. http://www.repubblica.it/2007/10/sezioni/spettacoli_e_cultura/sergente-paolini/ascolti-la7/ascolti-la7.html.

Cento Bull, Anna, and Adalgisa Giorgio, eds. *Speaking Out and Silencing: Culture, Society and Politics in Italy in the 1970s*. London: Legenda, 2006.

Certeau, Michel de. *The Writing of History*. Translated by Tom Conley. New York: Columbia University Press, 1988.

Cixous, Hélène. "The Laugh of the Medusa." *Signs: Journal of Women in Culture and Society* 1, no. 4 (1976): 875–93.

Claycomb, Ryan. *Lives in Play: Autobiography and Biography on the Feminist Stage*. Ann Arbor: University of Michigan Press, 2012.

———. "(Ch)Oral History, Documentary Theatre, the Communal Subject and Progressive Politics." *Journal of Dramatic Theory and Criticism* 17, no. 2 (2003): 95–121.

Cordileone, Amy, and Rachel Tuggle Whorton. "Site-Specific Theatre: New Perspectives on Pedagogy and Performance." *Research in Drama Education: The Journal of Applied Theatre and Performance* 20, no. 3 (2015): 298–301. https://doi.org/10.1080/13569783.2015.1059267.

Crenshaw, Kimberlé. "Mapping the Margins: Intersectionality, Identity Politics, and Violence against Women of Color." *Stanford Law Review* 43, no. 6 (July 1991): 1241–99. https://doi.org/10.2307/1229039.

Curino, Laura. "La vicenda del testo." *Prove di Drammaturgia* 1 (March 1996). https://archivi.dar.unibo.it/files/muspe/wwcat/period/pdd/num03/03.html.

Curino, Laura, and Roberto Tarasco. *Santa Bàrbera*. Bergamo, Italy: Teatro Donizetti and the Assessorato alla Cultura del Comune di Bergamo, 2008.

Curino, Laura, Roberto Tarasco, and Gabriele Vacis. *Passione*. Novara: Interlinea, 1998.

Curino, Laura, and Gabriele Vacis. *Adriano Olivetti: Il sogno possibile*. Milan: IPOC, 2010.

———. *Camillo Olivetti: Alle radici di un sogno*. Milan: Baldini & Castoldi, 1998.

Curti, Stefano. "A 'Floating' Audience for Marco Paolini's TV Show on Venice History, Sept. 10." *Playbill*. Sept 9, 1998. https://www.playbill.com/article/a-floating-audience-for-marco-paolinis-tv-show-on-venice-history-sept-10-com-77240.

Dagrada, Elena. "Television and Its Critics: A Parallel History." In *Italian Cultural Studies: An Introduction*, edited by David Forgacs and Robert Lumley, 233–47. Oxford: Oxford University Press, 1996.

Davidson, James West. "The New Narrative History: How New? How Narrative?" *Reviews in American History* 12, no. 3 (1984): 322–34.

Dawson, Gary Fisher. *Documentary Theatre in the United States: An Historical Survey and Analysis of Its Content, Form, and Stagecraft*. Westport, CT: Greenwood, 1999.

Denzin, Norman K. *Interpretive Autoethnography*. 2nd ed. London: Sage, 2014. https://doi.org/10.4135/9781506374697.

Diamond, Elin. *Performance and Cultural Politics*. London: Routledge, 1996.

———. "Performance in the Archives." *Theatre History Studies* 28 (2008): 20–26.

Dixon, Steve. *Digital Performance: A History of New Media in Theater, Dance, Performance Art, and Installation*. Cambridge, MA: MIT Press, 2007.

Dunnage, Jonathan. *Twentieth-Century Italy: A Social History*. London: Longman, 2002.

Edwards, Phil. *More Work! Less Pay! Rebellion and Repression in Italy, 1972–77*. Oxford: Oxford University Press, 2009.

Enia, Davide. *Mio padre non ha mai avuto un cane*. Palermo: Duepunti Edizioni, 2010.

Farrell, Joseph, and Paolo Puppa. *A History of Italian Theatre*. Cambridge: Cambridge University Press, 2006.

Ferdman, Bertie. *Off Sites: Contemporary Performance beyond Site-Specific*. Carbondale: Southern Illinois University Press, 2018.

Fischer, Donatella. "Introduction." In *The Tradition of the Actor-Author in Italian Theatre*, edited by Donatella Fischer, 1–8. London: Legenda, 2013.

Fischer-Lichte, Erika. "Culture as Performance." *Modern Austrian Literature* 42, no. 3 (July 1, 2009): 1–10.

Fo, Dario. *Mistero buffo: Giullarata popolare*. Verona: Bertani, 1977.

Fo, Dario. *Mistero buffo: Giullarata popolare*. Edited by Franca Rame. Turin: Einaudi, 2003.

Fo, Dario, and Vittorio Franceschi. *Compagni senza censura*. Milan: Mazzotta, 1970.

Fo, Dario, and Franca Rame. *Female Parts: One Woman Plays*. London: Pluto Press, 1981.

Foot, John. *The Man Who Closed the Asylums: Franco Basaglia and the Revolution in Mental Health Care*. London: Verso, 2015.

Forgacs, David. *Italian Culture in the Industrial Era, 1880–1980: Cultural Industries, Politics, and the Public*. Manchester: Manchester University Press, 1990.

"Formations des animateurs." *Association Technique pour l'Action Culturelle (Atac)* 74 (February 1976).

Foucault, Michel. "Of Other Spaces." Translated by Jay Miskowiec. *Diacritics* 16 (Spring 1986): 22–27.

———. *Power/Knowledge: Selected Interviews and Other Writings, 1972–1977*. Translated by Colin Gordon. Brighton, UK: Harvester, 1980.

Francioso, Monica. "Impegno and Ali Baba: Celati, Calvino, and the Debate on Literature in the 1970s." *Italian Studies* 64, no. 1 (2009): 105–19.

Fuentes, Marisa J. *Dispossessed Lives: Enslaved Women, Violence, and the Archive*. Philadelphia: University of Pennsylvania Press, 2016.

Garde, Ulrike, and Meg Mumford. *Theatre of Real People: Diverse Encounters at Berlin's Hebbel Am Ufer and Beyond*. London: Bloomsbury Methuen Drama, 2016.

Gingrich-Philbrook, Craig. "Autoethnography's Family Values: Easy Access to Compulsory Experiences." *Text and Performance Quarterly* 25, no. 4 (October 2005): 297–314. https://doi.org/10.1080/10462930500362445.

Ginsborg, Paul. *Storia d'Italia, 1943–1996: Famiglia, società, stato*. Translated by Marcello Florese. Turin: Einaudi, 1998.

Ginzburg, Carlo. *The Cheese and the Worms: The Cosmos of a Sixteenth-Century Miller*. Translated by John and Anne C. Tedeschi. Baltimore: Johns Hopkins University Press, 2013.

———. "Clues: Morelli, Freud, and Sherlock Holmes." In *The Sign of Three: Dupin, Holmes, Pierce*, edited by Umberto Eco and Thomas Albert Sebeok, 81–118. Bloomington: Indiana University Press, 1983.

———. *Il formaggio e i vermi: Il cosmo di un mugnaio del '500*. Turin: Einaudi, 1976.

———. "Microhistory: Two or Three Things That I Know about It." Translated by John and Anne C. Tedeschi. *Critical Inquiry* 20, no. 1 (1993): 10–35. http://www.jstor.org/stable/1343946.

———. *The Night Battles: Witchcraft and Agrarian Cults in the Sixteenth and Seventeenth Centuries*. Translated by John and Anne Tedeschi. Baltimore: Johns Hopkins University Press, 1983.

———. "[The Possibilities of the Past]: A Comment." *Journal of Interdisciplinary History* 12, no. 2 (1981): 277–78. https://doi.org/10.2307/203029.

———. "Spie: Radici di un paradigma indiziario." In *Crisi della ragione*, edited by Aldo Giorgio Gargani, 57–106. Turin: Einaudi, 1979.

Glynn, Ruth. "Trauma on the Line: Terrorism and Testimony in the *anni di piombo*." In *The Value of Literature in and after the Seventies: The Case of Italy and Portugal*, edited by Monica Jansen and Paula Jordão, 317–35. Utrecht: University of Utrecht Igitur Publishing and Archiving, 2006.

Glynn, Ruth, and Giancarlo Lombardi. *Remembering Aldo Moro: The Cultural Legacy of the 1978 Kidnapping and Murder*. London: Legenda, 2012.

Goffman, Erving. *The Presentation of Self in Everyday Life*. Garden City, NY: Doubleday, 1959.

Goodman, Lizbeth, and Gabriella Giannachi. “A Theatre for Urban Renewal.” *New Theatre Quarterly* 7, no. 25 (1991): 27–34. https://doi.org/10.1017/S0266464X00005169.

Gramsci, Antonio. “Angelo Musco.” *Avanti!*, March 29, 1918, sec. Cronache teatrale. http://www.quartaparetepress.it/2012/03/30/gramsci-cronache-teatrali-dallavanti-angelo-musco/.

Grasso, Aldo. *Storia della televisione italiana*. Milan: Garzanti, 2000.

“Grillo sentito sul crac Parmalat ‘Ho portato pure Fiat e Telecom.’ ” *La Repubblica*, January 16, 2004, sec. Economia. http://www.repubblica.it/2004/a/sezioni/economia/parmalat6/grillo1/grillo1.html.

Grotowski, Jerzy. *Towards a Poor Theatre*. Edited by Eugenio Barba. New York: Routledge, 2002.

Guccini, Gerardo. *La bottega dei narratori: Storie, laboratori e metodi*. Rome: D. Audino, 2005.

———. “Lettera a Laboratorio Teatro Settimo sull’esplorazione e le carte.” *Prove di Drammaturgia* 1 (March 1996). https://archivi.dar.unibo.it/files/muspe/wwcat/period/pdd/num03/num03.html.

———. “Racconti della memoria: Il teatro di Ascanio Celestini.” *Prove di Drammaturgia* 2 (2003): 20–21.

———. “Recitare la nuova performance epica.” *Acting Archives Review: Rivista di studi sull’attore e la recitazione* 1, no. 2 (2011): 65–67.

———. “Teatro di narrazione.” *Hystrio* 1 (January 2005): 3–6.

Guccini, Gerardo, and Michela Marelli. *Stabat mater: Viaggio alle fonti del teatro di narrazione*. Bologna: Le ariette libri, 2004.

Guccini, Gerardo, and Claudio Meldolesi. “Editoriale: L’arcipelago della ‘nuova performance epica.’ ” *Prove di Drammaturgia* 10, no. 1 (2004): 3–4.

Guzzetta, Juliet. “At Work, at Home: Women, Labor, and Laura Curino’s Olivetti Plays.” In “From Otium and Occupatio to Work and Labor in Italian Culture,” special issue, *Annali d’Italianistica* 32 (2014): 291–306.

———. “The Lasting Theatre of Dario Fo and Franca Rame.” *Theatre History Studies* 37, no. 1 (2018): 257–77. https://doi.org/10.1353/ths.2018.0013.

———. “A Presentation of Herself: Laura Curino’s Passions in Everyday Life.” *Spunti e Ricerche* 25 (2011): 116–30.

———. “A Voice of Her Own: Feminism and Subjectivities for a Modern Santa Bàrbera.” In *A Window on the Italian Female Modernist Subjectivity: From Neera to Laura Curino*, edited by Rossella M. Riccobono, 187–201. Newcastle, UK: Cambridge Scholars, 2013.

Haider, Asad, and Salar Mohandesi. “Workers’ Inquiry: A Genealogy.” *Viewpoint Magazine* 3 (2013). http://viewpointmag.com/2013/09/27/workers-inquiry-a-genealogy/#fn1–2809.

Haller, Hermann W. *The Other Italy: The Literary Canon in Dialect*. Toronto: University of Toronto Press, 1999.

Harnois, Catherine. “Re-presenting Feminisms: Past, Present, and Future.” *NWSA Journal* 20, no. 1 (2008): 120–45.

Hartman, Saidiya V. *Scenes of Subjection: Terror, Slavery, and Self-Making in Nineteenth-Century America*. Oxford: Oxford University Press, 1997.

Haycraft, John. *Italian Labyrinth: Italy in the 1980s*. London: Secker & Warburg, 1985.

Heddon, Deirdre. "Performing the Archive Following in the Footsteps." *Performance Research* 7, no. 4 (January 1, 2002): 64–77. https://doi.org/10.1080/13528165.2002.10871893.

Hibberd, Matthew. "The Reform of Public Service Broadcasting in Italy." *Media, Culture and Society* 23, no. 2 (2001): 233–52.

Hilwig, Stuart J. *Italy and 1968: Youthful Unrest and Democratic Culture*. Basingstoke, UK: Palgrave Macmillan, 2009.

———. "The Revolt against the Establishment: Students versus the Press in West Germany and Italy." In *1968: The World Transformed*, edited by Carole Fink, Philipp Gassert, and Detlef Junker, 321–50. Cambridge: Cambridge University Press, 1998.

Hipkins, Danielle. "'Whore-Ocracy': Show Girls, the Beauty Trade-Off, and Mainstream Oppositional Discourse in Contemporary Italy." *Italian Studies* 66, no. 3 (November 2011): 413–30. https://doi.org/10.1179/007516311X13134938224529.

Hobsbawm, E. J. "The Revival of Narrative: Some Comments." *Past and Present*, no. 86 (1980): 3–8.

Homan, Sidney. "Introduction: What It Can Mean to Play Offstage—and Why." In *Playing Offstage: The Theater as a Presence or Factor in the Real World*, edited by Sidney Homan, vii–xiv. London: Lexington Books, 2017.

Horn, Gerd-Rainer. *The Spirit of '68: Rebellion in Western Europe and North America, 1956–1976*. Oxford: Oxford University Press, 2007.

"Il gioco del teatro: Convegno 'l'animazione trent'anni dopo.' Vetrina del teatro ragazzi e giovani." April 21, 1998, box 1996–99, Laura Curino Private Collections: Settimo Torinese, Turin.

"Il gioco del teatro: Vetrina del teatro ragazzi e giovani." April 17, 2000, box 2000, Laura Curino Private Collections: Settimo Torinese, Turin.

Jackson, Anthony, and Jenny Kidd. *Performing Heritage: Research, Practice and Innovation in Museum Theatre and Live Interpretation*. Manchester: Manchester University Press, 2011.

Jenkins, Keith. *Rethinking History*. New York: Routledge, 1991.

Jenkins, Ronald Scott. *Dario Fo and Franca Rame: Artful Laughter*. New York: Aperture, 2001.

———. Preface to *Body of State: The Moro Affair, a Nation Divided*, by Marco Baliani, translated by Nicoletta Marini-Maio, Ellen Victoria Nerenberg, and Thomas Simpson, vii–x. Madison, NJ: Fairleigh Dickinson University Press, 2012.

Kemp, Sandra, and Paola Bono, eds. *The Lonely Mirror: Italian Perspectives on Feminist Theory*. Translated by Giuliana De Novellis. London: Routledge, 1993.

King, Russell. *The Industrial Geography of Italy*. London: Routledge, 2015.

Klimke, M., and J. Scharloth. *1968 in Europe: A History of Protest and Activism, 1956–1977*. New York: Palgrave Macmillan, 2008.

Laboratorio Teatro Settimo. "Atélier di Cultura Teatrale" (1982). Correspondence, box 1982, Laura Curino Private Collections: Settimo Torinese, Turin.

———. "Cosa sarà il nuovo spettacolo?" (January 6, 1976). Box 1976, Laura Curino Private Collections: Settimo Torinese, Turin.

———. "Fase 0, 1, 2: Progetto Città Laboratorio" (1980–81). Box 1980, Laura Curino Private Collections: Settimo Torinese, Turin.

———. "Laboratorio Teatro Settimo" (1977). Box 1977, Laura Curino Private Collections: Settimo Torinese, Turin.

———. "L'Arcircolo PEPE Pamphlet" (1978). Box 1978, Laura Curino Private Collections: Settimo Torinese, Turin.

———. "LTU3: Appunti per l'avvio del terzo laboratorio di trasformazione urbana. La ricerca storica" (1981). Box 1981, Laura Curino Private Collections: Settimo Torinese, Turin.

———. "Qual'é la storia del Laboratorio Teatro Settimo?" (1982). Box 1982, Laura Curino Private Collections: Settimo Torinese, Turin.

———. *Theatre's Heterotopias* (1978). Box 1978, Laura Curino Private Collections: Settimo Torinese, Turin.

Ladurie, Emmanuel Le Roy. *Montaillou: The Promised Land of Error*. Translated by Barbara Bray. New York: George Braziller, 2008.

———. *The Peasants of Languedoc*. Translated by John Day. Urbana: University of Illinois Press, 1977.

Lago, Alessandro Dal. *Clic! Grillo, Casaleggio e la demagogia elettronica*. Naples: Cronopio, 2013.

Landis, Kevin, and Suzanne Macaulay. *Cultural Performance: Ethnographic Approaches to Performance Studies*. London: Palgrave Macmillan, 2017.

La Ruina, Saverio. *Teatro: Dissonorata, La Borto, Italianesi*. Pisa: Titivillus, 2014.

Letourneux, Frédérique. *Les métiers de l'animation*. Paris: L'Étudiant, 2007.

Levi, Giovanni. "On Microhistory." In *New Perspectives on Historical Writing*, edited by Peter Burke, 93–113. Cambridge, UK: Polity, 1991.

Libreria delle donne di Milano, ed. *Non credere di avere dei diritti: La generazione della libertà femminile nell'idea e nelle vicende di un gruppo di donne*. Turin: Rosenberg & Sellier, 1987.

Lumley, Robert. *States of Emergency: Cultures of Revolt in Italy from 1968 to 1978*. London: Verso, 1990.

Madison, D. Soyini. *Critical Ethnography: Method, Ethics, and Performance*. Thousand Oaks, CA: Sage, 2011.

Malpede, Karen. *Women in Theatre: Compassion and Hope*. New York: Drama Book Publishers, 1983.

Mamprin, Lodovico, Gian Renzo Morteo, and Loredana Perissinotto. *Tre dialoghi sull'animazione*. Rome: Bulzoni, 1977.

Marini-Maio, Nicoletta, and Ellen Victoria Nerenberg. "Critical Introduction. Corpses and Coups: On Body of State." In *Body of State: The Moro Affair, a Nation Divided*, by Marco Baliani, 1–21. Translated by Nicoletta Marini-Maio, Ellen Victoria Nerenberg, and Thomas Simpson. Madison, NJ: Fairleigh Dickinson University Press, 2012.

Martin, Carol. *Theatre of the Real*. London: Palgrave Macmillan, 2013.

Martin, Jacqueline, Georgia Seffrin, and Rod Wissler. "The Festival Is a Theatrical Event." In *Theatrical Events: Borders, Dynamics, Frames*, edited by Vicki Ann Cremona, Peter Eversmann, Hans van Maanen, Willmar Sauter, and John Tulloch, 91–110. Amsterdam: Rodopi, 2004.

Maza, Sarah. "Stories in History: Cultural Narratives in Recent Works in European History." *American Historical Review* 101, no. 5 (1996): 1493–1515.

McCall, Leslie. "The Complexity of Intersectionality." *Signs: Journal of Women in Culture and Society* 30, no. 3 (2005): 1771–1800.

Meersman, B., S. Patsalidis, M. Glauner, B. Orel, and R. Dennemann. "Theater Festivals and Their Audiences: A Forum." *Theater* 41, no. 1 (January 1, 2011): 79–103. https://doi.org/10.1215/01610775-2010-024.

Mehtonen, Païvi. "Poetics, Narration, and Imitation: Rhetoric as Ars Applicabilis." In *The Rhetoric of Cicero in Its Medieval and Early Renaissance Commentary Tradition*, edited by Virginia Cox and John O. Ward, 289–312. Leiden: Brill, 2006.

Mignone, Mario B. "Dario Fo, Jester of the Italian Stage." *Italian Quarterly* 85 (Summer 1981): 47–62.

Milan Women's Bookstore Collective. *Sexual Difference: A Theory of Social-Symbolic Practice*. Bloomington: Indiana University Press, 1990.

Miller, Lynn C., Jacqueline Taylor, and M. Heather Carver. *Voices Made Flesh: Performing Women's Autobiography*. Madison: University of Wisconsin Press, 2003.

Morteo, Gian Renzo, and Anna Sagna. *L'animazione come propedeutica al teatro*. Turin: Giappichelli, 1977.

Musso, Giuliana. "Nati in casa." In *Senza corpo: Voci dalla nuova scena italiana*, edited by Debora Pietrobono, 17–52. Rome: Minimum fax, 2009.

Myerhoff, Barbara. "'Life Not Death in Venice': Its Second Life." In *The Anthropology of Experience*, edited by Victor Witter Turner and Edward M. Bruner, 261–86. Urbana: University of Illinois Press, 1986.

Negri, Antonio. "Reviewing the Experience of Italy in the 1970s." *Le Monde Diplomatique*, n.d. http://mondediplo.com/1998/09/11negri.

Nencioni, Giovanni. *Di scritto e di parlato: Discorsi linguistici*. Bologna: Zanichelli, 1983.

Nilsen, Don L. F. "The Evolution of Stand-Up Comedy: From the Middle Ages to Post-modernism." *Journal of Evolutionary Psychology* 21, nos. 1–2 (2000): 35–39.

Nosari, Pier Giorgio. "I sentieri dei raccontatori di storie: Ipotesi per una mappa del teatro di narrazione." *Prove di drammaturgia* 1 (2004): 11–14.

Novara, Francesco, Renato Rozzi, and Roberta Garruccio. *Uomini e lavoro alla Olivetti*. Milan: Mondadori, 2005.

Padovani, Cinzia. *A Fatal Attraction: Public Television and Politics in Italy*. Lanham, MD: Rowman & Littlefield, 2005.

Padovani, Cinzia, and Michael Tracey. "Report on the Conditions of Public Service Broadcasting." *Television and New Media* 4, no. 2 (2003): 131–53.

Palandri, Enrico. "The Difficulty of a Historical Perspective on the 1970s." In *Speaking Out and Silencing: Culture, Society and Politics in Italy in the 1970s*, edited by Anna Cento Bull and Adalgisa Giorgio, 115–20. London: Legenda, 2006.

Palieri, Serena. "A proposito di femminismo." *L'Unità*, April 16, 2009. http://www.unita.it/italia/a-proposito-di-femminismo-1.28317.

Panigada, Maria Grazia. "Introduction." In *Santa Bàrbera*, by Laura Curino and Roberto Tarasco. Bergamo, Italy: Teatro Donizetti and the Assessorato alla Cultura del Comune di Bergamo, 2008.

Paolini, Marco, and Oliviero Ponte di Pino. *Quaderno del Vajont: Dagli album al teatro della diga*. Turin: Einaudi, 1999.

Paolini, Marco, and Gabriele Vacis. *The Story of Vajont*. Translated by Thomas Simpson. Boca Raton, FL: Bordighera, 2000.

Passerini, Luisa. *Storia e soggettività: Le fonti orali, la memoria*. Florence: La Nuova Italia, 1988.

———, ed. *Storia orale: Vita quotidiana e cultura materiale delle classi subalterne*. Turin: Rosenberg & Sellier, 1978.

———. *Torino operaia e fascismo*. Bari: Gius. Laterza & Figli SpA, 1984.

Pearson, Mike, and Michael Shanks. *Theatre/Archaeology*. London: Routledge, 2001.

Peirce, Gualtiero. "Corpo a corpo fra video e teatro." *La Repubblica*, May 11, 1998, sec. Spettacoli.

Peltonen, Matti. "Clues, Margins, and Monads: The Micro-Macro Link in Historical Research." *History and Theory* 40, no. 3 (2001): 347–59. http://www.jstor.org/stable/2677970.

P.G. "Che la festa cominici . . . sulla piazza settimese." *La Stampa*. July 21, 1981, Sera ed., sec. Spettacoli.

Pirandello, Luigi. *L'umorismo e altri saggi*. Florence: Giunti, 1994.

Pollock, Della. *Remembering: Oral History Performance*. New York: Palgrave Macmillan, 2005.

Ponte di Pino, Oliviero. *Il nuovo teatro italiano, 1975–1988: La ricerca dei gruppi, materiali e documenti*. Florence: La Casa Usher, 1988.

Portelli, Alessandro. *The Battle of Valle Giulia: The Art of Dialogue in Oral History*. Madison: University of Wisconsin Press, 1997.

———. *The Death of Luigi Trastulli and Other Stories: Form and Meaning in Oral History*. Albany: SUNY Press, 1991.

———. *The Order Has Been Carried Out: History, Memory, and Meaning of a Nazi Massacre in Rome*. New York: Palgrave Macmillan, 2003.

———. Preface to *Radio clandestina: Memoria delle Fosse Ardeatine*, by Ascanio Celestini, 9–17. Rome: Donzelli, 2005.

Postlewait, Thomas. *The Cambridge Introduction to Theatre Historiography*. Cambridge: Cambridge University Press, 2009.

Povoledo, Elisabetta. "In Italy, Memories Are Made of This." *New York Times*, September 12, 2005, sec. Arts. https://www.nytimes.com/2005/09/12/arts/in-italy-memories-are-made-of-this.html.

———. "Italian Monologues with a Message." *International Herald Tribune*, March 16, 2007.

Pozzi, Emilio. "Prefazione." In *Il teatro in televisione: Regia e registi dalle prime trasmissioni in diretta all'alta definizione*, edited by Giorgio Tabanelli, 11–16. Rome: RAI ERI, 2002.

Puppa, Paolo. "The Actor-Narrator." In *The Tradition of the Actor-Author in Italian Theatre*, edited by Donatella Fischer, 158–65. London: Legenda, 2013.

———. *Il teatro dei testi: La drammaturgia italiana nel Novecento*. Turin: UTET libreria, 2003.

"Quando il teatro scende in piazza e la trasforma." *La Stampa*. July 16, 1982, Sera ed., sec. Spettacoli.

Rame, Franca, and Dario Fo. *Tutta casa, letto e chiesa*. Milan: F. R. La comune, 1981.

———. *A Woman Alone and Other Plays*. Translated by Gillian Hanna, Ed Emery, and Christopher Cairns. London: Methuen Drama, 1991.

Ravengai, Samuel. "Performing the Archive and Re-archiving Memory: Magnet Theatre's Museum and Reminiscence Theatre." *South African Theatre Journal*

28, no. 3 (September 2, 2015): 209–21. https://doi.org/10.1080/10137548.2015.1046398.

Reekie, Gail. "Michel de Certeau and the Poststructuralist Critique of History." *Social Semiotics* 6, no. 1 (January 1, 1996): 45–59. https://doi.org/10.1080/10350339609384463.

Revelli, Nuto. *L'anello forte*. Turin: Einaudi, 2018.

R.M. "Cavalcata eroica del teatro in piazza." *Il Manifesto*. July 17, 1981, sec. Le Immagini.

Rokem, Freddie. *Performing History: Theatrical Representations of the Past in Contemporary Theatre*. Iowa City: University of Iowa Press, 2002.

Rosa, Alberto Asor. *Scrittori e popolo*. Rome: Samonà e Savelli, 1966.

Sauter, Willmar. "Introduction: Festival Culture in Global Perspective." *Theatre Research International* 30, no. 3 (October 2005): 237–39. https://doi.org/10.1017/S0307883305001495.

Scabia, Giuliano. *Marco Cavallo: Da un ospedale psichiatrico la vera storia che ha cambiato il modo di essere del teatro e della cura*. Merano: Edizioni Alpha Beta Verlag, 2011.

Schechner, Richard. "Magnitudes of Performance." In *The Anthropology of Experience*, edited by Victor Witter Turner and Edward M. Bruner, 344–69. Urbana: University of Illinois Press, 1986.

———. *Performance Studies: An Introduction*. London: Routledge, 2013.

Schneider, Rebecca. *Performing Remains: Art and War in Times of Theatrical Reenactment*. New York: Routledge, 2011.

Scott, Joan Wallach. Foreword to *Autobiography of a Generation: Italy, 1968*, by Luisa Passerini, translated by Lisa Erdberg, xi–xiv. Hanover, NH: University Press of New England, 1996.

Scuderi, Antonio. "Dario Fo and Oral Tradition: Creating a Thematic Context." *Oral Tradition* 15, no. 1 (March 2000): 26–38.

———. "Dario Fo and Performance Theory." *Italian Culture* 12 (1994): 239–46.

"Settimo riscopre le piazze." *Gazzetta del Popolo*, July 15, 1981, sec. Cinema, teatro, musica, mostre.

Simonelli, Giorgio. *Ci salvi chi può: Cronache della TV italiana dal 2000 a oggi*. Turin: Effatà, 2009.

———. *I peggiori anni della sua vita: La televisione italiana nel nuovo millenio*. Turin: Effatà, 2004.

Soriani, Simone. *Dario Fo: Dalla commedia al monologo, 1959–1969*. Pisa: Titivillus, 2007.

———. "Dario Fo, il teatro di narrazione, la nuova performance epica: Per una genealogia di un 'quasi-genere.'" *Forum Italicum* 39, no. 2 (Fall 2005): 620–48.

———. "In principio era Fo." *Hystrio*, no. 1 (January 2005): 17–22.

———. "Mistero buffo, dal varietà al teatro di narrazione." In *Coppia d'arte: Dario Fo e Franca Rame con dipinti, testimonianze e dichiarazioni inedite*, edited by Concetta D'Angeli and Simone Soriani, 103–30. Pisa: Pisa University Press, 2006.

———. *Sulla scena del racconto*. Arezzo: Zona, 2009.

Southgate, Beverley C. *History Meets Fiction*. New York: Routledge, 2014.

Spadaro, Damiana. *Il teatro in televisione da Eduardo De Filippo a Dario Fo. Il teleteatro: Sviluppo, tecniche e esperienze*. Florence: Firenze Atheneum, 2004.

Spry, Tami. "Performing Autoethnography: An Embodied Methodological Praxis." *Qualitative Inquiry* 7, no. 6 (2001): 706–32. https://doi.org/10.1177/107780040100700605.

Spunta, Marina. *Voicing the Word: Writing Orality in Contemporary Italian Fiction*. Bern: Peter Lang, 2004.

Steedman, Carolyn. *Dust: The Archive and Cultural History*. New Brunswick, NJ: Rutgers University Press, 2002.

Stomeo, Anna. *Intrecci: Teatro-educazione—new media*. Lecce: Amaltea Edizioni, 2006.

Stone, Lawrence. "The Revival of Narrative: Reflections on a New Old History." *Past and Present*, no. 85 (1979): 3–24.

Tabanelli, Giorgio, ed. *Il teatro in televisione: Regia e registi dalle prime trasmissioni in diretta all'alta definizione*. Rome: RAI ERI, 2002.

Taylor, Diana. *The Archive and the Repertoire: Performing Cultural Memory in the Americas*. Durham, NC: Duke University Press, 2003.

Teatro Odin. "Transcript from Televised Interview of 'Un'ora con Jerzy Grotowski.'" January 5, 1976, box 1976. Laura Curino Private Collections: Settimo Torinese, Turin.

Tompkins, Joanne. *Theatre's Heterotopias: Performance and the Cultural Politics of Space*. London: Palgrave Macmillan, 2014.

Toraille, Raymond. *L'animation pedagogique*. Paris: Éditions Esf, 1973.

Townshend, Charles. *Terrorism: A Very Short Introduction*. Oxford: Oxford University Press, 2011.

Tronti, Mario. *Operai e capitale*. Turin: Einaudi, 1966.

Trouillot, Michel-Rolph. *Silencing the Past: Power and the Production of History*. Boston: Beacon, 1995.

Turner, Victor. "Dewey, Dilthey, and Drama: An Essay in the Anthropology of Experience." In *The Anthropology of Experience*, edited by Victor Witter Turner and Edward M. Bruner, 33–44. Urbana: University of Illinois Press, 1986.

Turner, Victor Witter. *The Ritual Process: Structure and Anti-structure*. Chicago: Aldine, 1969.

Ugolini, Fabio. "Settimo Torinese: Quarant'anni fa il Laboratorio Teatro Settimo." *12alle12*, April 9, 2014. https://12alle12.it/settimo-torinese-quarantanni-fa-il-laboratorio-teatro-settimo-56452.

Vacis, Gabriele. *Awareness: Dieci giorni con Jerzy Grotowski*. Milan: BUR, 2002.

———. "Il disegno e la casa." *Prove di drammaturgia* 1 (March 1996). https://archivi.dar.unibo.it/files/muspe/wwcat/period/pdd/num03/num03.html.

Valentini, Valentina. *New Theatre in Italy: 1963–2013*. Translated by Thomas Simpson. New York: Routledge, 2017.

Veneziani, Massimo. *Controinformazione: Stampa alternativa e giornalismo d'inchiesta dagli anni Sessanta a oggi*. Analisi. Rome: Castelvecchi, 2006.

White, Hayden. "Interpretation in History." *New Literary History* 4, no. 2 (1973): 281–314. http://www.jstor.org/stable/468478.

———. "Introduction: Historical Fiction, Fictional History, and Historical Reality." *Rethinking History* 9, nos. 2–3 (2005): 147–57. https://doi.org/10.1080/13642520500149061.

Wood, Sharon. "Women and Theater in Italy: Natalia Ginzburg, Franca Rame, and Dacia Maraini." *Romance Languages Annual* 5 (1993): 343–48.

Zavoli, Sergio. *La notte della repubblica*. Milan: Mondadori, 1992.

INDEX

Page numbers in italics indicate figures.